If I Forget Thee

If I Forget Thee

The Story of a Nation's Rebirth

by

LORD RUSSELL OF LIVERPOOL

C.B.E., M.C.

CASSELL · LONDON

CASSELL & COMPANY LTD
35 Red Lion Square · London WC1
and at
MELBOURNE · SYDNEY · TORONTO · CAPE TOWN
JOHANNESBURG · AUCKLAND

———

© Lord Russell of Liverpool 1960
First published 1960

Printed in Great Britain
by Unwin Brothers Ltd.
Woking and London
F.1259

If I forget thee, O Jerusalem,
let my right hand forget her cunning.
If I do not remember thee,
let my tongue cleave to the roof of my mouth.

Psalm cxxxvii, 5-6

It is, indeed, not the birth of a nation, for the Jewish nation, through centuries of oppression and captivity, have preserved their sentiment of nationality as few people could; but if it is not the birth of a nation, I believe we may say it is the rebirth of a nation.

Extract from a speech by Lord Robert Cecil at the London Opera House, 2 December 1917

ACKNOWLEDGMENTS

I SHOULD like to express my thanks to the following:

First and foremost to my wife whose idea it was that I should write this book, and who helped to type the manuscript and correct the proofs; to Mrs. Weizmann for supplying the photograph of Oswald Birley's portrait of her late husband; to Mr. Barnet Litvinoff of the Jewish National Fund Office for the loan of certain documents; and to the Librarian and Assistant Librarians of the House of Lords for helping me to trace many references to the Parliamentary Debates during the period covered by this book.

For permission to quote extracts from their publications I am indebted to Hamish Hamilton Ltd. (*Trial and Error* by Chaim Weizmann); to The Jewish Publication Society of America (*Theodor Herzl* by Alex Bein); to The Esco Foundation and the Yale University Press (*Palestine*, Vols. I and II); to Sir Norman Bentwich and Ernest Benn Ltd. (*Israel*); to Harry Sacher and George Weidenfeld & Nicolson Ltd. (*Israel, the Establishment of a State*); to the Controller of H.M. Stationery Office (certain official pamphlets and documents); and to the Editor of *The Times* (certain letters which appeared in their correspondence columns).

For the use of maps on which those appearing in this book are based my thanks are also due to the Controller of H.M. Stationery Office, 'Provisional scheme of Partition as proposed by the Palestine Royal Commission, 1937' (Command Paper 5479), and 'Palestine' (Command Paper 3530); the Royal Institute of International Affairs and the Controller of H.M. Stationery Office, 'Palestine and Syria in 1915' (*Great Britain and Palestine*, 1915–1945, Information Papers No. 20); and George Weidenfeld & Nicolson Ltd., 'The Partition Boundaries, 1947' (*The First Ten Years* by Walter Eytan).

CONTENTS

ILLUSTRATIONS

MAPS

Preface

Now that the State of Israel has survived a perilous first decade and has grown in stature, in that short time, even beyond the expectation of many of her friends, it seemed to me opportune that a short account should be written of the political events leading up to the formation of the new State. That is the object of this book.

There will, doubtless, be some who will ask why this account of the events begins with Theodor Herzl's entry into active Zionism. Clearly it had to start somewhere, but I have chosen that point of departure because it was then that Zionism became a political movement and a world-wide organization came into being.

An active movement had been in existence for the resettlement of Jews in Palestine since 1882. As a longing of the Jewish people to return to the land of their fathers it dates from the first days of the Diaspora. Its inspiration was Biblical, and the idea of a return to Palestine has been nurtured by Rabbinical teaching throughout the long centuries of exile and persecution, and enshrined in Talmudic law and in legend. This idea, this longing was kept well to the fore in the home, in the school and in the synagogue.

It was, however, during the last decade of the nineteenth century that Jews in general were first made to realize that a return to their National Home might be brought about by other means than direct divine intervention. Many others had paved the way for this, but it was Herzl who put Zionism on the map.

CHAPTER I

The Long Journey Begins

In 1886, when Edouard Drumont's book *La France Juive* was published, anti-Semitism in France was on the increase. Drumont was persuaded that the social and economic depression in France was brought about by what he called 'international Jewry'. It was not the first time that the Jews had been made a scapegoat nor was it to be the last. Drumont, however, was a peculiarly unpleasant type of anti-Semite for he attacked the Jews, as the Crusaders had attacked the infidels, in the defence of Christendom, and with sickening hypocrisy assured his readers that 'God had taken the book under His care, because He knew, no doubt, that it was inspired by love of justice'.

He saw all history through anti-Semitic eyes and condemned the emancipation of the Jews in 1791 as a blunder. The Jews in France were not Frenchmen but guests who exploited the expanding economic system for their own benefit and to achieve world domination. They were corrupting the spirit of France. *La France Juive* was the best of all best-sellers in the nineteenth century and in the course of one year ran into a hundred editions.

In 1890 the *Wiener Neue Freie Presse*, the leading Austrian newspaper of the day, got a new Paris correspondent in the person of Theodor Herzl. A Hungarian by birth, he had moved to Vienna with his family in 1878, at the age of eighteen, and had been on the Viennese staff of the *Freie Presse* for two or three years before his posting to Paris. Anti-Semitism was always very strong in Vienna but Herzl was used to it and thought very little about it, nor had he been greatly perturbed at the recent outbreak of pogroms in Russia and the renewal of anti-Semitism in Germany.

I

He had read Drumont's *La France Juive* but it had not shocked him as much as might have been expected. In 1892 he had an opportunity, however, of seeing Drumont in the flesh, when he attended and reported the Burdeau–Drumont trial, and for the first time heard the cry of Drumont's followers, '*A bas les Juifs*', echoing through the streets of Paris.

The trial took place at a time of great excitement. A fortnight earlier a duel, the first of a series, had been fought between a Jewish captain in the French Army and a prominent anti-Semite, the Marquis de Morès. The officer, Captain Mayer, had been killed. The incident created a storm in France and abroad, and even the Minister for War and the Military Governor of Paris felt bound to deplore such conduct though they did not go so far as to condemn anti-Semitism for what it was. Captain Mayer's funeral was attended by a crowd of fifty thousand, and during the next few weeks the French newspapers wrote of little else, and Herzl himself, a month later, wrote a long report on anti-Semitism for the *Freie Presse*.

It was not until the Dreyfus trial, however, that he became deeply stirred. When the first reports of the trial came in Herzl had taken little interest in them. He was busily engaged in writing a play, *The New Ghetto*, and failed to realize the importance of the case which appeared to him, as to almost everyone else, to be an ordinary spy trial in which Alfred Dreyfus was the villain who had betrayed his country by selling her secrets to a foreign power and potential enemy, Germany.

But as the trial wore on Herzl formed the opinion that it was a crowning act of French anti-Semitism, and, as he wrote in one of his reports for the *Neue Freie Presse*, that Dreyfus was being 'persecuted because he was a Jew'. In it Herzl described the public degradation of Dreyfus which took place on the parade ground of the École Militaire on Saturday, 5 January 1895. He had himself heard the howling mob outside the gates shouting '*A mort, à mort les Juifs*', and the cries echoed in his memory and were still ringing in his ears when he wrote again about the trial in 1899. 'The Dreyfus case', he wrote, 'embodies more than a judicial error: it embodies the desire of the vast majority of the French to condemn a Jew, and in this one Jew to condemn all Jews. "Death to the Jews!" howled the mob, as the decorations were being ripped from the Captain's coat . . . and where did this happen? In

France. In republican, modern, civilized France, a hundred years after the Declaration of the Rights of Man. The French people, or at any rate the greater part of the French people, does not want to extend the rights of man to Jews. The edict of the great Revolution has been revoked. Until that time', he continued, 'most of us believed that the solution of the Jewish question was to be patiently awaited as part of the general development of mankind. But when a people who in every other aspect are so progressive and so highly civilized can take such a turn, what are we to expect from other peoples who have not yet reached the level of civilization which France attained a hundred years ago?'

It has often been suggested that had it not been for the fact that Herzl was a newspaper correspondent at the time of the Dreyfus trial he would never have become actively interested in Zionism. That is probably an over-simplification. It may well have been the last straw, but he had been greatly upset some years earlier by Eugen Dühring's book, *The Jewish Problem as a Problem of Race, Morals and Culture*. Dühring regarded the Jewish race as utterly worthless and recommended a return to the ghetto. When Herzl had read the book, at the age of twenty-one, its effect on him was, in the words of his biographer,[1] like that of 'a blow between the eyes', and it was 'the beginning of a great process of change'. Herzl himself said, in later years, that his 'serious and troubled' preoccupation with the Jewish problem dated from that time.

Nevertheless, the Dreyfus trial undoubtedly had a profound effect on him, and it was only four months later that he first approached Baron de Hirsch, an immensely rich Jewish philanthropist who had already bought large areas of land in the Argentine for Jewish colonization, but he was unable to persuade the Baron to give financial assistance to his scheme for solving what he called 'the Jewish question'.

During the winter of 1895–6 Herzl had been busy working out this plan and the result was his famous pamphlet *The Jewish State (Der Judenstaat): An attempt at a modern solution of the Jewish question*. It was a detailed, practical scheme but it did not precisely state whether Palestine or the Argentine was to be the location of the new Jewish National Home, although a preference for Palestine, 'our unforgettable historic homeland', was indicated. The plan envisaged two organizations. The

---

[1] *Theodor Herzl* by Alex Bein.

Society of Jews and the Jewish Company whose functions were, respectively, to acquire sovereignty over a country, under the protection of the European Powers, and to arrange and supervise the migration and settlement of Jews.

He proposed that for the 'Holy Places of Christendom a status of internationally secured extra-territoriality could be instituted'. As the implementation of the plan proceeded, Herzl predicted, there would follow a weakening and a retreat of anti-Semitism. The pamphlet ended with this clarion call for action. 'Let me repeat once more my opening words: the Jews who will it shall have their State. We shall at last live as free men on our own soil, and die peacefully in our own homeland. The world will be freed by our liberation, enriched by our wealth, made greater by our greatness, and that which we seek for our own welfare will stream out mightily and beneficially upon all mankind.'[1]

At the time of the pamphlet's publication the Palestine colonizing movement, although there were already eighteen settlements in the country, was in the doldrums. Herzl's *Judenstaat* burst over the scene like a tornado. Reaction against it was, in some quarters, violent and, in some cases, surprising. The Jewish press in Germany, for instance, was extremely antagonistic. The rest of the opposition was mainly anti-Semitic and not unexpected. Herzl's own employers sought to prevent publication, and when it was published it was not even mentioned in the *Neue Freie Presse*. One German newspaper which was under Jewish influence, the *Allgemeine Zeitung* of Munich, described it in a review as the prospectus, poor in ideas, rich in imbecilities, of a company for the creation of a Jewish Switzerland. It also received widespread criticism from 'orthodox' sources because of its indifferent attitude to religion. The orthodox Jews at that time believed that they should wait for 'the visible signs of God's direct intervention'. The Liberal or Reform Jews' 'ultimate ideal was not the re-establishment of nationality'.

The suspicion amongst some members of the Hoveve Zion, who were the pre-Herzl Zionists, was probably the offspring of jealousy. It was not the first time in national or charitable movements that rival organizations have failed to see that both were really working for the

[1] *The Jewish State* by Theodor Herzl, translated into English by Sylvie d'Avigdor (David Nutt, 1896).

same cause. Who was this new prophet? asked some of them. Why all this vulgar advertisement? Why does he not insist on Palestine? Would not this scheme offend the philanthropists and alarm Turkey? Herzl's ideas might well retard rather than accelerate the resettlement of Jews in Palestine which was the main aim of Hoveve Zion. The opposition was indeed formidable, especially as much of it came from Jewish sources.

But the effect on many others was electric. To Zionist youth it gave a new hope and a new impetus. The ancient longing had not the same meaning for the young as it had for the old; Herzl had given it a new meaning. The flutter of eagles' wings which, Herzl said, he had felt over his head when he wrote *Der Judenstaat*[1] now became audible to these young men and changed them from traditional supporters into enthusiastic pioneers.

By the oppressed Jewish population in Bulgaria, Galicia, Germany and Russia, Herzl was acclaimed as a second Moses, come from Midian 'to liberate the Jews from their wretchedness'.

Chaim Weizmann, who later became Israel's first President, has described in his autobiography the effect of Herzl's pamphlet as profound. 'Not the ideas but the personality which stood behind them appealed to us. Here was daring, clarity and energy. The very fact that this westerner came to us unencumbered by our preconceptions had its appeal. . . . We were right in our instinctive appreciation that what had emerged from the *Judenstaat* was less a concept than a personality. The *Judenstaat* by itself would have been nothing more than a nine days' wonder. If Herzl had contented himself with the mere publication of the booklet— as he orginally intended to do before it became clear to him that he was no longer his own master but the servant of the idea—his name would be remembered today as one of the oddities of Jewish history. What has given greatness to his name is Herzl's role as a man of action, as the founder of the Zionist Congress, and as an example of daring and devotion.'[2] Nevertheless, Weizmann was critical of Herzl's approach to the problem which he thought was 'simpliste and doomed to failure'.[3]

---

[1] *Theodor Herzl* by Alex Bein, p. 184.
[2] *Trial and Error* by Chaim Weizmann (East and West Library), pp. 61-2.
[3] Ibid. p. 63.

Other distinguished Jews, however, rallied to him, including Max Nordau[1] and David Wolffsohn. Through the latter Herzl got in touch with the German organization of Hoveve Zion, but Chaim Weizmann does not seem to have thought much of either of them. He has described Nordau as being an ardent Zionist only during the sessions of the various Zionist Congresses, although he had to admit that on these occasions he proved a veritable spellbinder and what he said was as if 'a bugle call sounded all over the world, and the world took note'.

Wolffsohn, Weizmann considered, was well-meaning, generous, hard-working, but without Herzl's personality, vision, or organizing ability. Nevertheless, despite these recorded deficiencies, both Nordau and Wolffsohn rendered signal service to the Zionist cause.

During the next few months which followed the publication of *Der Judenstaat*, writers, politicians, businessmen, students, visionaries and even adventurers rallied round the new champion of the Jews. In the two last-named categories the outstanding examples were both non-Jews. The visionary was chaplain to the British Embassy in Vienna, the Reverend Hechler. His hobby was collecting Bibles and models of the ancient Temple of Jerusalem, and he had written a book prophesying that Palestine would once again become Israel in about 1897. Hechler became an enthusiastic supporter, and it was through his good offices that Herzl got in touch with the Grand Duke of Baden and, through him, with the Kaiser. The adventurer was the Ritter von Nevlinski, an impoverished Polish nobleman who had been compelled, through debt, to give up what had looked like being a brilliant diplomatic career. He proved to be of great use to Herzl and taught him much, but Herzl never felt quite sure of him, and alternately despised and respected him.

Stimulated by so much criticism, and encouraged by so much enthusiastic support, Herzl decided on action. In the introduction to his pamphlet he had stated that with its publication he considered his task completed. Happily he changed his mind and did not rest on his laurels. In the eight years of his short life that still remained he succeeded in establishing the Zionist movement as a political force.

[1] Max Nordau was a famous writer and journalist, and was Paris correspondent of the *Vossische Zeitung* when Herzl held the same position with the *Neue Freie Presse*.

It was not long before Herzl realized that his Jewish State was not going to be brought into being by the generosity of rich Jews. It was this early approach of Herzl to the problem which the youthful Weizmann had considered so unrealistic and misguided. The rich Jews, or most of them, were not anxious to get involved in any political plan for the re-establishment of Israel as the Jewish National Home.

A visit to England by Herzl to obtain support from leading British Jews met with no success, although Herzl was given a warm reception at a mass meeting held in Whitechapel. Before he reached Paris, Colonel Goldsmith, one of the British Jewish leaders, had warned Baron Edmond de Rothschild against Herzl, who intended to seek an interview with the French head of the Rothschild family. Consequently this interview, also, proved to be abortive. Edmond de Rothschild refused to take over the leadership of world Zionism, and regarded the whole idea of setting up a Jewish State by political means as highly dangerous. He feared that it would only arouse hostility against the Jews, and he preferred his own idea of gradual colonization. Weizmann appears to have shared this view, to some extent, for he has written, 'To me Zionism was something organic which had to grow like a plant, had to be watched, watered, and nursed if it was to reach maturity. I did not believe that things could be done in a hurry.'

The support which Herzl had received throughout from ordinary people and the cold shoulder given him by the wealthy, more assimilated Jews, convinced him that the Jewish question must be taken away 'from the control of the benevolent individual', and he decided, therefore, to convene a world-wide congress which should meet at stated intervals to discuss and formulate policy and to establish an elected body to execute such policy in the interval between the congresses. Simultaneously he founded a new official journal named Die Welt.

The suggestion of a congress met with almost universal support, and in Basle, because the Jewish community of Munich objected to it being held in their own city, the First Zionist Congress opened on Sunday, 29 August 1897. Before the great day arrived, however, Herzl had put in a lot of hard work, for he was determined that the Congress should be a success and it could, so easily, be a failure. As the hour drew near there was a feeling of great excitement and an air of expectancy, for no

7

one knew exactly what was going to happen. Some were afraid lest things might be said and done which would cause dissension among the different Zionist camps. Some were anxious lest Russia should become alarmed, Baron de Rothschild antagonized, or the orthodox community affronted.

Herzl, however, sensed all these perils and avoided all the pitfalls. As his biographer has written, 'He saw all the difficulties clearly. He had to go forward, and at the same time take into consideration the most extraordinary diversity of interests and viewpoints. He had to avoid offending the orthodox Jews; but he must also keep pace with the free-thinking Liberals. He had to take into account the patriotic sentiments of the assimilationists and half-assimilationists, whose support he would like to win; he also had to bear in mind the views of the Christian Churches with regard to the Holy Places. And in all this he had to stand by his principles, if he was not to compromise his aims. His natural moderation and self-control were put to the utmost test. It may be said that the difficult task could not have been carried out more skilfully than it was.'[1]

The Congress declared itself to be the chief organ of the Zionist movement and adopted the following plan of action:

The aim of Zionism is to create for the Jewish people a home in Palestine secured by public law.[2] The Congress contemplates the following means to the attainment of this end:

(1) The promotion, on suitable lines, of the colonization of Palestine by Jewish agricultural and industrial workers.

(2) The organization and binding together of the whole of Jewry by means of appropriate institutions, local and international, in accordance with the laws of each country.

(3) The strengthening and fostering of Jewish national sentiment and consciousness.

(4) Preparatory steps towards obtaining government consent, where necessary, to the attainment of the aim of Zionism.

This form of words was not arrived at without much argument and considerable compromise. Where there was vagueness, it was intentional. 'Home' was deliberately used instead of 'State', for it was

---

[1] *Theodor Herzl* by Alex Bein, p. 228.

[2] The words used in Herzl's speech were *offentlich rechtlich*, the literal translation of which is 'openly legal'.

thought that the Turkish Government would not relish the latter word. But Herzl was well content. He had wanted agreement and he had got it. He had not lost the substance for the shadow. The Congress had produced a policy, a programme, an executive committee, a flag, and even a national anthem. It was no mean achievement, and it had put Zionism on the map.

CHAPTER II

After the Congress

HERZL lost no time in getting down to work for there was much to be done. Being finally persuaded that it was a waste of time trying to enlist the support of rich Jews for his programme, even those who had given generously towards Jewish colonization in Palestine, he decided to approach those in power. Failing to get an audience with the Sultan of Turkey, Abdul Hamid, he succeeded in 1898 in having two audiences with the German Emperor.

At their first meeting in Constantinople the Kaiser appeared to be favourably disposed, but there does not seem to be any doubt that this was, at any rate, partly due to the fact that he found the prospect of getting rid of some of his Jewish subjects, by emigration to Palestine, not entirely unattractive. At their second meeting, however, which took place in Palestine a fortnight later, the atmosphere was several degrees cooler, and in a Court communiqué which was issued to the Press after its conclusion the audience was dismissed in one depressingly non-committal paragraph. 'Later the Kaiser received . . . a Jewish deputation which presented him with an album of pictures of the Jewish colonies in Palestine. In reply to an address by the leader of the deputation His Majesty remarked that he viewed with benevolent interest all efforts directed towards the improvement of agriculture in Palestine so long as these accorded with the welfare of the Turkish Empire, and were conducted in a spirit of complete respect for the sovereignty of the Sultan.'

Herzl had gone to Turkey straight from the Second Zionist Congress which had again been held in Basle. That much ground had been covered by the movement during the twelve months' interval was evident by the increased number of delegates who attended and the new groups which some of them represented. Among the new delegates was Chaim Weizmann, then only twenty-four years old. Furthermore, and this was considered an encouraging sign, the Russian Zionists were strongly represented.

Herzl had insisted, as early as the previous November, that the movement must have a financial organization. 'It must be liberated', he wrote in *Die Welt*, 'from the graciousness of benefactors and the kindness of foundations.' There were many others who shared this view, and when a resolution was proposed at the Congress to set up a bank for this very purpose it was carried with enthusiasm.

Nevertheless, there were disappointments as well as successes, and a number of other subjects were, much to Herzl's disgust, bitterly contested. He deplored the tendency 'to bring division into the national ideal' while it was still in its infancy, and he warned the delegates of the dangers of internecine strife. This was not the first time that such a warning had been necessary, and it was not to be the last.

Although, on the whole, he appeared to have been satisfied with the results obtained, the words with which Herzl wound up the last session of the Second Congress had not such a ring of confidence as was sounded at the first. 'We have set out,' he said. 'The moral wandering of the Jews has begun. Whither will it lead us? Into better times let us hope.'

After his two meetings with the Kaiser, Herzl worked hard to obtain an audience with the Sultan, but when this eventually materialized in May 1901 nothing concrete came out of it, and a second meeting in the following year produced no better results.

During the Fifth Congress, which was held in December of the same year, Herzl ran into even stormier weather than at the Third and Fourth. Neither had been exactly plain sailing. Nothing spectacular having been achieved during the past four years the Russians had begun to grow impatient and wanted to see some results.

Although there had been considerable opposition at the last three Congresses there had, so far, been no official opposition. Now, however, some of the malcontents decided to form one, and it was in this way that the Democratic-Zionist Fraction was formed. One of its members, who later earned the gratitude of world Jewry for the great part he played in bringing the Balfour Declaration into being, and became

Israel's first President, was Weizmann. The Fraction, as it was commonly called, wanted the leadership of the movement to be more democratic and desired cultural activity to be pursued throughout the Diaspora.[1] The accent was on youth. Before the Congress disbanded this new group showed, in no uncertain manner, that it was determined to get its own way or know the reason why. As a protest against what they considered high-handed action by Herzl its members all left the hall and remained outside in high dudgeon for at least an hour. The group doubtless thought that it ought to impress the Congress at the earliest possible moment that it was a new force in the movement to be reckoned with, but it was a rather childish exhibition of temper, and although an open break was avoided, due entirely to Herzl's tact and forbearance, it would be useless to deny that the group's behaviour on that occasion left rather a nasty taste in his mouth. Nevertheless, this Congress was not without its achievements, for it saw the establishment of the Jewish National Fund for the purchase of land in Palestine for the Jewish people and completed the structure of the Zionist Organization.

Meanwhile, despite earlier disappointments, Herzl had not given up all hope of winning one of the British branch of the Rothschild family over to the idea of a Jewish State. At that time Lord Rothschild distrusted alike both the old Zionists and the new. Nevertheless, he was buying land for the Jews in Palestine. The opportunity for an interview with him came with Herzl's visit to London in 1902 to give evidence before the Royal Commission on Alien Immigration. Lord Rothschild was the son of Lionel Rothschild, the first Jew to sit in the British Parliament. He was not, therefore, predisposed to anything which, in his opinion, might endanger the hard-won emancipation of the Jews in the British Isles. He was the head of the Rothschild banking firm, one of the Directors of the Bank of England and President of the United Synagogue, a man of great power and influence and a pre-eminent figure in English Jewry. He had, hitherto, refused to meet Herzl whom he regarded as a demagogue, and he had even opposed Herzl being called to give evidence before the Royal Commission. His only reason for granting Herzl an interview on this occasion was so that he could try to prevent him making any dangerous statements to the Commission.

[1] Diaspora is the Jewish word for the Jews dispersed throughout the world.

The interview began stormily but, after lunch, it was resumed in a more friendly atmosphere. The question of Herzl's plan for a Jewish colony in British territory was then raised. Rothschild suggested Uganda, but Herzl said that for various reasons he could only use the Sinai Peninsula, Egyptian Palestine or Cyprus. To Herzl's surprise Rothschild expressed agreement with these suggestions.[1] After he had explained his plan to Rothschild regarding Sinai, El-Arish and Cyprus he submitted it next day to the Chairman of the Royal Commission, Lord James, who pointed out that it could only be carried out with the assistance of Lord Rothschild.

That same afternoon Herzl had another longer interview with Rothschild and put forward details of a colonization company for the development of those territories. Rothschild appeared to be seriously interested and asked for further particulars as he wanted to discuss it with the Secretary of State for the Colonies, Mr. Joseph Chamberlain.

Three days later, on 12 July, Herzl sent Rothschild, as requested, an outline of the plan for Chamberlain together with details of the financial aspect. With it Herzl sent this letter: 'To avoid all misunderstanding, now and for the future, I wish to make it clear that I have submitted this plan only because you are against Palestine. You are the greatest effective force that the Jews have had since their dispersion, and I consider it my duty to place my advice at your disposal if you are at all interested in doing something for our unfortunates. . . . But apart from this human interest of mine there exists also a political interest. A great Jewish settlement in the eastern Mediterranean strengthens our position in regard to Palestine. . . . Whether I myself can co-operate in the carrying out of this plan, i.e. whether I can place the Zionist Organization at its disposal depends on the decision of my party.'[2] Rothschild required more time to examine the Sinai plan more closely, particularly as regards the financial requirements.

A week after his visit to England had ended Herzl left for Constantinople, having been summoned by the Sultan. His friend and colleague, Wolffsohn, went with him. Their reception was friendly, Herzl was told to consider himself as the Sultan's guest and a Court carriage was

---

[1] This account of the interview is given in *Theodor Herzl* by Alex Bein. Unfortunately it is impossible to check it as there are no Rothschild papers. They were all burned.

[2] *Theodor Herzl* by Alex Bein, pp. 330–1.

placed at his disposal. But the visit proved fruitless and was summed up by Herzl in *Die Welt* in the following words. 'The negotiations have again led to no results. However . . . contact has by no means been broken off. On the contrary we may still hope that the advantages which would accrue from a publicly recognized, legally secured settlement of the Jews in accord with our plan will still, at some later date, be appreciated by the Turkish Government. The Zionist Organization must, meanwhile, prepare itself for that moment, our propaganda must be carried on unceasingly, and the material means accumulated. The more capable of action our movement becomes, the sooner and more certainly shall we reach our goal.'

Nevertheless, it seemed clear that the direct road to Palestine was not yet open, but there was still a way round via El-Arish. If the Jews became established there Herzl thought that the Sultan might change his views, for they would then be his neighbours with whom it might be as well to have friendly relations.

It was not long, however, before Herzl received a rather cold douche from Lord Rothschild who wrote warning him against being over-ambitious and hasty. The idea of Palestine was too far-fetched; it was a dream, a castle in the air. Herzl replied that if Rothschild only had an inkling of the unspeakable conditions in which many Jews were living, particularly in Eastern Europe, he would be more sympathetic. But Rothschild still preferred his own idea of scattered settlement; 'otherwise', he wrote, 'there will only arise a new ghetto with all the disadvantages of a ghetto.'

All the way along the line the luckless Herzl continued to be attacked from both flanks by the rich assimilated Jews, on the one hand, who thought little of Zionism anyhow although they were prepared to be philanthropic to their less fortunate brethren, and on the other hand by the young dissidents who had started the Fraction.

Few, if any, are likely to dispute Herzl's lasting contribution to the Zionist movement, namely, the creation of a central parliamentary association. Even those who were the sharpest critics of his leadership and, in their own opinion, fair critics, have stated definitely and categorically that this, Herzl's cardinal achievement, must never be forgotten.

It may be wondered why these men were so critical. Weizmann himself has given one of the reasons in his autobiography.[1] 'We were not revolutionaries, but it would have been even more inaccurate to call us reactionaries. We were a struggling group of young academicians, without power and without outside support; but we had a definite outlook of our own. We did not like the note of elegance and pseudoworldliness which characterized official Zionism, the dress suits and frock coats and fashionable dresses. On me the formalism of the Zionist Congresses made a painful impression, especially after one of my periodic visits to the wretched and oppressed Russian Jewish masses. Actually it was all very modest, but to us it smacked of artificiality, extravagance and the *haut monde*. It did not bespeak for us the democracy, simplicity and earnestness of the movement, and we were uncomfortable.'

It is difficult today to get under the skin of those young men, and the temptation to think that this discomfort of which Weizmann has written may have been partly due to an inferiority complex should, perhaps, be resisted.

The group, however, consistently objected to what they considered Herzl's penchant for running after the rich and powerful. It was not merely because they thought that this was a waste of time, although they did, but also because, to use Weizmann's own words, 'it was accompanied most unfortunately but perhaps inevitably by a shift of the leadership to the right. Herzl played to the rich and the powerful, to Jewish bankers and financiers, to the Grand Duke of Baden, to Kaiser Wilhelm II, to the Sultan of Turkey and later to the British Foreign Secretary. We, on the other hand, had little faith in the benevolence of the mighty.' This touching belief on the part of so many Zionist leaders that salvation could only come from the Left was to receive a rude shock forty-three years later. Nevertheless it was, perhaps, natural that the Fraction, some of whose leaders were Russian Jews, should hold such views for they came from a land where, as Herzl surprisingly wrote in a typically British under-statement, success was 'peculiarly difficult for the Jews'.

It has already been stated that in Herzl's original concept of a Jewish State the question of venue was unimportant. Soon, however, he became convinced that to the majority of Jews a National Home

[1] *Trial and Error.*

15

meant Palestine, the 'land of their fathers'. After his visit to that country in 1898 this conviction strengthened, and it was of Palestine that he wrote in his famous novel *Altneuland*.[1]

This novel when it appeared was widely criticized. Asher Ginsberg,[2] a Jewish writer and Hebrew scholar living in Hampstead, and an untiring critic of Herzl and all his works, condemned it because it 'lacked Jewish character'. The old-new land which Herzl so graphically described was, in Ginsberg's opinion, 'a colourless Utopia', devoid of the Hebrew language and literature. Nevertheless, whatever the critics may have thought, it was prophetic in its assessment of the technical development which is such a remarkable feature of the State of Israel today. One of the characters in the book, David Litvak, describing this development to a number of new immigrants, is made to say: 'The real creators of Altneuland were the irrigation engineers. Drainage of swamps, irrigation of the desert regions, and above all the system of power-houses—there was the answer.'

All this difference of opinion as to what kind of place the new State was to be, a spiritual and cultural vacuum or a vibrant, vital reality, was to come to the boil in the following year at the Sixth Zionist Congress over the question of Uganda. In the autumn of 1902 Herzl had a meeting with Joseph Chamberlain arranged by Leopold Greenberg. This interview took place on 22 October and had far-reaching results. Chamberlain was then Colonial Secretary and had been since 1895, retaining the post when Lord Salisbury's Government was replaced by that of Mr. Balfour. Chamberlain had previously been a Liberal. He had shown considerable understanding of the Jewish problem and, in a letter to the *Roumanian Bulletin* in July 1902, he had indicated that he regarded the Jewish question as a national one. Chamberlain was, therefore, receptive ground for Herzl who did not have to waste much time on preliminaries. He explained that the ultimate objective was Palestine and on this he was still negotiating with the Sultan of Turkey. He had not yet given up all hope, but parleying with an Oriental was never a quick and easy task. 'I have time to negotiate,' he said, 'but my people have not. Many of them in Eastern Europe are starving and live in wretched conditions. I must bring them immediate help.' Herzl

[1] *Old-New Land.*
[2] More generally known as Ahad Ha'am.

16

then submitted his plan for the colonization of Cyprus and the Sinai Peninsula, including El-Arish, by Jewish settlers under a Jewish administration. Chamberlain replied that only Cyprus came within his jurisdiction; the Foreign Office dealt with the Sinai Peninsula. Cyprus was not hopeful. Both the Greeks and Mohammedans would, for once, unite over that and Chamberlain, as Colonial Secretary, would have to support them.

Chamberlain, however, appeared interested in El-Arish but pointed out that difficulties would be encountered there as well. Herzl emphasized that there was unoccupied land in El-Arish and Sinai. If England could give them that she would receive the gratitude of ten million Jews. The Colonial Secretary said that a great deal would depend on the attitude of Lord Cromer, the British Consul-General in Egypt who was also Vice-Regent of that country. Meanwhile, he would arrange a meeting between Herzl and the Foreign Secretary, Lord Lansdowne, if Herzl could come back the following day. Everything was arranged as promised, and when Herzl called on Chamberlain next day he was told that the interview had been fixed for 4.30 p.m. and that the 'way had been prepared'. All Herzl had to do was to put the whole matter to him and reassure Lord Lansdowne that he was not contemplating a Jameson raid on Palestine from El-Arish.[1] Before the interview with Lord Lansdowne Herzl had lunched with Lord Rothschild who was astounded when he heard of the meeting between his guest and Chamberlain and the impending talks with the Foreign Secretary.

Herzl's interview with Lord Lansdowne passed off very successfully. The Foreign Secretary listened carefully and, at the end of their meeting, asked Herzl to let him have a written memorandum. Meanwhile Lord Lansdowne would find out what Lord Cromer thought about it. Herzl arranged with the Foreign Secretary that his friend and confidential agent, Greenberg, should go and see Lord Cromer immediately, and Lord Lansdowne promised to arrange this. Greenberg saw Lord Cromer and met with some success, and was able to report in person to Herzl that Lord Cromer had been very friendly at their talks, and had given

[1] On 29 December 1895 Dr. Jameson launched his famous 'Raid' on Johannesburg. Apart from its dismal failure, it had been a great embarrassment to H.M. Government. Chamberlain was then Colonial Secretary, and the Government denounced and repudiated it. Jameson was eventually tried by a British criminal court and duly convicted and sentenced.

him all the necessary information, and a letter of introduction to the Egyptian Prime Minister. Herzl's plan had been placed before Lord Cromer and not turned down.

Both he and the Egyptian Prime Minister, however, had reminded Greenberg of the miserable failure of an attempted Jewish colony started in 1891 near the ancient city of Midian. There was, in fact, little resemblance between it and the new plan, but it proved, in the end, to be a definite stumbling-block, and the memorandum which Herzl had sent to Lord Lansdowne met with an unfavourable response. The scheme fell through because, in the judgment of Lord Cromer, a large enough supply of water could not be spared. The Commission which Herzl had got together to visit the district and report on its suitability had observed that although, under existing conditions, the country was quite unsuitable for settlers from European countries, in the event of a sufficient water-supply being forthcoming the conditions of soil, hygiene and climate were such that part of what was then a desert would be capable of supporting a considerable population. In short, the whole question was one of water-supply.

It was about this time, also, that Joseph Chamberlain first suggested Uganda, but until the negotiations about Sinai and El-Arish were concluded, Herzl did not want to consider any place so far removed from Palestine. He did not have to wait long, however, for these negotiations to break down. The Egyptian Government decided, on the advice of the irrigation expert of the Anglo-Egyptian Administration, that the quantity of water needed was so great that they could not permit a diversion of it from the Nile. Furthermore, the laying of pipes would interfere with the Suez Canal traffic for several weeks.

It was just before the final breakdown of the negotiations that Western Europe began to hear of the terrible pogroms which went on in Russia during Easter week. In one town, Kishineff, under the eyes of the city's administration, a mob which had been systematically incited to violence with anti-Semitic slogans carried out the first of a series of bloody pogroms which were to sweep across the country. The reports which reached the Western world of barbarity, rape and bloodlust filled everyone with horror. In Kishineff itself forty-five Jews were murdered, six hundred seriously wounded, five hundred slightly wounded, and fifteen hundred houses plundered and destroyed.

In spite of this disappointment in Egypt Herzl decided to continue the negotiations for El-Arish alone, which would not need any Nile water, and to continue to ask for Cyprus. He sent a message to Chamberlain asking him once more, having regard to the serious situation in Russia which had started another wave of Jewish emigration, to take up the question of Cyprus. Herzl's idea was that colonization could start there and later, if the resistance of the Egyptian Government were withdrawn, it could be extended to the Sinai Peninsula.

On 20 May Greenberg had an hour's talk with the Colonial Secretary who said that in principle he was prepared to help. Kishineff had demonstrated how right Herzl had been to demand regulated emigration of the Jews from Eastern Europe. But where were they to go? Greenberg reminded Chamberlain that although the ultimate goal was Palestine, El-Arish and Cyprus could be used in this emergency. Chamberlain was quite definite about it being a sheer waste of time to approach Lord Cromer a second time. Cyprus, too, was out of the question. Once again, however, he mentioned Uganda. It had a good climate and other favourable conditions for the creation of a new colony of at least a million Jews. He told Greenberg that when he had previously mentioned it to Herzl, it had not been greeted with enthusiasm. Chamberlain fully realized the importance of Palestine in Jewish minds and, for that reason, understood the significance of the El-Arish plan. Nevertheless, he said, 'If nothing comes of it I hope that Herzl will take my other suggestion seriously.' The colony, he promised, would be granted self-administration and the Governor could be a Jew. At that moment the territory was under the Foreign Office but could easily be transferred to the Colonial Office. Greenberg duly reported the details of the interview to Herzl and stated that he thought that it would be no small gain from a political point of view to be able to say that the British Government had offered them a place of refuge. Herzl by telegram assented to this view.

Without delay he had a draft charter drawn up for Uganda. It was to be called New Palestine and to be established 'for the encouragement of the Jewish national idea and the promotion of the welfare of the Jewish people'. The concession was to be offered to the Jewish Colonial Trust. Max Nordau, who had been asked by Herzl to prepare an address for the coming Zionist Congress on the immigration question, was not enamoured with the idea of Uganda. He foresaw, more accurately than Herzl, the tremendous opposition which the scheme would arouse amongst the Jews from Eastern Europe who were so strictly brought up in Jewish tradition and history.

It was not long before Herzl heard from Lord Lansdowne who wrote to say he understood that the Jewish Colonial Trust wished to send a number of gentlemen to the East Africa Protectorate to find out on the spot whether there was any vacant land suitable for the purpose in question. If that were so, Lord Lansdowne would be very happy to give them every facility to enable them to discuss with His Majesty's Commission the possibility of meeting the view which might be expressed at the forthcoming Zionist Congress in regard to the conditions upon which a settlement might be possible. If a site could be found which the Trust and the Commissioner considered suitable and which commended itself to H.M. Government, Lord Lansdowne would be prepared to entertain favourably proposals for the establishment of a Jewish colony or settlement on conditions which would enable them to observe their national customs. Lansdowne also offered, subject to the consent of the relevant officials, a Jewish governorship and internal autonomy, thus acknowledging the undertaking previously given by Chamberlain. This letter from Lord Lansdowne had been sent in reply to a request from Greenberg asking for an answer to Herzl's outline of a charter for East Africa, so that it could be laid before the impending Zionist Congress which was due to open in August.

On 21 August Herzl reported the offer to the Actions Committee. He was bitterly disappointed at the Committee's reception of it and made a note in his diary to the effect that it did not even occur to the Committee that his hard work and success in England and Russia 'merited so much as a word or a smile of thanks'.

As it was obviously going to be a controversial issue the Actions Committee decided to adjourn until the following day when it would be discussed and put to the vote. Before it reassembled, however, Herzl called a number of the Zionist leaders to an emergency meeting, amongst whom were a number of prominent Russians, his friend and colleague, David Wolffsohn, and the English writer, Israel Zangwill. He produced Lord Lansdowne's letter and the impression created was tremendous. Nevertheless, an agitated discussion ensued for four hours during which Herzl left the meeting so as not to influence the other participants by his presence. When the Actions Committee met again in the evening it appears that there was no formal discussion of the East African project, but Herzl concluded that he was empowered to lay the offer before the Congress.

When it was announced by Herzl to the full Congress at its first session it was greeted by a storm of applause, for everyone appreciated the magnanimity of the British offer. As the Congress progressed, however, considerable opposition developed, especially from the Russians, and this grew in intensity throughout its length. Although Herzl had emphasized in his opening speech that Uganda was not intended to be a substitution for Palestine, but a temporary stepping-stone, it made little impression on the delegates.

There was little cause for such antagonism at that stage for the only resolution before the Congress on the subject concerned the despatch of a commission of investigation to carry out a survey, and it was by no means a foregone conclusion that it would report back favourably. It also seemed inexplicable to Herzl that amongst the principal Russian opponents of the scheme were included the delegates from Kishineff which had been the scene of a recent pogrom although, of course, he knew that they were against it, because they considered it a break in tradition and a reversal of the 'Basle programme'. They suspected that it was a compromise withdrawal from what they regarded as a fundamental principle. Having regard to the terrible persecution then taking place in Russia, it would have been reasonable to expect most of the delegates to have taken the view that half a loaf was better than no bread, particularly if the full ration was to be issued later.

Herzl, who was physically handicapped throughout the Congress by recurring heart attacks, fought like a Trojan to carry the day and did succeed in carrying a resolution entrusting to a commission of nine the task of 'co-operating with the smaller Actions Committee . . . in sending an expedition to the territory to be investigated'. When this resolution was put to the vote the majority of Russians voted against it and about a hundred other delegates abstained. Nevertheless, it was carried by 117 votes. All the 'Noes' then left the hall in a body and went into private conclave. Pocketing his pride, Herzl went and spoke to them, and on the following day a compromise was at last reached, and a declaration was made in open Congress by the dissidents to the effect that their mass withdrawal had not been intended as a hostile demonstration but was 'the spontaneous expression of a profound spiritual shock'.

The discontent, however, still rankled, for the Russians were not satisfied with Herzl's assurance that, despite appearances to the contrary, Palestine remained the main and ultimate goal.

The extent to which tense feelings had been worked up was seen, four months later, when an attempt was made on Nordau's life. He had never been heart and soul behind the Uganda project although he had supported it at the Congress principally out of loyalty to his old friend and leader. Nevertheless, on 19 December, at a ball organized by the Zionist Society of Paris, a young student, crying 'Death to Nordau, the East African', fired two shots at him at point-blank range, both of which happily missed the great orator. That the miscreant was later found to be mentally unbalanced does not disguise the degree of heat which had been engendered in the prolonged struggle by those whose slogan was 'Palestine or nowhere'.

It is hardly surprising, therefore, that Nordau wrote to Herzl on 20 December: 'Yesterday evening I got an instalment of the debt of gratitude which the Jewish people owes me for my selfless labours on its behalf. I say this without bitterness, only with sorrow. How unhappy is our people to be able to do such deeds.' In his reply to this letter Herzl wrote: 'The would-be murderer's revolver was loaded in Russia.' In a leading article in Herzl's paper, *Die Welt*, some strong words were used, but they can hardly be said to have been unjustified. The writer was Dr. Werner. 'Although the shots may have been fired by a demented man', he wrote, 'who was therefore only partly responsible for his act, no such mitigating observation can be made concerning the unscrupulous agitation which had heated his faith to the point of fanaticism and thus made him capable of such action. These people have assumed a frightful responsibility and have inflicted untold harm on Zionism.'

The attempted crime caused a profound stir throughout the Zionist world, and the anti-East Africans were loudly denounced as traitors and accused, not unjustly, of sowing the seeds of disunity in the movement.

Herzl might well have been spared all this turmoil, bitterness and disappointment, as the whole project eventually fell through, for the Commission reported, in May 1905, that the territory in question was unsuitable for any large number of agricultural settlers. Mercifully he did not have to suffer this last humiliation, for he had died ten months earlier. He had worn himself out, for, as he himself said, he had given his heart's blood for his people. Let another great leader, Chaim Weizmann, who was both an admirer and severe critic of the man, speak his epitaph. 'He was the first—without rival—among Western leaders.... With his magnificent gifts and his complete devotion, he rendered incalculable service to the cause. He remains the classical figure in Zionism.'[1]

In his will Herzl had asked to be buried quietly in Vienna next to his father 'and to remain there until the Jewish people shall transport my remains to Palestine'. Fifty years later his wish was realized. His body was flown from Vienna in a plane belonging to the Israeli Air Force and laid to rest on Mount Herzl, a hill on the outskirts of Jerusalem now become a national shrine. A few years before he died he had written: 'God breaks the instruments that have served His purpose. . . . No Moses ever enters the Promised Land.'

★ ★ ★ ★ ★

Disunity amongst the Zionists did not end with the death of Herzl, and a divergency, not so much of objective but of the method of its attainment, continued between the two opposing groups who became known as 'political' and 'practical' Zionists.

The 'politicals', on the one hand, took the view that the primary objective should be to obtain political guarantees for the aims of the Basle Charter before proceeding with further Jewish settlement in Palestine which was, after all, part of the Ottoman Empire, and where the purchase of land for this purpose was forbidden by law. The 'practicals', on the other hand, took what Dr. Weizmann, by then a leading member of the Democratic Fraction, called 'a more organic view of Zionism'. The 'practicals' were not, he maintained, opposed to Zionist political activity, but they considered that, by itself, it was not enough and they thought that it should go hand in hand with settlement

---

[1] *Trial and Error*, p. 75.

of the Jews on Palestinian land. In this way a cultural renaissance would take place, including the revival of Hebrew as a living language, which the Russian Zionists thought was most important, and of Hebrew literature. This, they considered, would have a spiritual influence and a unifying effect.

Dr. Weizmann was particularly keen on this cultural aspect and, above all, he desired the establishment of a Hebrew University. This may well have dated from his student days in Berlin where the idea, then it could only have been a dream, was first mooted by a Heidelberg professor and struck Weizmann's fancy and stirred the Jewish student youth. Whatever its origin, he pursued the idea with never-flagging energy until his death, and on 1 April 1925 had the pride and satisfaction of seeing the Hebrew University of Jerusalem, magnificently sited on Mount Scopus, formally opened by Lord Balfour.

It was most important that these two separate and, to some extent, opposing streams of endeavour should be canalized into one motive force. The first steps that were taken to join these two bodies together was when an administrative committee was formed, with Herzl's old friend and firm supporter, David Wolffsohn, in the chair, composed of three 'politicals' and three 'practicals'. This Committee remained in existence until the Eighth Zionist Congress assembled in 1907 when the 'practicals' gained ascendancy and a new Presidium, as it was called, was formed under the chairmanship of a Professor Warburg, an agricultural expert who had been one of the members of the Wolffsohn Committee.

It was Weizmann's personality that brought about this change, and the opinions which he expressed during the Congress fell on the very receptive ears of the Socialist Zionists and the young pioneers, and found wide acceptance. He told the delegates that even if Herzl's dream charter were possible it would be without value unless it rested on the very soil of Palestine, on a Jewish population rooted in that soil, and on institutions established by and for Palestinian Jews. A charter was a mere scrap of paper. It could not be brought into being by force and it could only be made realistic by work on the spot. It was, of course, necessary for the Zionists to keep their case before world opinion, he told the Congress, but the presentation of their case would not really be effective unless there was immigration, colonization, and education.

In order to further the settlement of Jews in Palestine a Dr. Ruppin[1] was chosen to open an office in Jaffa and organize a Colonial Department to give advice and information to prospective immigrants, and assistance in the purchase of land.

Jewish settlers had been coming to Palestine in ever-increasing numbers since the middle of the nineteenth century. Most of those who had immigrated during the last quarter of the century had acquired land along the western coastal strip north of Jaffa, and they were the pioneers of the citrus fruits industry. During the first decade of the twentieth century a new crop of settlements had sprung up in lower Galilee.

Until about 1908 most of the money to buy this land for these immigrants had been provided by Baron Edmond de Rothschild. After that date the Zionist Organization came into the picture and, up to the outbreak of World War I, many new small colonies were formed and devoted to mixed farming and, particularly, dairy produce, market gardening and poultry. By 1914 there were some twelve thousand Jewish settlers in the country occupying not less than a hundred thousand acres, and organized in forty separate agricultural areas.

There had also been a large increase in the total Jewish population of Palestine. In 1882 it was little more than thirty-four thousand, and was more or less confined to the four old cities of Jerusalem, Hebron, Safad and Tiberias, and few of them used Hebrew as an everyday language. By 1914 the population had risen to about ninety thousand and, with the increase of colonization, Hebrew was revived and gradually became the common tongue of the Jewish settlers, as it remains today the official State language.

The basis for a Jewish National Home was thus enlarged culturally and materially. A temporary halt was soon to be made, however, due to circumstances entirely beyond the Jews' control. Little did they know that Palestine and the rest of the world was on the eve of great events, or that the disruption of the Ottoman Empire would, before many years had passed, bring about the fulfilment of ancient prophecy and the realization of Herzl's Jewish State.

[1] Dr. Ruppin later was put in charge of colonization as an official of the Jewish Agency until his death in 1943. He was the founder of Tel-Aviv, now the commercial capital of Israel.

CHAPTER III

World War I

WHEN Germany violated the neutrality of Belgium in August 1914, thus starting the First World War, there can have been few, if any, who foresaw that a year before it ended, the Jewish claim for a National Home in Palestine would have been officially and publicly recognized by one of the great Allied Powers.

Still less did this seem possible when, after Turkey entered the war on the side of the Central Powers on 31 October, the Turkish military commander in Syria and Palestine, Jemal Pasha, began a reign of oppression and persecution against Arabs and Jews alike. Against the Jewish population, who were apparently suspected by Jemal Pasha of working underground for the Allies, special measures were taken, and all Jews who were allied nationals were given the alternative of becoming naturalized Turks and serving in the Ottoman Army, or being deported. That is why there are some Israelis alive today who fought, when young men, on Germany's side as Turkish soldiers.

It is often said that Great Britain's need for a new policy in the Middle East, after the collapse of her traditional alignment with the Turks, was the main factor in her decision to support the Zionist policy in World War I. Lloyd George has said so although, as he has also said, many of those who supported the new policy which eventually led up to the Balfour Declaration, did so from conviction as well as expediency.

Before describing the events which led up to the British Government's decision to make the Balfour Declaration, and the negotiations which preceded it, it is necessary to consider:

(1) The secret treaties among the Allied Powers with regard to the division of the Ottoman Empire in the event of an Allied victory, and

(2) The famous correspondence in 1915 between the Sharif of Mecca and the British High Commissioner in Egypt, Sir Henry McMahon, concerning the terms upon which the Sharif would be prepared to stage an Arab revolt against their Turkish masters.

Turkey's declaration of war against the Allies was a resounding diplomatic defeat for Great Britain whose policy had for many years been to support Turkey as a counterpoise to Russia's designs on the Dardanelles and in order to maintain a friendly power east of the Suez Canal. Although German diplomats had worked patiently in Constantinople for years to bring this about, the British still hoped that Turkey would remain neutral in the event of a European war. No longer could they rely on Turkey to protect British interests in the Near and Middle East; there was even a danger that Syria and Palestine might be made the base for a Turco-German attack on the Suez Canal.

There was also some apprehension lest an attempt might be made by the Sultan Caliph to proclaim a Holy War. Steps were, therefore, taken to guard against these two contingencies. Troops were concentrated in Egypt, diplomatic negotiations were opened with Hussein, the Sharif of Mecca, and an exchange of letters took place between him and Sir Henry McMahon, regarding the terms on which the Sharif was willing to join with Great Britain against Turkey.

It was the Sharif, however, who made the first move, and on 14 July 1915 he made definite proposals and defined the area in respect of which he suggested that the British should recognize Arab independence. The area mentioned was too extensive in British eyes, and in his reply Sir Henry stated that 'it would appear to be premature to consume our time discussing such details in the heat of war', particularly as much of the area was still under British occupation, and many of the Arabs who lived there were lending their arms to German and Turk alike, to the new despoiler, and the old oppressor.

The tenor of the correspondence changed with the varying fortunes of war. In the months immediately preceding the dispatching of Hussein's first letter, a number of successes had attended British arms. In February 1915 the Turco-German attack on the Suez Canal had been decisively repulsed, and in April the Allied offensive in Gallipoli was

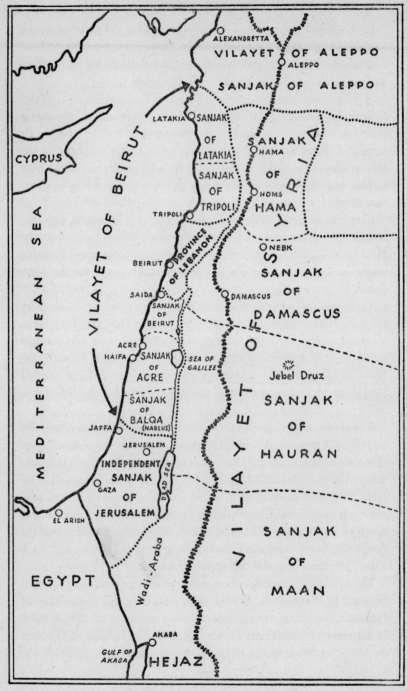

PALESTINE AND SYRIA IN 1915

progressing so well that the Arab world apprehended that Constantinople might fall in the near future.

When the Sharif received the British High Commissioner's reply at the end of August, however, the British attack on Achi Baba from Suvla Bay had broken down, and in his reply Hussein refused to modify his demands and the negotiations appeared to be in jeopardy. It became clear that the Arabs' price had gone up, and as Sir Henry had good reason to believe that their choice between the Allies and the Central Powers would be determined by the nature of British assurances as to their future independence, he wrote on 24 October what is often known as the 'Key' letter.

The interpretation of this letter is of considerable importance because, as Palestine was not explicitly excluded from the area in which the British promised to help the Arabs attain independence, the Arabs have been vigorously contending, ever since 1921, that the British assurance envisaged Palestine as an independent Arab country. The relevant paragraph of the Key letter read as follows:

The two districts of Mersina and Alexandretta, and the portions of Syria lying west of the districts of Damascus, Homs, Hama and Aleppo cannot be said to be purely Arab, and should be excluded from the proposed limits and boundaries. With the above modifications and without prejudice to our existing treaties with the Arab chiefs we accept these limits and boundaries.[1]

It is significant that the first occasion on which the above claim was made by the Arabs was more than five years after the conclusion of the Hussein–McMahon correspondence. Had they really believed in its genuineness they would, surely, not have waited so long before raising it. Frequent pronouncements upon the letter have been made from time to time by responsible British statesmen and by Sir Henry McMahon himself, and all without exception have declared categorically that no pledges were made to the Palestine Arabs.

Mr. Winston Churchill, speaking in the House of Commons on 11 July 1922 said: 'On that occasion the point of view of His Majesty's Government was explained to the Emir Feisal (son of the Sharif) who expressed himself as prepared to accept the statement that it had been the intention of His Majesty's Government to exclude Palestine. When

[1] Those proposed in the Sharif's first letter.

I assumed responsibility for Middle Eastern affairs I went carefully into the correspondence referred to, and my reading of it is the same as that of the Foreign Office, as was recently stated in the Declaration of British Policy in Palestine. I am quite satisfied that it was fully the intention of His Majesty's Government to exclude Palestine from the area of Arab independence as it was to exclude the more northern coastal tracts of Syria.'

The claim was also refuted in a White Paper published on 3 June in the same year.[1] 'It is not the case, as has been represented by the Arab Delegation, that during the war His Majesty's Government gave an undertaking that an independent national government should be at once established in Palestine. This representation mainly rests upon the letter dated 24 October 1915 from Sir Henry McMahon, His Majesty's High Commissioner in Egypt, to the Sharif of Mecca, now King Hussein of the Kingdom of the Hedjaz. That letter is quoted as conveying the promise to the Sharif of Mecca to recognize and support the independence of the Arabs within the territories proposed by him. But this promise was given subject to a reservation made in the same letter, which excluded from its scope, among other territories, the portions of Syria lying to the west of the district of Damascus. This reservation has always been regarded by His Majesty's Government as covering the Vilayet of Beirut and the independent Sanjak of Jerusalem. The whole of Palestine west of the Jordan was thus excluded from Sir Henry McMahon's pledge.'

Lord Milner, who had been a member of the War Cabinet, also speaking on the alleged promise to give independence to the Arabs in Palestine said: 'I was a party to the Balfour Declaration. I do not believe that it is inconsistent with any pledges which have been given to King Hussein or to anybody else. It is my conviction that when all the documents are published it will be clearly established that in the promises which we made to King Hussein a definite reservation was made of the country about which we are now speaking.'[2]

But it was not until 1937, after the publication of the Palestine Royal Commission's Report, that Sir Henry McMahon in a letter to the London *Times* removed all doubt as to the British Government's

---

[1] H.M.S.O. Command Paper 1700 (1922), p. 20. The Churchill White Paper.
[2] House of Lords Official Report, 27 June 1923. Debate on Palestine.

intention and the Sharif's understanding of it. Until then his silence
had been used to support the Arab argument.

Many references have been made in the Palestine Royal Commission Report
and in the course of recent Debates in both Houses of Parliament to the
'McMahon Pledge', especially to that portion of the pledge which concerns
Palestine, and of which one interpretation has been claimed by the Jews and
another by the Arabs.

It has been suggested to me that continued silence on the part of the giver of
that pledge may itself be misunderstood. I feel, therefore, called upon to make
some statement on the subject, but I will confine myself in doing so to the point
now at issue, i.e. whether that portion of Syria now known as Palestine was or
was not intended to be included in the territories in which the independence of
the Arabs was guaranteed in my pledge. I feel it my duty to state, and I do so
definitely and emphatically, that it was not intended by me in giving this pledge
to King Hussein to include Palestine in the area in which Arab independence was
promised. I had also every reason to believe at the time that the fact that
Palestine was not included in my pledge was well understood by King Hussein.

Furthermore, Sir Gilbert Clayton, a former Chief Secretary of Palestine, who was closely associated with McMahon, has said: 'I was in daily
touch with Sir Henry McMahon throughout the negotiations with
King Hussein, and I made the preliminary drafts of all the letters. I can
bear out his statement that it was never the intention that Palestine
should be included in the general pledge given to the Sharif. The intro-
ductory words of Sir Henry's letter were thought at the time, perhaps
erroneously, clearly to cover the point. It was, I think, obvious that the
peculiar interests involved in Palestine precluded any definite pledges
in regard to its future at so early a stage.'[1]

A statement was also made in the House of Commons on 21 July
1937 by the Colonial Secretary, then Mr. Ormsby-Gore,[2] who had
served in 1916 in the Arab Bureau in Cairo on Sir Henry McMahon's
staff. He rose to testify to the fact that it had never been in the mind of
anyone on that staff that Palestine west of the Jordan was in the area
within which the British Government then undertook to further the
cause of Arab independence. That this was so is proved by subsequent
events, as Mr. Ormsby-Gore explained. Immediately after the Arab
revolt and during the months that followed, the British Government

[1] House of Lords Official Report, 20 July 1937.
[2] Later Lord Harlech.

was advised in such matters principally by Sir Mark Sykes. After the McMahon correspondence, and the outbreak of the revolt in the Hedjaz, he was instructed by his Government to get in touch with the French and other Allied Governments in regard to the future of that part of the world. Negotiations were lengthy, with the result that England and France (France then having claimed the whole of Palestine) acceded to an arrangement which was embodied in the Sykes–Picot Agreement which is dealt with below.

From his intimate knowledge of the circumstances existing at that time Mr. Ormsby-Gore categorically stated: 'His Majesty's Government, neither then nor now, can or will admit that Palestine west of the Jordan was included in the pledge given to the Sharif, and they always had in mind the fact that special considerations must appertain in regard to the future governing of the Holy Land. The unique character of Palestine was recognized by the Arab Delegates to the Peace Conference. It is recognized all over the world.'

Still further light was thrown on this controversy in 1939 in a letter to the London *Times* published while the St. James's Palace Conference was in session. The writer was Colonel C. E. Vickery, who had been sent from Cairo in 1920 to visit King Hussein and had read the original copy of the letter from Sir Henry McMahon which had caused so much controversy.

The following are extracts from this letter:

It happened that the King had arrived at Jeddah the day before I received my instructions, and I asked for my audience which was at once accorded. It was not my custom to take an interpreter with me for these audiences and I was received by the King alone on the top story of his Jeddah house. For an hour or more I listened to the bitter complaints of King Hussein of the way he had been treated in defiance of pledged and written word; again and again I brought the discussion round to the 1915 letter and tried to provoke the Sharif into showing it to me.

It must have been at midday when I had been with him three hours . . . that the King suddenly clapped his hands and bade the slave who came in to bring his portfolio. This was done and unlocked by King Hussein himself. He fumbled through some papers and finally threw one at me, saying, 'Read this, oh light of my eye.' I read the letter through very slowly; it was not written in very scholarly Arabic and had no English translation in the margin, and it was quite evident that Palestine was not included in the proposals to the King. I can say most definitely that the whole of the King's demands were centred around Syria and only around Syria. . . . He stated most emphatically that he did not concern himself at all with Palestine and had no desire to have suzerainty over it for himself or his successors. He did, however, frequently and vehemently point out to me the following excerpt of the letter, and as it is to be published the accuracy of my memorandum can be established. [Here the sentence was set out in Arabic.] 'On behalf of the great British Government I accept your demands.' This may have been worded unfortunately, for there was no doubt in my mind that it referred to the requests for munitions of war which he demanded with great frequency. Nothing could persuade the Sharif that it did not refer to everything that he has asked for in the acquisition of territories to form the Arabian Empire which had inspired every waking moment of his life.

Finally, in February 1939, during the St. James's Palace Conference, which was attended by Arab and Jewish delegates, it was decided to set up a committee to consider 'the McMahon–Hussein correspondence' and to furnish the Conference with a report on it. In this report it was stated that 'Sir Henry McMahon never had any intention of including Palestine in the area of Arab independence: and furthermore never had any reason to suppose that his intention was not perfectly clear to the Sharif'. The committee also stated that it was evident 'that His Majesty's Government were not free to dispose of Palestine without regard for the wishes and interests of the inhabitants of Palestine', and that this fact 'must be taken into account in any attempt to estimate the responsibilities, which, upon any interpretation of the correspondence, His Majesty's Government have incurred towards those inhabitants as a result of the correspondence'.

Furthermore, Great Britain was not free in October 1915 to act in Palestine without regard to French interests, for at that time France was claiming the Mediterranean littoral as far south as the Egyptian border and as far east as Damascus, and it was not until the spring of 1916 that these extreme claims were modified as the result of the discussions culminating in the so-called Sykes–Picot Agreement referred to above. King Hussein must have realized the possibility, and even the extreme probability, of the existence of a French claim to Palestine even if he did not know it was a fact, and having regard to all the circumstances, including the extensive British and religious interests in Palestine, the wording of Sir Henry's vital letter of 24 October ought to have suggested to him, and to anyone else who read it, that Palestine was excluded from, or to put it at the very lowest, not manifestly included in the area of Arab independence.

It cannot be denied that the wording of the letter is not as specific and unmistakable as it was thought to be at the time. Nevertheless, the weight of evidence both direct and circumstantial supports the British contention that Palestine was excluded from the Arab territories which were promised independence.

*　　*　　*　　*　　*

Next to be considered are the Constantinople Agreement and the Sykes–Picot Agreement, both of which are of considerable interest for they provide further independent evidence that Palestine was excluded from any contemplated Arab State or confederation of Arab States.

The first negotiations took place between Russia, France and Great Britain, and later Italy, and the results of these diplomatic exchanges were embodied in the Constantinople Agreement. Russia had pressed for a decision on the Dardanelles very soon after the outbreak of hostilities, and in March 1915 the British agreed to Russia's annexation of Constantinople and control of the Straits, if the Allies won, subject to two specific conditions: namely that Russia should consent to supervision of certain zones in Persia, and to the establishment of an independent Moslem power in Arabia with full control of the Moslem Holy Places. The ground had been prepared for this earlier in the year, for a message from Sir Edward Grey,[1] conveyed by the Russian Ambassador to his Government, asked for its views on the settling of Jews in Palestine, and brought a reply to the effect that Russia was willing to approve any project concerning Palestine which gave freedom of access to all orthodox institutions and existing rights, and would offer no objection to the settlement of Jewish colonists in the country.

It then became necessary, after the pledge had been given to King Hussein, to consult with the French regarding their interests in Syria. In November 1915 Sir Edward Grey had given instructions that negotiations should be begun in London with Monsieur Georges Picot, representing the French Government, with a view to reconciling British, French and Arab claims in the Syrian area. Monsieur Picot began by insisting that the whole of Syria down to the Egyptian

[1] The British Secretary of State for Foreign Affairs.

Theodor Herzl in his study in Vienna
(The study is preserved intact in Jerusalem)

Leopold Amery   Lord Milner

frontier must be assigned to France, but after consultation with his Government he agreed to it being administered by the Arabs under French influence. After these preliminary discussions Sir Mark Sykes was brought in and authorized to act on behalf of H.M. Government. The final arrangements agreed to were as follows: Iraq and Syria with the exception of Palestine, were to be divided into four Zones—designated respectively A, B, Blue and Red:

Zone A was to consist of the interior of Syria from and including the cities of Damascus, Homs, Hama and Aleppo on the west, to and including the Mosul district on the east. In this Zone both countries were prepared to recognize semi-independent Arab States or a confederation of Arab States under an Arab chief, but the French were to have the right of supplying foreign advisers and officials and enjoying economic privileges.

Zone B was to consist of the area lying south of Zone A bounded on the west by a line running approximately from Gaza to Aqaba and reaching Transjordan eastwards to the Red Zone, a northerly arm jutting out in Persia, and a southerly arm towards the Persian Gulf. In this Zone, also, semi-independent Arab States or a confederation of them would be set up, but the rights enjoyed by the French in Zone A would be accorded to the British in Zone B.

Blue Zone was to consist of Alicia in Asia Minor and all of coastal Syria west of Zone A with the cities of Damascus, Homs, Hama and Aleppo just outside the border. In this zone France was to have such political control as she thought fit after agreement with the Arabs there.

Red Zone was to consist of the province of Basra and Baghdad in Persia, and the British were to have similar control to the French in the Blue Zone.

A fifth Zone, designated the Brown Zone, consisted of Palestine, which was to be placed under international control. The same wording was used in the agreement between Great Britain, France and Russia. 'With a view to securing the religious interests of the Entente Powers, Palestine, with its Holy Places, is separated from Turkish territory and subjected to a special régime to be determined by agreement between Russia, France and Great Britain.'

It was decided to keep this agreement secret and neither the Sharif nor the Italians were informed. The failure to let Hussein know has proved since to have been an error of the first magnitude, for had he been let into the secret it would have cleared up, once and for all, any points which had been left undefined in the correspondence between himself and the British High Commissioner in Egypt. Be that as it may, the agreement remained a secret until November 1917 when the Bolsheviks, who had found a copy of it in the Foreign Office archives in Petrograd, published it to the world.

★   ★   ★   ★   ★

Meanwhile, as the war progressed, the hopes of Jewish nationalism began to rise. After a long delay a British offensive was at last got under way against the Turks. The British General Staff had, hitherto, opposed what they regarded as a side show, but in June 1917 General Allenby, who had been commanding the Third Army in France, was sent out to take command of the Egyptian Expeditionary Force, and in October he launched a strong attack on the Turkish Army. His troops captured Beersheba on 31 October, and Jerusalem was surrendered to the British Commander by the Turkish representative on 9 December. Coming barely more than a month after the Balfour Declaration, the entry of the British troops into the Holy City was hailed by Jews throughout the world with great joy.

The Balfour Declaration was a great event in the history of Zionism, for it was the first public recognition of the Jewish claim for a National Home for more than eighteen hundred years. When the war broke out Zionists throughout the world were split into opposing sides; some supported the Allies and others sided with the Central Powers. The Central Office of the Zionist Organization was situated in Berlin, but the six members of the Executive Committee separated and carried on with their duties in four different countries. Two of them, including Professor Warburg, remained in Berlin to look after Central Europe. A third, who was in America when hostilities opened, remained there until the war ended, and a fourth opened a new office in Copenhagen. Sokolow, the famous Hebrew writer and journalist, managed to reach England where he was soon joined by the Russian Zionist leader, Dr. Tschlenow.

It was in England, however, that the policy which culminated in the Balfour Declaration was formulated, and it was with the British

Government that all the negotiations took place. This was not entirely inappropriate for many British Jews were in favour of Herzl's idea of a Jewish National Home as, indeed, were many of Britain's leading politicians. But during the first half of the war there could be no unanimity amongst Zionists as to which of the opposing sides they should support. Jewish leaders in the British Isles not unnaturally favoured the Allies. The Jews from Eastern Europe could hardly be expected to support the Allies when Russia was numbered amongst them,[1] nor was it surprising that until the United States of America's entry into the war, after the sinking of the *Lusitania*, American Zionists followed their own Government in adopting a policy of neutrality.

Dr. Chaim Weizmann took a foremost part in the negotiations. In 1904 he had immigrated to England and become a lecturer in chemistry at Manchester University. When war broke out in August 1914 he was holidaying with his wife and son in Switzerland, but they all returned to England as quickly as possible. Passing through Paris he visited Baron Edmond de Rothschild who advised him to get in touch with British statesmen as soon as possible. The Baron was sure that the war would soon spread to the Middle East, and the defeat of the Turks and the dissolution of the Ottoman Empire might be the prelude to great events in Jewish history.

Doubtless with the idea of facilitating Weizmann's approach to some important member of the British Government, de Rothschild arranged for him to see Lord Bertie who was then British Ambassador in Paris. The visit did not, apparently, achieve its purpose, to judge from the following entry which Lord Bertie made in his diary for that day. 'Edmond de Rothschild sent a co-religionist established in Manchester to "talk" about what I think an absurd scheme, though they say it has the approval of Grey, Lloyd George, Samuel and Crewe. . . . It contemplates the formation of Palestine into an Israelite State, under the protectorate of England, France or Russia; preferably England.'

[1] At Weizmann's second meeting with Balfour, which took place in December 1914 the latter wondered how a friend of England could be so anti-Russian, when Russia was doing so much to help England win the war. Weizmann giving an account of this meeting has written: 'I gave him a description of what was taking place behind the Russian lines, especially when the Russians advanced into new territory—pogroms, and the expulsions which made every Russian victory a horror for the Jews—this while hundreds of thousands of Jews were fighting in the Russian Army. It was news to him!' *Trial and Error*, p. 196.

It was not long, however, before Weizmann got his opportunity, for in December 1914 he had his first meeting with Lloyd George, then still Chancellor of the Exchequer. Their meeting took place at one of the famous breakfasts and Herbert Samuel, afterwards Lord Samuel, and Josiah Wedgwood were also present. Both these other guests were to be future supporters, but Weizmann had no idea at this first meeting that they were already favourably disposed. For some reason Weizmann had expected Samuel to be 'the type of Jew who by his very nature was opposed to Zionism'. It caused him no little surprise, therefore, to learn that Samuel was in the course of preparing a memorandum for the Prime Minister on the subject of a Jewish State in Palestine.

When the Prime Minister saw it he does not appear to have thought any more of it than Lord Bertie thought of the scheme propounded by Weizmann, for Asquith wrote thus in his diary for 28 January 1915: 'I received from Herbert Samuel a memorandum headed, "The Future of Palestine". He goes on to argue, at considerable length and with some vehemence, in favour of the British annexation of Palestine, a country the size of Wales, much of it barren mountain and part of it waterless. He thinks we might plant in this not very promising territory about three or four million European Jews and that this would have a good effect on those who are left behind. It reads almost like a new edition of *Tancred* brought up to date. I confess I am not attracted to this proposed addition to our responsibilities, but it is a curious illustration of Dizzy's favourite maxim, "Race is everything", to find this almost lyrical outburst from the well-ordered and methodical brain of Herbert Samuel.'[1]

During the years 1915 and 1916 support for the policy of restoring the Jews to Palestine grew considerably in British Governmental circles. Strangely enough the main opposition came from the Jews themselves. Most wealthy influential British Jews were in the opposing camp. Perhaps the greatest antagonist was Edwin Montagu, then in the Cabinet as Secretary of State for India. 'He saw the spectre of anti-Semitism in every country if its Jews permitted themselves to dream of a territorial centre or a national political existence outside their present citizenships. Such aspirations in English Jews he looked upon as a traitorous disloyalty to their native land. In the case of Jews living under less happy

[1] See Viscount Samuel's autobiography.

conditions he believed their relations with the countries of their birth would only be worsened.'[1]

This attitude of mind was not shared by most British Jews, and it was difficult for non-Jews to understand it. Nevertheless, the fact that British Jews were themselves divided on such an important historic issue was bound to have its effect on the Government's views, although in the Cabinet and the Imperial War Cabinet there were several strong supporters, among them Lloyd George, Balfour, Milner and Smuts. By 1917 some of the Government's advisers were also sympathetic, very largely due to Sir Mark Sykes's influence and persuasion. Weizmann deserves much of the credit for winning Sykes over.

The so-called Balfour Declaration was, in fact, a letter written by him as Foreign Secretary to Lord Rothschild on behalf of H.M. Government. Nevertheless, it is right and proper that it should bear his name for it was he, more than anyone, who fought the opposition in the Cabinet. Although, perhaps, Weizmann did not realize how much his first meeting with Balfour in Manchester in 1906 during the General Election had impressed the British statesman, their second meeting in December 1914 left the matter in little doubt.

This second meeting took place on Lloyd George's suggestion, and Balfour's first words revealed how much the idea of a Jewish National Home had been in his thoughts. 'You know I was thinking of that conversation of ours, [he was referring to the 1906 meeting] and I believe that when the guns stop firing you may get your Jerusalem.' Lady Blanche Dugdale, his sister and biographer, has confirmed that the appeal of Zionism had continued to affect her brother ever since that first meeting, for the Zionist ideology had 'appealed to him as a philosopher and impressed him as a student of history'. For many years prior to his interest in the Zionist movement as a political force, he had held strong views that the Jews' contribution to world culture and religion had been ill-requited by Christendom.

Balfour told Weizmann of a conversation which he had had with Frau Wagner, the composer's widow, during the Bayreuth musical festival two years before the war on the position of German Jews. Frau Wagner had complained how Jews had captured the stage, the press, the universities and commerce, and expressed resentment at being

[1] *Arthur James Balfour* by Blanche Dugdale, p. 214.

obliged to receive all culture at Jewish hands. Dr. Weizmann replied that her sentiments revealed the very crux of the Jewish tragedy, that the Jews who were giving their energy and brains to Germany were doing so as Germans, not as Jews. They were enriching Germany, not Jewry, and must sink their Judaism to put their brains at Germany's disposal. The Zionists could not accept them as Jews, yet the Germans did not recognize them as Germans. Mr. Balfour was quite unable to understand why some Western Jews should be opposed to the idea of a Jewish National Home. 'Why can I afford to be a Zionist and not they?' he asked Dr. Weizmann, who answered that nobody would challenge Mr. Balfour's position, but that anti-Semitism lurked even in Great Britain. However good an Englishman a Jew might be, he was constantly challenged. Nevertheless, at their second meeting, Balfour and Weizmann never got down to fundamentals and the Jewish leader, describing the conversation which took place, has said that they never got beyond abstract ideas and principles. It ended with Balfour asking whether there was any practical help he could give. Weizmann answered, 'Not while the guns are roaring, but when the military situation becomes clearer I will come again.' Balfour pressed him to return.[1]

During the year 1915 there was increasing evidence that opinion in important influential circles in England was veering towards sympathy with the Zionist cause. Meanwhile, every effort was quietly being made by British Zionists to create a favourable political atmosphere and, more important still, to permeate the Middle East section of the Foreign Office which had then, as it has now, a definite pro-Arab leaning. A journalist in Manchester, named Herbert Sidebotham, who later wrote a book entitled *Great Britain and Palestine*, suggested in a leading article in the *Manchester Guardian* that if Turkey went under, 'the most vital spot in our communications with the East would be exposed to land attack from which the most powerful navy could not possibly secure us'. He proposed that a buffer State be established in Palestine as a means of protecting the Suez Canal and Egypt, and argued that the only people capable of forming such a State was the Jewish nation. 'We began this war', the article continued, 'on behalf of the conceptions of international law and justice whose most conspicuous violation at that time was the invasion of neutral Belgium. Even if Belgium were all,

<hr>

[1] *Arthur James Balfour* by Blanche Dugdale, Vol. II, p. 224.

there would still be among British people no regrets, no doubts. But great as the ideal of relieving Belgium from the invader may be, the ideal of restoring the Jewish State of Palestine is incomparably greater, as a new birth is a greater thing than a recovery from sickness. . . . Before the magnitude of this war most ideals seem to shrink in size. But one ideal is the peer even of this war in magnitude and grandeur. It is the ideal of restoration of the Jews to a country which, small and poor as it is, they made as famous as Greece and as great as Rome. . . . Nor is there any achievement that would exhibit the contrast between English and German political ideals so favourably to us, and so eloquently vindicate our own, as the establishment of a Jewish State under the British Crown.'[1]

Even Lord Cromer, who had been disinclined to be very helpful in Egypt at the time of the Sinai–El-Arish propositions, wrote in July 1916 that Zionism was on the brink of being launched into the current of affairs. Before long politicians would be unable to brush it aside as the fantastic dream of a few idealists.

During the Spring of 1916 H.M. Government began canvassing the Allies on this important subject, and the British Ambassador approached Russia, where no objection to a Jewish settlement of Palestine was made, subject to the provision that Russian orthodox religious interests in the Holy Land must be adequately safeguarded. The French, however, at that early stage were not enthusiastic.

It was about this time, however, the late summer of 1916, that Sir Mark Sykes became aware of the British interests in Zionism. The idea greatly appealed to him, for he was in favour of a renaissance in the Middle East and thought that this might be a new means of bringing about co-operation between the Arabs and the Jews in Palestine, which he considered an essential step. When a new Government was formed in the United Kingdom at the end of 1916 Lloyd George became Prime Minister, and Balfour Foreign Secretary. Sykes was then chosen to conduct negotiations with the Zionist leaders and, after a few preliminary meetings with Weizmann, the talks themselves began.

The proposals put forward during the talks by the Zionist leaders contained certain fundamental provisions.

---

[1] This extract is taken from a leading editorial article written by Sidebotham, but not signed, which appeared in the *Manchester Guardian*.

(1) The right of the Jewish people over Palestine should receive international recognition.

(2) The Jewish settlement in Palestine should be recognized as a nation in the juridical sense, with a large measure of self-government, the right to use Hebrew, and to levy taxes.

(3) A charter should be granted to a Jewish company with the preferential right to acquire state and private lands, to obtain concessions on public works, to enjoy the right of free immigration and facilities for the naturalization of immigrants.

(4) The whole area of historic Palestine should be united under one administration.

(5) The Holy Places should enjoy the privileges of extra-territoriality.

Sykes's conception of the programme which should be followed is set out below.

(1) The Jewish settlement should be organized under a chartered company, formed by the Zionists under British protection.

(2) This company should have the right of settlement in a part of Palestine with certain enclaves under international control.

These proposals were discussed at length, and it was finally decided that the Zionists themselves should let the French know that they preferred British control to condominium. Sokolow was chosen to get in touch with the French and tell them of their preference. He had a satisfactory interview with the French Foreign Minister, and after it was over the French Government confirmed its attitude by letter. 'You were good enough to present the project to which you are devoting your efforts, which has for its object the development of Jewish colonization in Palestine. You consider that, circumstances permitting and the independence of the Holy Places being safeguarded, it would be an act of justice and of reparation to assist, by the protection of the Allied Powers, in the renaissance of the Jewish nationality in that land from which the people of Israel were exiled so many years ago. The French Government which entered this present war to defend a people wrongfully attacked, and which continues the struggle to assure the victory of right over might, can but feel sympathy for your cause, the triumph of which is bound up with that of the Allies.'[1]

[1] *History of Zionism* by Nahum Sokolow, Vol. II, p. 53.

Sokolow succeeded also in obtaining, not without some difficulty, support for the Zionist aims from the Federation of Jewish Communities in Italy, and even the Pope went so far as to agree not to oppose so long as the Holy Places were fully protected.

Meanwhile, in Sokolow's absence, Weizmann continued negotiations in London. Balfour was not too happy about Palestine being put under sole British control, until he visited the United States of America in April 1917 and met Louis Brandeis, later Justice Brandeis, who was the guiding spirit of American Zionism. Brandeis told the British Foreign Secretary that he and all other American Zionists wanted to see a British administration in Palestine and, by the end of the month, as Lady Blanche Dugdale has written, 'the Foreign Office recognized with some slight dismay that the British Government was virtually committed'. It must, at all events, have come to a definite decision to support the Zionist programme before 20 May, for on that day Weizmann made an announcement at a special conference of the English Zionist Federation to this effect: 'I am entitled to state to this assembly that His Majesty's Government is ready to support our plans.'

Nevertheless, he considered it advisable to warn the assembly that if they were expecting the early establishment of a Jewish State they might be disappointed. It was constantly being said, he told them, that the objective of the Zionist movement was immediately to create a Jewish State in Palestine. In America they had even determined what form of State it would be, a Jewish Republic. Whilst heartily welcoming all these statements as a genuine manifestation of the Jewish national will, the English Zionists did not consider them to be safe statesmanship. In their opinion, and it must be obvious to everyone who was deeply involved in the movement, conditions were not yet ripe for the setting up of a State. States must be built up slowly, gradually, systematically and patiently. While, therefore, the creation of a Jewish Commonwealth in Palestine was the final objective, for which the whole of the Zionist Organization was working, the way to achieve it lay through a series of intermediate stages. One of these, which Weizmann hoped would soon come about as a result of the war, was that Palestine would come under the protection of Great Britain. Under her wing, it was hoped, the Jews would be able to develop and set up the administrative machinery which, while not interfering with the legitimate interests of the non-

Jewish population, would enable the ultimate objective of a Jewish State to be achieved.

But despite all the appearances of fine weather, clouds soon began to appear on the horizon, and it was not long before the storm broke. It was of this that Weizmann had spoken during his speech of 20 May. America, Britain, France and Italy were all supporting the idea of a Jewish National Home in Palestine. How humiliating it was, therefore, that the Jews were not united at this great moment in their history. How lamentable it was that there still existed a small minority which disputed the very existence of the Jews as a nation.

The first assault was launched by the Board of Deputies of British Jews and the Anglo-Jewish Association, both of which organizations objected principally to the Jewish settlement in Palestine being recognized as having a national character in the political sense. They regarded Jews as being only a religious community and unable, therefore, to create in Palestine 'a secular Jewish nationality recruited on some loose and obscure principle of race and ethnographic peculiarity'. These words appeared in a very lengthy letter which the Presidents of those two organizations, Mr. Alexander and Mr. Montefiore, wrote to the London *Times*, and which was published on 24 May 1917.

Dr. Weizmann gave short shrift to the arguments put forward by these gentlemen. The fact that the Jews are a nationality, he pointed out, was attested by the conviction of the overwhelming majority of Jews throughout the ages right up to the present time. He also reminded the opposition that this conviction had at all times been shared by non-Jews in every country, a fact which he was surprised they appeared to have forgotten. Furthermore, he emphasized another fact which seemed to have escaped their memory: no one was demanding that the Jews who had settled in Palestine should be granted any special privileges to the detriment of the non-Jewish inhabitants.

The London *Times*, a few days later, published a reply from Lord Rothschild. As a sincere believer both in the justice and benefits likely to accrue from the Zionist cause and aspirations, he asked leave to reply to the letter of Messrs. Alexander and Montefiore. Lord Rothschild thought it was most unfortunate that such a controversy should have been raised at that moment. The opponents of Zionism, 'a mere

fraction of the Jewish opinion of the world', sought to interfere in the
wishes and aspirations of the great majority of Jews. He and his Zionist
friends could not understand how the establishment of an autonomous
Jewish State under the ægis and protection of one of the Allied Powers
could, for a moment, be considered as in any way subversive to the
status of loyalty of millions of Jews who had identified themselves
thoroughly with the citizenship of the countries in which they lived.

There are many who, like Lord Rothschild, have never been able
to understand this double-loyalty bogy which was worrying Mr.
Alexander and Mr. Montefiore so greatly, yet it is a fact that in some
countries it has lived on to the present time.

During the summer of 1917 Mr. Balfour had been keeping in touch
with Lord Rothschild, who was the titular head of the Zionist movement in Britain, and was pressing, on behalf of British Zionists, for a
declaration to be made to Jews throughout the world guaranteeing that
the Allies would make it one of the conditions of the peace settlement
with Turkey that there should be a National Home for the Jews in the
land from which they had been driven as a people, but with which
their name would always be associated.

Three different drafts were considered, and the official one, finally
presented to the Foreign Office by Lord Rothschild on 18 July, was a
combination of two of them and read as follows:

H.M. Government, after considering the aims of the Zionist Organization,
accepts the principle of recognizing Palestine as the National Home of the
Jewish people, and the right of the Jewish people to build up its national
life in Palestine under a protection to be established at the conclusion of peace,
following upon the successful issue of the war.

H.M. Government regards as essential for the realization of this principle the
grant of internal autonomy to the Jewish nationality in Palestine, freedom of
immigration of Jews, and the establishment of a Jewish National Colonizing
Corporation for the resettlement and economic development of the country.
The conditions and forms of the internal autonomy and the charter for the
Jewish National Colonizing Corporation should, in the view of H.M. Govern-
ment, be elaborated in detail and determined with the representatives of the
Zionist Organization.

Four members of the Cabinet, by whom this proposal now fell to be
considered, Lloyd George, Balfour, Lord Milner and Lord Robert
Cecil were entirely in sympathy with the Zionist ideal and so also,

according to Lloyd George, were nearly all the leaders of public opinion at home and in the Dominions.

The two greatest opponents within the Cabinet were Lord Curzon and Edwin Montagu, himself a Jew. Curzon, who professed himself in sympathy with some resettlement of the Jews in Palestine, very much doubted the possibility of its being carried out on a large scale owing to the barrenness of the land. Misled by the lukewarmness of some of his wealthier Jewish friends for the idea of a Jewish National Home, he very much doubted whether the stamina of the Jews would be strong enough to undergo the physical hardships which would have to be endured by the pioneers who were to build up the new Israel. He prepared a memorandum for the Cabinet setting out his doubts and apprehensions. Having regard to what the Jews have done in Palestine since those days, the document makes strange reading today. Had he lived to see the modern Israeli doing things the hard way he would have discovered how inaccurate was his appraisal of Jewish toughness.

The arch antagonist, however, was Montagu, then Secretary of State for India. He belonged to that small and dwindling minority of Jews, mostly wealthy, who had inspired that long letter in *The Times*, and who regarded the Jews as a religious community only and not as a people. He objected to the use of the phrase 'the home of the Jewish people', which Lord Milner had inserted in one of the provisional drafts, for he maintained that it would prejudice the position of every Jew elsewhere. Lloyd George, describing Montagu's attitude in his book, *The Truth about the Peace Treaties*, stated that Montagu strongly objected to any declaration in which the expression 'Jewish National Home' was used, for he regarded himself as a Jewish Englishman. Moreover, he was not a practising Jew and, as he once told Lord Morley, he had been striving all his life to escape from the ghetto.

At last he withdrew his opposition to the proposed Declaration on the grounds that it was a necessary military expedient, but his fears of the effect which it would have on the status of English Jews like himself appear to have received recognition, for the final form of the Declaration contained a passage which safeguarded the rights and political status enjoyed by Jews in other countries.

The new draft, which had been prepared by Lord Milner, after being approved by the Foreign Office and finally by the Prime Minister, was submitted to President Wilson for his comments. It read as follows:

> His Majesty's Government view with favour the establishment in Palestine of a National Home for the Jewish race and will use its best endeavours to facilitate the achievement of this object, it being clearly understood that nothing shall be done which may prejudice the civil and religious rights of existing non-Jewish communities in Palestine or the rights and political status enjoyed in any other country by *such Jews who are fully contented with their existing nationality and citizenship*.

While the document was at the White House the leaders of the Zionist Organization of America were allowed to see it, and they took objection to the words shown above in italics, for they considered that such phraseology equated Zionism with discontent of present status. They also preferred the word 'people' to 'race'. When the American President intimated his approval, he did so with the Zionist Organization of America's proposed amendments.

It was then shown, in its new form, to the leading Jews in England as well as to the Zionists. Both Weizmann and Sokolow were disappointed about the substitution of the words, 'the establishment of a National Home for the Jewish people' for their original draft, 'recognizing Palestine as the National Home of the Jewish people'. These two expressions meant two very different things.

When the revised formula was presented to the Cabinet by Balfour, who was supported by Lord Milner, he strenuously urged its members to approve it. Lloyd George, who presided over this meeting as Prime Minister, has given this account of it. Balfour told them that although the movement was opposed by a number of wealthy Jews in England it had behind it the support of a majority of Jews in America, in Russia and in many other countries. He could see nothing inconsistent between the establishment of a Jewish National Home in Palestine and the complete assimilation and absorption of Jews into the nationality of other countries. Just as English emigrants to the U.S.A. became either in the first or subsequent generations American nationals, so in the future, should a Jewish citizenship be established in Palestine, Jews would become either Englishmen, Americans, Germans or Palestinians. The motive force of the Zionist movement was the national consciousness held by certain members of the Jewish race. They regarded themselves as one of the great historic races of the world, whose original home was in Palestine, and they had a passionate longing to regain once more their National Home. Balfour then read out a very sympathetic declaration by the French Government, which had been conveyed to the Zionists, and told the Cabinet that President Wilson was also favourably inclined.

Edwin Montagu and Curzon having at last withdrawn their opposition, the Declaration was approved and conveyed by letter to Lord Rothschild on 2 November.

Foreign Office,
November 2nd, 1918.

Dear Lord Rothschild,

I have much pleasure in conveying to you, on behalf of His Majesty's Government, the following declaration of sympathy with Jewish Zionist aspirations, which has been submitted to, and approved by, the Cabinet.

'His Majesty's Government view with favour the establishment in Palestine of a national home for the Jewish people, and will use their best endeavours to facilitate the achievement of this object, it being clearly understood that nothing shall be done which may prejudice the civil and religious rights of existing non-Jewish communities in Palestine or the rights and political status enjoyed by Jews in any other country.'

I should be grateful if you would bring this declaration to the knowledge of the Zionist Federation.

Yours sincerely,
Arthur James Balfour.

Although it was hailed by Jews throughout the world as the ushering in of a new era in their history, the question of whether its wording ultimately envisaged a Jewish State has been bitterly and endlessly argued ever since. Many of the leading British and Dominion statesmen and several prominent journalists, to judge from their speeches and their writings, thought that it did. So did the American President.

This is what Lloyd George had to say about it: 'There has been a good deal of discussion as to the meaning of the words "Jewish National Home" and whether it involved the setting up of a Jewish National State in Palestine. . . . The words actually used by Mr. Balfour, when he submitted the Declaration to the Cabinet for its approval, were not challenged at the time by any member present, and there could be no doubt as to what the Cabinet then had in their minds. It was not their idea that a Jewish State should be set up immediately by the Peace Treaty without reference to the wish of the majority of the inhabitants. On the other hand,when the time arrived for according representative institutions to Palestine, if the Jews had meanwhile responded to the opportunity afforded them by the idea of a National Home and had become a definite majority of the inhabitants, that Palestine would have to be artificially restricted in order to ensure that the Jews should be a permanent minority never entered into the heads of anyone engaged in framing the policy. That would have been regarded as unjust and a fraud on the people to whom we were appealing.'

According to Lloyd George's own account of the historic Cabinet meeting, Balfour understood the words 'National Home' to mean some form of British, American or other protectorate under which full facilities would be given to the Jews to work out their own salvation and to build up, by means of education, agriculture and industry, a real centre of national culture and focus of national life. It did not necessarily involve the early establishment of an independent Jewish State, which was a matter for gradual development in accordance with the ordinary laws of political evolution.

At a meeting of the Imperial Cabinet in 1921, Winston Churchill defined Great Britain's responsibilities in relation to Palestine under the Balfour Declaration as 'to do our best to make an honest effort to give the Jews a chance to make a National Home there for themselves', and to give them independence, 'if, in the course of many years they become a majority in the country'. Nevertheless, according to Churchill, an equal pledge had been made not to turn the Arab off his land or invade his political and racial rights. If, however, as he wrote on another occasion, 'there should be created in our lifetime by the banks of the Jordan a Jewish State under the protection of the British Crown which might comprise three or four millions of Jews, an event will have occurred in the history of the world which would, from every point of view, be beneficial, and would be in harmony with the truest interests of the British Empire'.[1]

The following declaration was signed in 1919 by twenty-two Privy Councillors, seventy-four Members of Parliament, including Neville

[1] *Illustrated Sunday Herald*, 8 February 1920.

Chamberlain, thirty-four representatives of the Christian Churches and 147 men and women representing all branches of science, literature, education and arts.

Among all the national claims which must be satisfied if the world is to have a durable peace, there is none more worthy of the sympathy and assistance of all right-thinking men than the claim of the Jewish people to rebuild its national life in Palestine. Through twenty centuries of exile the Jews have never lost hope of a return to their historic land, with which everything that is best in their distinctive culture and outlook is clearly bound up. Theirs is surely the most ancient of national wrongs, and in righting it humanity will both perform an act of simple justice and sow a seed of incalculable promise for their future. Politically, the resettlement of Palestine by Jews and its development into a Jewish Commonwealth will introduce a needed factor of stability and ordered progress into the life of the Near-East. Not less important, in our view, for the highest interests of humanity is the gain which human thought and social ideals may hope to derive from the free self-expression of the Jewish genius in its national setting. The Great Powers associated in the war for justice and freedom have promised to facilitate the establishment in Palestine of a National Home for the Jewish people. We are convinced that this promise must be amply and unequivocally translated into fact if the world settlement is to correspond with the ideals of the Allies and the United States.[1]

The Declaration was also publicly endorsed by President Wilson, and by France and Italy. The President, interpreting the Declaration to the American public, said, 'I am persuaded that the Allied nations, with the fullest concurrence of our Government and our people are agreed that in Palestine shall be laid the foundations of a Jewish Commonwealth.'

On the many occasions when doubts have been expressed by the British on the wisdom of the Balfour Declaration it would have been only right and proper to remember the actual war position at the time of its negotiation. Writing some years after the war, Lloyd George suggested that it should be remembered that in 1917 the issue was still very much in doubt. Most British people were convinced, though not all, that their country would pull through victoriously, but the Germans thought so too, and had some reason for so thinking. They had defeated the Roumanians, the Russian army was completely demoralized. The French army was exhausted and temporarily unequal to resume the offensive. The Italians had sustained a shattering defeat

[1] Documents relating to the Palestine Problem, 1945.

Foreign Office,

November 2nd, 1917.

Dear Lord Rothschild,

I have much pleasure in conveying to you, on
behalf of His Majesty's Government, the following
declaration of sympathy with Jewish Zionist aspirations
which has been submitted to, and approved by, the Cabinet

"His Majesty's Government view with favour the
establishment in Palestine of a national home for the
Jewish people, and will use their best endeavours to
facilitate the achievement of this object, it being
clearly understood that nothing shall be done which
may prejudice the civil and religious rights of
existing non-Jewish communities in Palestine, or the
rights and political status enjoyed by Jews in any
other country"

I should be grateful if you would bring this
declaration to the knowledge of the Zionist Federation.

Y. [signature]

[signature] Arthur James Balfour

The Balfour Declaration, 1917

Arthur James, Earl Balfour of Whittingham, 1848–1930

at Caporetto, the unrestricted submarine warfare had sunk millions of tons of Allied shipping and there were, as yet, no American divisions in the front line.

That was the situation when Britain decided to enlist the support of world Jewry and, what is more, the Germans were simultaneously making serious efforts to do the very same thing. Some gratitude should, therefore, be felt toward the Jews for, as Lloyd George told the Peel Commission,[1] when giving evidence before it in 1937, the Zionist leaders gave the British a definite promise that if the Allies committed themselves to giving facilities for the establishment of a National Home in Palestine for the Jews, they would do their best to rally Jewish sentiment and support throughout the world to the Allied cause and, furthermore, they kept their word in the letter and the spirit, and as Lloyd George wrote in 1938, 'The only question that remains now is whether we mean to honour ours.'

In its report the Peel Commission pointed out that the Balfour Declaration was issued in 1917 in order to enlist Jewish support for the Allies, and this was not sufficiently appreciated in Palestine. The Arabs did not appear to realize, firstly, that the present greatly improved position of the Arab world as a whole was mainly due to the great sacrifices made by the Allied and Associated Powers in the war, and secondly, that in so far as the Declaration helped to bring about the Allies' victory it also helped to bring about the liberation of all the Arab countries under Turkish rule.

From the long-drawn-out wail emitted by Arab nationalists and others ever since, it might be imagined that it was the Arab and not the Turkish rule in Palestine that the Mandatory Power replaced in 1920. It is only necessary to study its history to discover how little truth there is in the claim that Palestine has been governed by the Arabs or been an Arab country for the last 1300 years. In his authoritative *History of Palestine*, after summing up the political history of the country since it was a province of the Roman Empire, the author has written: 'In this motley procession of emperors, queens, kings, sultans and caliphs, at intervals of centuries a Jew was twice governor of Palestine prior to the Great War. Palestine was the victim of tyrants when all rulers were

---

[1] The Royal Commission for Palestine which reported in 1937 and of which Lord Peel was the Chairman.

absolute, the sport of lecherous monarchs when West vied with East in licentiousness. The world's unending buffer state, never in these last two thousand years has it been free to assert its own spirit, or let that spirit grow.'[1]

At the time of its announcement no official objection was made to the Balfour Declaration by any Arab leader not even by Sharif Hussein or his son, Feisal, though it may well be that at that particular moment they felt that discretion was the better part of valour. Dr. Weizmann, however, appears to have apprehended an unfavourable reaction from that quarter, for in a speech at Manchester, just a month after the Declaration, he said: 'We all hope and believe that out of this welter of blood and destruction a better world will arise. If misunderstandings existed in the past between Arabs and Jews we have not created them; they have been created by those who were the masters of Palestine, by the deadening hand of the Turk who can only rule over his Empire by playing off one part of the population against the other. All that, we hope, will disappear now. Is it not imperative, is it not logical, that we who have suffered so much from physical force should try and reconstitute in Palestine an age of justice and right for everybody? It is strange indeed to hear the fear expressed that the Jew in Palestine may become an aggressor, that the Jew who has always been the victim, the Jew who has always fought the battle of freedom for others, should suddenly become an aggressor because he touches Palestinian soil.'

The long and never wearying argument as to what the Declaration meant, however, still goes on unendingly. Did it envisage the foundation of a Jewish State in which the Jews would be the predominant element, or merely contemplate setting up a home as a refuge for Jews oppressed in other lands, and a cultural centre for Judaism? In this connexion the actual wording is important. The Zionists wanted 'the establishment *of* Palestine as *the* National Home', whereas in the Balfour Declaration the following words were used, 'the establishment *in* Palestine of *a* National Home'. Is it correct to say, as many have since said, that the words recognized no more than the right of the Jews to share the country with others and left the political character and future development of the 'National Home' completely obscure? Palestine was to become an asylum for oppressed refugee Jews. The introduction

---

[1] *History of Palestine* by Jacob de Haas.

of the word 'national' would seem to raise a presumption of a home with some substance in international law.

The subsequent ratification of the Declaration by the major Allied Powers made it an international war aim, and it would have been making a mountain out of a molehill to have issued what purported to be a major declaration of policy, if all that was intended was to announce to the world that when Turkey was defeated Jews from all over the world would be allowed to settle in Palestine, where they had already established settlements under the Ottoman Empire for many decades.

What was the motive behind the British Government's new Palestine policy as declared in Balfour's letter to Rothschild? Was it idealism or expediency? The truth of the matter appears to be that the issue of the Declaration was brought about by means of a combination of both. Lloyd George wrote in his book, *Truth about the Peace Treaties*, 'It was important for us to seek every legitimate help we could get. We came to the conclusion from information we received from every part of the world that it was vital we should have the sympathy of the Jewish communities.'

Two suggestions have often been made:

(1) That the Declaration was made to induce the rich American Jews to use their influence to make the United States Government enter the war.

(2) That the offer was made by Britain for imperialistic reasons.

Dr. Weizmann, and who should know better, has dismissed both these accusations as being groundless. He has ascribed the promise as a 'recognition of the yearning of an old race' and has pointed out that 'the British Government agreed on one condition: that Palestine should *not* be the charge of Great Britain'.[1] It could hardly, therefore, be said that Britain acted for 'imperialistic reasons'.

Writing in the *Liverpool Daily Post* a fortnight before Balfour's letter to Rothschild was sent, the Editor, Sir Edward Russell,[2] wrote a leading article with the heading 'Prospects of Palestine'. The article began with these words:

One of the by-products of the world crisis, and not the least important, is the revival of activity on behalf of Jewish nationalism. The concurrence of by far

[1] 'Palestine Today' in *International Affairs*, September–October 1936, p. 673.
[2] Later Lord Russell of Liverpool.

the largest number of the Jewish people in the national idea invests it with a very general interest. It is an open secret that negotiations have been proceeding for some time between the leaders of the movement and the representatives of the Allied Powers, with a view to securing the reconsideration of Palestine as the national home of the Jewish people. The preponderance of Jewish opinion in its favour is a factor which is certain to have won for the project a sympathetic reception from Powers the *raison d'être* of whose alliance has been the championship and restoration of despoiled nationalities. That the fact that the ancient homeland of Jewry has come once more within the orbit of hostilities offers the Allies a great opportunity to right a historic national wrong, none can gainsay; and the hope is widespread that there may be a settlement in manner acceptable to liberal Europe in general and the Jewish people in particular.

Lord Curzon, who originally opposed the Declaration, stated in the House of Lords on 29 June 1920, that the chief reason for it was strategic. Winston Churchill in the House of Commons on 4 July 1922, stated that the motive was to obtain Jewish support both moral and financial all over the world, particularly in the U.S.A. and Russia, whereas Mr. Ormsby-Gore, who was connected with the Arab Bureau in Cairo and for twenty years concerned with the Jewish National Home policy, declared in the House of Commons on 21 July 1937 that the outstanding motive was the ideal of the restoration of the Jews to their ancient homeland.

Balfour always maintained that Lloyd George's imagination was kindled in the first place because he knew the Bible. There is no doubt that Lloyd George's interest in Zionism went back, as did Balfour's, to the days of the Uganda project when, as a young man, he was asked to make a draft of the proposed Jewish settlement under Britain's protection.

Balfour was, undoubtedly, moved by the ideal of the Jewish restoration although at times he frankly defended the policy on the grounds of its strategic and propaganda values to Great Britain, but practical motives are not necessarily inconsistent with idealistic impulses. He was brought up in an atmosphere of traditional Victorian piety and his mother, Lady Blanche Balfour, who was a sister of Lord Salisbury, chose for their church at Whittinghame a parish minister of the extreme evangelical school. Many times must Balfour have heard these words read in his parish church: 'The Jew must first return to Zion and then will come the final consummation.'

His views on this subject were probably never so clearly expressed as in the House of Lords on 21 June 1922, when he defended his policy during a debate on the question of whether Great Britain should accept the Mandate from the League of Nations. 'I do not deny that this is an adventure. Are we never to have adventures? Are we never to try new experiments? I hope Your Lordships will never sink to that unimaginative depth, and that experiment and adventure will be justified if there is any case or cause for their justification. Surely, it is in order that we may send a message to every land where the Jewish race has been scattered, a message which will tell them that Christendom is not oblivious of their fate, is not unmindful of the service they have rendered to the great religions of the world, and most of all to the religion that the majority of Your Lordships' House profess, and that we desire to the best of our ability to give them that opportunity of developing, in peace and quietness under British rule, those great gifts which hitherto they had been compelled from the very nature of the case only to bring to fruition in countries which know not their language and belong not to their race. That is the ideal which I desire to see accomplished, that is the aim which lay at the root of the policy I am trying to defend; and, though it be defensible indeed on every ground, that is the ground which chiefly moves me.'

The first real opposition to the Declaration by the Arabs was made at the Peace Conference. The fate of Palestine was the subject of lengthy negotiations linked up with the problem of the dismemberment of the Ottoman Empire, and the final clauses of the Turkish Treaty were not decided until 26 April 1920 at the San Remo Conference. The Supreme Council had just allotted the control of Palestine to Great Britain under a Mandate. A proviso to the Mandate was that the Mandatory Power should be responsible for giving effect to the Balfour Declaration.

In the intervening two and a half years much had happened to complicate the Palestine problem.

The Arab case rested upon two main grounds:

(1) The Balfour Declaration and the Mandate, they said, violated previous commitments given to them during the war period in return for the part they played in the overthrow of the Turks.

(2) The Mandate violated the principle of self-determination, i.e.

the right of any settled population to remain in possession of its land and to decide the political character of the country in accordance with the will of the majority of its inhabitants.

The Sykes–Picot Agreement[1] was attacked as 'not only the product of greed at its worst, that is to say, of greed allied to suspicion and so leading to stupidity: it also stands out as a startling piece of double dealing'.[2] It was, also, the Arabs alleged, a shocking breach of faith having regard to the arrangements worked out by the Allies *pari passu* with the negotiations between Great Britain.

The Sykes–Picot Agreement is undoubtedly open to criticism, but T. E. Lawrence, who cannot be accused in this context of being pro-Jew or anti-Arab, has pointed out that its terms were not inherently in conflict with the McMahon–Sharif of Mecca understanding. But this aspect of the argument has already been adequately dealt with above. Lawrence's belief that his Government had let down the Arabs had nothing whatever to do with the Balfour Declaration, or with British intentions in regard to Zionism, and he did not think that there were any insuperable discrepancies in the various promises purported to have been made to the Arabs by Great Britain. In a letter to Professor William Yale, he wrote on 22 October 1929, 'It is my deliberate opinion that the Winston Churchill settlement of 1921–2 (in which I shared) honourably fulfils the whole of the promises we made to the Arabs, in so far as the so-called British spheres are concerned.'[3] Furthermore, in a draft preface that he wrote for an abridged edition of *The Seven Pillars of Wisdom*, Lawrence stated that he must put on record his conviction that England came out of the 'Arab affair with clean hands'.[4]

Lawrence rendered great service to the Zionist cause, and Weizmann has paid tribute to this in his autobiography.[5] Although he was strongly pro-Arab he was never anti-Zionist, for he thought, like Feisal, that the Jews could be of great help to the Arabs and that the Arabs might greatly benefit by the establishment of a Jewish National Home in Palestine.

For a time, at least, there was considerable hope that both sets of

[1] See p. 34 above.   [2] *The Arab Awakening* by George Antonius, p. 248.
[3] *The Letters of T. E. Lawrence* by D. Garnett, p. 671.
[4] Ibid.   [5] *Trial and Error*.

promises could be implemented without any great difficulty. The Zionist Organization after the Balfour Declaration had issued a statement on Palestine in which it stated that 'nothing shall be done which may prejudice the civil and religious rights of existing non-Jewish communities in Palestine', and the Sharif's son, Feisal, wrote as follows in a memorandum: 'In Palestine the enormous majority of the people are Arabs. The Jews are very close to the Arabs in blood, and there is no conflict of character between the two races. In principles we are absolutely at one.' Nevertheless, he went on to say, they would prefer to have a trustee appointed to hold the balance. At the meeting of the Supreme Council, at which he put forward demands for the implementation of Allied promises of independence, he stated that Palestine should be left on one side for the mutual consideration of all interested parties.

Feisal had met Weizmann in Transjordan while he was in Palestine with the Zionist Commission which the British Government sent there in the spring of 1918. It was the Commander-in-Chief, General Allenby, who suggested that Weizmann should see the Emir, who was considered by Allenby to be the only representative Arab whose opinion was of more than local importance. The Zionist leader explained that the Commission of which he was a member was most anxious to do all it could to allay Arab fears and suspicions, and hoped that the Emir would assist. Feisal said that he was eager to see the Jews and Arabs working in harmony during the Peace Conference when the war was ended, and that, in his opinion, the destiny of the two peoples was linked with the Middle East and must depend on the goodwill of the great Powers.

Subsequent events were to prove that Feisal meant what he said, for in January 1919 an agreement was entered into by the two men, the Emir, representing and acting on behalf of the Arab Kingdom of the Hedjaz, and Dr. Weizmann, acting on behalf of the Zionist Organization. The agreement pledged the parties to cordial co-operation between the Arab State and Palestine to the acceptance of the Balfour Declaration, and the encouragement of the immigration of Jews into Palestine on a large scale and their rapid settlement on the land. When signing the document the Emir made one reservation which was added as a footnote. 'If the Arabs are established as I have asked in my manifesto of January 4th addressed to the British Secretary of State for

Foreign Affairs, I will carry out what is written in this agreement. If changes are made I cannot be answerable for failing to carry out this agreement.' It is true, as it has often since been contended by the Arabs, that when he concluded this agreement Feisal was not directly representing the Palestinian Arabs, but the Arabs always regarded Syria as one country and in Syria the Emir's leadership had been accepted. Unfortunately, as the Peel Commission stated in its report, the agreement marked the one brief moment in the whole story at which a genuine harmony was established between Arab and Jewish statesmanship. If King Hussein and his son Feisal got back their Arab States, they would concede little Palestine to the Jews.

Speaking of this eighteen months later, Balfour reminded the Arabs that the great Powers, and especially Great Britain, had liberated them from tyranny and that it was Great Britain which had established the independent Arab sovereignty of the Hedjaz and desired in Mesopotamia to prepare the way for the future of a self-governing autonomous Arab State. He hoped that, remembering all that, they would not grudge that 'small notch' of what were then Arab territories being given to the people who for all those hundreds of years had been separated from it.

Further evidence, if it were needed, of Feisal's sympathy for Zionist aspirations, is contained in a letter written by the Emir in March 1919 to Professor Felix Frankfurter who was an American member of the Zionist Delegation to the Peace Conference. The Emir wrote to Frankfurter, as an American Zionist, in order to give him a similar assurance of goodwill as he had given to Weizmann. The Arabs, he wrote, especially those who were educated, looked with deepest sympathy on the Zionist movement. There was room in Syria for Arabs and Jews, indeed it was even doubtful whether either could be a real success without the other. Such differences as existed between them were not of principle but of detail. He and his people looked forward to a future in which they could be mutually helped so that their respective countries might once again take their places in the community of civilized peoples of the world.

In its report the Peel Commission stated that, 'The present difficulties of the problem of Palestine were all inherent in it from the beginning. Time has not altered, it has only strengthened them.' For one brief fleeting moment it had looked as though they would be surmounted, but that was not to be. Once gone it could never be recaptured.

★　★　★　★　★

Between the end of the war and the appointment of the first High Commissioner for Palestine in 1920, the country was under a military administration which can hardly be said to have been in sympathy with the aims of Zionism, and most of whose members, with two notable exceptions, considered that the Balfour Declaration was a mistake, when eventually they heard about it. H.M. Government, however, did all it could in the early stages to further the declared object of the Declaration and early in 1918, shortly after the conquest of Palestine, permission was given for a Zionist Commission to visit the country.

It was headed by Dr. Weizmann, and its main functions were to act as liaison between the administration and the Jewish community and to prepare the way for the 'establishment of the Jewish National Home'. As the Mandatory Power had not yet been appointed, there were representatives from France and Italy on the Commission as well as British members. Mr. Ormsby-Gore assisted by Captain James de Rothschild was attached to the Committee as Political Officer representing H.M. Government.

When Weizmann arrived with his Commission he discovered that the Balfour Declaration had never reached many of Allenby's officers, even those of high rank. Furthermore, what was left of the sparse Jewish population spoke no English and cut a poor figure with the British who seemed to Weizmann to regard them as 'the sweepings of the Russian and Polish ghettos'. The Russian revolution was only a few months past and to many British officers in Palestine, as Weizmann observed, Russians, Jews and Bolsheviks were different words for the same thing.

Brigadier-General Deedes,[1] who was one of the few on General Allenby's staff who understood what was going on, explained that many British officers had been influenced by insidious propaganda which had been brought to Palestine by the British Military Mission which had been serving in the Caucasus on the staff of the Grand Duke Nicholas. It was in the form of a pamphlet and purported to contain

[1] Later Sir Wyndham Deedes and the first President of the Anglo-Israeli Association.

59

extracts from the 'Protocols of the Elders of Zion'. Dr. Weizmann has described the effect of this document in his autobiography.[1] 'It would be a mistake to imagine that the views of the whole British army were tainted by the ideas expressed in the Protocols of the Elders of Zion; but at a time when the horrors of the Bolshevik revolution were still fresh in everyone's mind the most fantastic rumours and slanders— operating frequently on existing background of prejudice—gained credence, and the extracts from the Protocols which I then saw had been obviously selected to cater for the taste of a certain type of British reader.'

Although the Commission was received with proper courtesy and respect its stay in Palestine achieved nothing. Relations between the Commission and the Administration improved as time went on, but the Arabs felt that the soldiers were with them and not with the Jews, and hostility to the new Allied policy grew daily. In Weizmann's own judgment, by the time the civil administration under Sir Herbert Samuel took over the gulf between the two peoples was already difficult to bridge.

[1] *Trial and Error*, p. 273.

CHAPTER IV

The First High Commissioner

THE British Mandate did not come into force until 29 September 1923. There had been a long period of delay between the end of the war and the final approval of the Mandate by the Council of the League of Nations on 24 July 1922. But there was a further delay even after that, for it was decided that the British Mandate for Palestine and the French Mandate for Syria should be put into operation simultaneously and the promulgation of the latter had been delayed by the Franco-Italian discussions.

Meanwhile, it was decided that the military occupation of the territory should be brought to an end, and on 1 July 1920 the new civil administration was set up with Sir Herbert Samuel at its head as High Commissioner. He was a Jew, and after he accepted the appointment, when it was offered to him by Lloyd George, there was some criticism in Great Britain. The critics, however, were mostly political opponents of the Prime Minister, and the bulk of public opinion was favourably disposed towards the appointment.

When Lloyd George had offered the post to Samuel on the day after the provisional assignment of the Mandate to Great Britain, Samuel had hesitated to accept it, for he thought that the appointment of a Jew as High Commissioner might create some difficulties, and he told the Prime Minister that he was doubtful whether it would be politically expedient, in all the circumstances, to send a Jew to Palestine as High Commissioner. Both Balfour and Curzon, however, had agreed that Samuel was 'the man for the job', for they thought it was essential to have someone who was interested in making the policy succeed.

After thinking it over, however, Samuel decided to accept and wrote the following letter to Lloyd George:

I have thought over the suggestion that I should undertake the administration of Palestine, which you made in conversation yesterday, and I have consulted Weizmann and Sokolow about it, as you said I was at liberty to do. I am quite clear that if the Government decide to invite me to fill that post it is my duty to accept it. The objection which I mention to you, that measures which the majority of the population would accept from a non-Jew would be resented if they came from a Jew could, I believe, be overcome. In the long run their attitude would depend upon the reasonableness of the measures themselves and upon the manner in which they were represented.

This letter does much to explain the character of the administration under Samuel which was characterized by moderation.

It was not only Samuel himself who had fears concerning the effect of appointing a Jew. Immediately after the announcement that Great Britain was to have the Mandate, serious riots had broken out in Jerusalem and ferocious attacks were made by Arabs on Jews. Five Jews had been killed and 211 wounded. The Arab casualties were thirty-four killed and twenty-one wounded. As usual order had to be restored by the British troops. On 12 May Curzon told Samuel that Allenby had told him, on hearing of Samuel's impending appointment, that he feared that the appointment of a Jew as the first Governor would be the signal for widespread disturbances, murders, and attacks on Jews and on Jewish settlements, and for Arab raids across the border. Samuel has recorded that Curzon told him that such a warning from such a source could not be ignored, and that while there could be no question of the Government changing its mind about the appointment, someone else should go to Palestine for the first year to relieve Samuel of the brunt of the difficulties. Curzon had, apparently, not yet told Lloyd George of Allenby's views. Brigadier-General Wyndham Deedes and Sir Gilbert Clayton, respectively head of political intelligence in Palestine and chief political adviser to Allenby in Egypt, did not agree with their chief and thought that uncertainty was more dangerous than the immediate appointment of Samuel. Sir Herbert was, therefore, appointed High Commissioner, made a Knight Grand Cross of the Order of the British Empire and sent to Palestine.

The Jewish population of Palestine were delighted, but although the

Zionist leaders placed great hopes on Samuel and thought him highly suitable for such a great task, they were somewhat apprehensive that it would add fuel to the flames of Arab anti-Jewish propaganda. The new High Commissioner was one of those who had no doubt about the meaning of the words 'National Home' in the Balfour Declaration, or the way in which it would become established. In a speech made on the second anniversary of the Declaration he drew a distinction between the long-term policy and the short. The immediate arrangement of a purely Jewish State in Palestine, he said, would entail minority rule, and this was contrary to democratic principles, and world opinion would be against it. Meanwhile, Jewish immigration and land settlement should be carried on to the maximum capacity which the resources and conditions of the country would permit, Jewish culture should be extended and developed, and the fullest measure of local self-government granted, so that with the minimum of delay the country might become a self-governing Commonwealth under the auspices of an established Jewish majority. When he became the first British High Commissioner for Palestine seven months later, his approach to the subject was, perhaps, a little more cautious, but it is only fair to add that it could hardly be anything else, for he was no longer speaking as a private individual, but as the representative of His Majesty, whose address to the inhabitants of Palestine stressed that the policy of the Allied and Associated Powers to secure the gradual establishment in Palestine of a National Home for the Jewish people would not in any way affect the civil or religious rights or diminish the prosperity of the general population of that country.

Announcing various measures to improve and further the economic development of the country, which would need funds and manpower to be provided by Jewish money and immigration, he reassured the Arabs by promising that the latter would be kept within reasonable limits and would not be allowed to swamp the country's natural resources or exceed the possibilities of employment. Nevertheless, the authorized quota for the admission of Jews for the first years was 16,500, enough to alarm the Arabs amongst whom there existed a rooted suspicion that they were going to be dispossessed of their land so that hordes of Jewish immigrants could be settled on it. Thus, from the very outset the twin bogies of land settlement and immigration began to rear their ugly heads.

Arab society in 1920 was still, more or less, based on feudal ideas. The majority of the Arab population were fellahin.[1] A few of these owned small plots of land but most of them cultivated the large establishments of absentee landlords belonging to the governing class of Effendi.[2] Poverty was widespread, and the birth-rate high and increasing yearly despite the almost complete absence of sanitation, hygiene, and public health facilities. Much progress was made in these fields during the first five years of the new administration, and it should not be forgotten that it was the Arab standard of life rather than the Jewish which received the most benefit. Nevertheless, there was a large gap to be closed and it would take a long time, for 'the Arabs were still living in the atmosphere of the past, still separated . . . by centuries from the educated, resourceful western-minded section of the Jews now entering the country in increasing numbers'.[3]

It was the closing of this gap with which the High Commissioner was most concerned. He chose for his right-hand man, Brigadier-General Sir Wyndham Deedes. Deedes was known to be sympathetic to the idea of a Jewish National Home, but many others who had held positions in the Military Government and whom Samuel retained were either indifferent or antagonistic. Some of them preferred to leave. Few Jews were appointed to senior offices, and when an Advisory Council of ten members was set up under the presidency of the High Commissioner it contained only three Jews.

Lord Samuel has stated in his *Memoirs*[4] that he was in no two minds about Deedes. He was clearly the man for the principal post, for having been a senior staff officer in the Intelligence Section of Allenby's General Staff he had a sound knowledge of the country and its problems. He also spoke fluent Turkish. As Governor of Jerusalem the new High Commissioner was fortunate in being able to retain Ronald Storrs, who had held the appointment under the Military Administration. He was an Oriental expert and spoke several languages including Arabic.

[1] Peasants.
[2] A Turkish title of respect generally applied to government officials and members of the learned professions. Literal meaning—'Lord'.
[3] Palestine Royal Commission's Report (July 1937), p. 46.
[4] *Memoirs* by the Rt. Hon. Viscount Samuel, P.C., G.C.B., G.B.E., p. 154.

Less than a month after the new Administration had taken over the government, a crisis arose in Syria which proved to be a source of embarrassment to the High Commissioner and led, incidentally, to Transjordan, which constituted more than half the total area of Palestine, being cut out of the area of the Jewish National Home as part of the plan to pay Britain's debt to Hussein. Feisal, Hussein's son, had fled from Syria after being defeated by the French near Damascus. Having been warned by the French Commander that his camp would be bombed unless he left the country, he had no alternative but to enter territory south of the Syrian border then governed by the British Administration.

This raised a difficult problem for the High Commissioner, who had to deal with it on his own initiative as there was no time to ask for guidance from the Foreign Secretary to whom he was still responsible.[1] It was, indeed, awkward. Both the French and Feisal were our Allies. It was important not to offend the French, and Feisal had been loyal and helpful during the war, and had been installed as Governor of Syria by Allenby. Samuel decided that when he arrived on Palestine territory Feisal should be received as a respected friend and not as a defeated fugitive. The High Commissioner, accompanied by Storrs, met the Emir at one of the stopping places on his way through, and gave him a message of sympathy and goodwill. Describing the incident in his *Memoirs*, Lord Samuel wrote, 'I was told afterwards that when the Emir saw the soldiers drawn up on the platform on his arrival he did not know whether they were there to arrest him, and after the mental strain of the previous days he almost broke down when he found that they were a guard of honour.'[2]

Another problem now arose, for when the French drove the Emir out of eastern Syria the southern part was left in the air. As this area was in the territory of the High Commissioner's administration some arrangements had to be made for its government. The High Commissioner had ample proof that the feeling in that part of Syria was in favour of it being a British sphere of influence rather than a French one. He decided, therefore, to send a small number of British officers to be stationed there.

[1] It was not until later that Palestine became a Colonial Office commitment.
[2] *Memoirs* by the Rt. Hon. Viscount Samuel, P.C., G.C.B., G.B.E., p. 159.

It was not long, however, before news was received that the Emir Abdullah, was marching up from the Hedjaz with a force of some twelve hundred troops to attack the French as a reprisal for his brother Feisal's expulsion four months earlier. Something had to be done, for Abdullah could clearly not be allowed to use British Palestine as a springboard for an attack on the French in Syria. Fortunately there appeared to be a convenient solution and Lord Samuel has described it thus: 'During the war, before the Arab revolt, a vast area had been promised by the British Government as the future area of Arab independence, and Transjordan was part of it. Our own administration there was a makeshift; let Abdullah, then, give up his campaign against the French and settle down in Transjordan; let him be recognized as ruler there and be given the help of a few British advisers, and the moderate subsidy essential for a proper government. We sent emissaries to make the proposal and to point out that if he persisted in attacking the strong French forces in Syria he would have no help from us, and would certainly suffer a disastrous defeat.'[1]

An agreement was negotiated in February 1921 under which Abdullah was recognized as administrator under the Mandate, and this was confirmed at a conference in which Churchill, Samuel and Lawrence took part, and was ratified in 1922 by the British Government which secured the League of Nations' approval of a memorandum pressing that Transjordan be exempted from all the clauses which dealt with the Holy Places and the Jewish National Home.

The separation of Transjordan from Palestine had serious effects upon the development of Jewish settlement in Palestine. It was sparsely populated and could have absorbed a large number of immigrants. Its elimination as an area of settlement dealt a severe blow to Jewish colonization. The Jewish Agency protested against the policy of prohibiting Jews from entering Transjordan. They contended that to do so was a breach of the articles of the Mandate which provided for the equality of rights in mandated areas irrespective of race or religion. Although the British were not obliged to facilitate Jewish immigration into Transjordan, the Agency argued that to prevent it was a violation of the Mandate, and it is not easy to disagree with this view. The Permanent Mandates Commission of the League of Nations was of the same

---

[1] *Memoirs* by the Rt. Hon. Viscount Samuel, P.C., G.C.B., G.B.E., p. 161.

opinion, and stated that if what was proposed was a general exclusion of Jews from Transjordan the terms of the Mandate were broken.

The Arab nationalists were becoming more active, and having given up hope of a union with Syria, following Feisal's expulsion, they began to agitate for the recognition of an independent Arab Palestine under a British Mandate, claiming the right of self-determination and the establishment of a national government responsible to a council elected by the Arabic-speaking people who were living in Palestine at the outbreak of the Great War.

Difficulties were also being experienced in Mesopotamia, and Lloyd George placed Near Eastern affairs in the hands of Churchill who organized a new Middle Eastern department and invited T. E. Lawrence to join it. Early in 1921 responsibility for the mandated territories, which had formerly been divided between the Foreign Office, the India Office and the War Office, came under the Colonial Office which then took over the administration of Mesopotamia and Palestine.

Churchill, now Secretary of State for the Colonies, went out to the Near East in March 1921 with a group of experts in Near Eastern affairs with the idea of improving relations with the Arabs who had been disturbed by the Peace Conference decisions. The intention was to work out a quasi-independent government for Palestine with the expectation that Arabs and Jews could be induced to co-operate in the government of the country. This pious hope had little chance of success, for when Churchill arrived in Palestine in March 1921 the Arab Executive Committee presented him with a memorandum which denounced the Balfour Declaration as contrary to the McMahon pledges. The Arab Committee made the following demands:

(1) Repudiation of the Jewish National Home policy.

(2) Creation of a national government in Palestine elected by inhabitants in their pre-war propositions.

(3) Cessation of Jewish immigration.

(4) Reconstitution of the pre-war system of laws until the establishment of a national government was completed.

(5) No distinction between Palestine and other Arab countries.

A minor anti-Jewish demonstration at Haifa greeted Churchill's arrival, but this was suppressed with a few casualties. Churchill, however, was not to be brow-beaten by such tactics, and stood firm. He told the Arab Executive Committee, in such a way that there could be no misunderstanding, that he neither wished nor was able to repudiate the Balfour Declaration or halt immigration. As Great Britain had promised to facilitate the development of the Jewish National Home in Palestine it could not be done without Jewish immigration. The Balfour Declaration had been approved by various Allied governments and it was just as much a fact as was the fall of the Ottoman Empire. It was only on the basis of the Balfour Declaration that Great Britain had received the Mandate. He reminded them of the second paragraph of the Mandate's preamble, 'Whereas the Principal Allied Powers have also agreed that the Mandatory should be responsible for putting into effect the Declaration originally made on 2 November 1917 by the Government of His Britannic Majesty and adopted by the said Powers in favour of the establishment in Palestine of a National Home for the Jewish people . . . and whereas recognition has thereby been given to the historical connexion of the Jewish people with Palestine and to the grounds for reconstituting their National Home in that country. . . .' Having received the Mandate on that basis, Churchill told the Arabs, it could not be carried out on any other.

Churchill was not content with saying that alone. He also pointed out that it was only right and proper that Jews who were scattered throughout the world should have a national centre and a National Home to which many would return. It was good for the world, good for the Jews, good for the British Government and good for the Arab inhabitants of the land.

He did something, however, to reassure the Arabs that it was not the intention of Great Britain to create a Jewish Government that would dominate them. The creation of self-government, he said, was a long way off. 'Step by step we shall develop representative institutions leading to full self-government but our children's children will have passed away before that is completed.'[1] Afterwards he received representatives of the National Council of the Jews of Palestine to whom he spoke similarly and reassured them that Great Britain was determined to fulfil the terms of the Balfour Declaration. They should, however,

[1] *The Times*, 2 April 1921.

exercise moderation, and he emphasized the importance of developing friendly relations with the Arabs.

Very shortly after Churchill's visit grave disturbances broke out, and serious rioting occurred in Jaffa and the surrounding district, lasting for four days. A raid was also made by the Arabs on the Jewish agricultural settlement of Khedera resulting in heavy casualties amongst both Arabs and Jews, killing ninety-five and wounding 219.

The immediate cause of the disturbances had nothing to do with Arab hostility to the Jews, but was a clash which took place between demonstrators of the Socialist Labour Party and a procession of the Jewish Labour Party on May Day which, on this occasion, happened to fall on Easter Sunday. The Socialist Labour Party, generally known in Palestine as M.P.S.,[1] was extremely left wing and its acknowledged aim was 'to prepare the soil of Palestine for Social Revolution'. On this Easter Sunday the demonstrators were carrying banners bearing Communist slogans such as 'Long Live Socialist Soviet Palestine'.

This Bolshevik demonstration would, under normal conditions, have produced nothing more than an ordinary street riot which the local police would have been able to control. On this occasion, however, it sparked off anti-Jewish hostility on the part of the Palestinian Arabs which had been smouldering for some time. As long as the Jews were an obscure minority, as they were when Palestine was under Turkish rule, there was no trouble. It was only when the Arabs believed that the Jews were becoming a danger, by their very numbers, that this suspicion bred the hostility which a minor provocative incident by a small party of undesirable Jews, turned into an outburst of popular anger against Jews in general.

It was the first Immigration Ordinance, issued by the High Commissioner two months after his arrival, which had caused alarm. The Arabs wrongly thought, and there was nothing which could correct the misunderstanding, that their land was to be expropriated for purposes of Jewish colonization, and that large-scale immigration would render the population of Palestine overwhelmingly Jewish.

In 1921, however, the Commission of Enquiry which investigated the disturbances found that practically the whole of the non-Jewish population was united in hostility to the Jews, and, furthermore, that

[1] The initials of Miflagat Poalim Sozialistim.

during the riots there was no discrimination on the part of the Arabs between different categories of Jews, whether they were old-established colonists, or newly arrived Bolshevik immigrants from Russia; they all became merged together as a target for the common hatred.

Two months after the first outbreak of violence a member of the Commission of Enquiry came across a band of decently dressed Arab children, whose average age was not more than six or seven, marching in procession along a street in Jaffa. They were brandishing sticks and shouting, 'We want to fight the Jews.' No attempt was made by several policemen present to interfere with the marchers in any way. As the Commission stated in its Report, the significance of the incident was that it clearly showed that so long as the popular feeling against the Jews ran high, it would not be possible to maintain law and justice effectively, because the mass of the people could not be trusted to do justice where a Jew was concerned.

The principal grievances cherished by the Arabs were said, by their representatives who gave evidence before the Commission, to be as follows:

(1) That Great Britain was adopting a policy mainly directed towards the establishment of a National Home for the Jews and not for the equal benefit of all Palestinians.

(2) That there was an undue proportion of Jews in the Government service.

(3) That the policy of the Zionist Commission was to flood Palestine with Jewish immigrants, possessing greater commercial and organizing ability than the Arabs, who would eventually gain ascendancy over the rest of the population.

(4) That immigrant Jews in Jaffa irritated the Arab population by their arrogance. Full of enthusiasm on arrival in their new home from a less pleasant environment in Eastern Europe, many of the younger people of both sexes perambulated the streets arm in arm, singing songs, holding up the traffic and behaving in what, to the Arabs, seemed a most provocative way.

(5) That, owing to insufficient precautions, immigrants with Bolshevik tendencies had been allowed to enter the country where

they tried to introduce social and economic unrest and promote the Bolshevik doctrine.

The Commission, when stating whether or not it considered any of the grievances justified, was in no doubt that they had 'contributed materially to the state of exasperation which found its outlet in the disturbances'. The Commission was convinced that without them there was no animosity towards the Jews as such, that there was no inherent anti-Semitism in the country and, moreover, that many educated Arabs 'would welcome the arrival of well-to-do and able Jews who could help to develop the country to the advantage of all sections of the community'.

Whatever other results the disturbances may have had, they undoubtedly had the effect of slowing down the process of establishing the National Home. When, on 14 May, the High Commissioner decided to suspend immigration, the two main Jewish organizations closed down their shutters and did not resume work until they had an assurance from the Colonial Office that immigration would be resumed. Still more steps were taken to reconcile the Arabs. On the occasion of the King's birthday, 3 June 1921, the High Commissioner devoted a large part of a speech which he delivered in Jerusalem to assuring the Arab leaders that Great Britain would never set up a Jewish Government to rule a non-Jewish majority, and said that all the Balfour Declaration meant was that 'the Jews, a people who were scattered throughout the world, but whose hearts always turned towards Palestine, should be enabled to find their home, and that some among them, within the limits that are fixed by numbers of interests of the present population, should come to Palestine in order to help by their resources and efforts to develop the country to the advantage of all the inhabitants'.

Sir Herbert doubtless gave all these assurances because he was already aware that any aggravation of Arab antagonism to the concept of the National Home would seriously undermine the foundations of the whole policy initiated by the Balfour Declaration and embodied in the Mandate, but although he did much to conciliate the Arabs, as so often happens, this appeasement did no more than put off the evil day. A Supreme Municipal Council was set up and given complete freedom, without government interference, to administer the large religious endowment funds which, in the days of Turkish rule, had been controlled from Constantinople. The rapid development of social services, moreover, though not carried out specifically for the purpose of conciliating the Arabs, was expected to have a moderating effect on their attitude towards the British administration.

In May 1922 the High Commissioner went home for consultations with the Colonial Office, and a month later the famous White Paper containing the latest statement of British policy in Palestine, commonly known as the Churchill Memorandum, was issued. The phraseology of that part of the Churchill Memorandum which defined the Jewish National Home was intended to conciliate, to some extent, Arab antagonism to it. In the words of the Peel Commission's Report, 'It was hoped that the statement of British policy in Palestine contained in the Memorandum, while firmly reassuring the Government's adherence to the Balfour Declaration, had robbed it of much of its significance by the moderate definition it contained of the National Home.'

Nevertheless, despite its moderation, it gave categorical recognition to certain fundamental principles underlying the policy of the National Home. Firstly, it declared it to be essential that the Jewish community in Palestine, in order that it should have full opportunity to display its capacities, should know that it was in Palestine 'as of right and not on sufferance', and for that reason the existence of a Jewish National Home in Palestine should be internationally guaranteed and recognized as resting on ancient historic connexions. Secondly, it recognized that the community had in fact 'national' characteristics. Thirdly, it acknowledged the right of the Jews to immigrate into Palestine subject only to the economic capacity of the country to absorb them. Finally, it asserted that there could be no question of rescinding the Balfour Declaration which was 'not susceptible of change'.

This statement was sent to the Palestine Arab Delegation and the Zionist Organization. The Arabs replied with a vigorous letter of protest, repeating all the old arguments regarding the McMahon 'pledges', protesting against its injustice to which it was not to be expected that the Arabs would give way. Until there was 'a real practical change in the policy of H.M. Government the Arabs must harbour the fears that the intention is to create a Jewish National Home to the disappearance or subordination of the Arab population, language, and culture in Pales-tine'. The Jews, in a short letter signed by Chaim Weizmann on behalf of the Organization's executive, assured H.M. Government that the Organization's activities would be conducted in conformity with the policy set forth in the statement. The letter stressed the fact that the Jews had always been anxious to proceed in harmonious co-operation with all sections of the people of Palestine, and would continue to spare no efforts to foster the spirit of goodwill necessary to ensure the future prosperity of the country.

On 24 July the Mandate was at last approved, although it did not come into force until 29 September 1923 jointly with the French Man-date for Syria. It went further than the Balfour Declaration had done for it recognized, in the third paragraph of the Preamble, the historical connexion of the Jewish people with Palestine and the grounds for re-constituting their National Home in that country.

That was, undoubtedly, why the British Government made it clear in a communication to the Council of the League of Nations that it accepted the responsibility of implementing it with the understanding that it would be carried out in the light of the 1922 Statement of Policy.[1]

The position of the Zionists in Palestine was also improved by the Mandate, as Article 4 recognized 'an appropriate Jewish Agency' as a public body for the purpose of advising and co-operating with the Administration of Palestine in all matters affecting the establishment of the Jewish National Home and the interests of the Jewish population in Palestine, and stated that the Zionist Organization would continue to be recognized as the appropriate Agency as long as its organization and constitution were considered suitable by the Mandatory Power.

The High Commissioner continued a policy of moderation and con-ciliation, mainly with the Arabs, for they were in the majority and more intransigent. But it brought about little or no beneficial result, for whichever side was favoured the other protested.

A further effort to gain Arab co-operation was made on 11 October 1923 when an offer was made to a fully representative gathering of Arab leaders assembled at Government House of an Arab Agency to deal with Arab matters. The High Commissioner told them that he

[1] H.M.S.O. Command Paper 1708 (1922).

realized that the special position accorded to a Jewish Agency under Article 4 had been the subject of frequent complaint, and that although it was not possible to alter the Mandate H.M. Government was perfectly prepared to recognize an Arab body on the same footing as that accorded to the Jewish Agency. The Government felt that this offer would demonstrate indubitably that it was determined to deal quite impartially with the different communities in Palestine, and to fulfil to the letter the obligations to both Arab and Jew to which the previous Government had publicly committed itself.

It is not possible from the available evidence to determine whether or not either the High Commissioner or his Government at home expected that this offer would be accepted. Having regard to the fact that the Arabs had refused to co-operate on two previous occasions, when the British Government had put forward proposals with a view to closer association of the Arab community with the Administration of Palestine, there seems to have been no reason why the Colonial Secretary or Sir Herbert should be at all sanguine.

The Arab refusal was clear and uncompromising. At the meeting, Musa Kazem Pasha, then Mayor of Jerusalem, gave a verbal refusal which was later confirmed in a letter from the President of the Executive of the Arab Congress. 'The object of the Arab inhabitants of Palestine is not an Arab Agency analogous to the Zionist Agency. Their sole object is independence. The Arab owners of the country cannot see their way to accept a proposal which tends to place them on an equal footing with the alien Jew.'

This reply must have made it crystal clear to all concerned that no amount of moderation, no conciliation, no appeasement would reconcile the Arabs to any régime which was determined to stand by the Balfour Declaration. H.M. Government certainly appear to have understood this at the time, although succeeding Governments, to judge from their policy, failed to remember the lesson.

In a telegraphic message from the Colonial Secretary to the High Commissioner he recalled the three proposals made by H.M. Government to the Arabs.

(1) The establishment of the Legislative Council on which Arabs would have been represented by ten elected members.

(2) The reconstruction of the Advisory Council so as to secure effective Arab representation.

(3) The recognition of an Arab Agency with further functions similar to those assigned to the Jewish Agency under the terms of the Mandate.

Towards all these proposals the Arabs had adopted the same attitude, namely refusal to co-operate, which had reluctantly driven H.M. Government to the conclusion that further efforts on similar lines would be a waste of time and the attempt would, therefore, not be repeated. Furthermore, the message stated, as all proposals for the closer association of the Arabs with the administration had been rejected, the Government had no alternative but to continue to administer the country in conformity with its understandings, even though it had to forgo the assistance it had hoped to obtain from the Arab community. The High Commissioner was authorized, therefore, to carry on the Administration of Palestine with the aid of an Advisory Council.[1] The appeasement, however, continued, and produced a few years of quiet, if nothing else. Hopes that the two communities would eventually agree to at least some form of peaceful co-existence ran high, but it is doubtful whether there was ever any sound reason for such optimism.

That it existed is confirmed by the reductions in the strength of the British armed forces and police in Palestine which were begun in Sir Herbert Samuel's time and continued under Field-Marshal Lord Plumer. The Permanent Mandates Commission in 1926 drew the British Government's attention to the risks run by not maintaining adequate local forces, and it repeated the warning three years later, in 1929, during its sixteenth session, but on that occasion the High Commissioner, Sir John Chancellor, who had by then succeeded Plumer, assured the Commission that the forces were adequate to deal with any situation that was likely to arise. This assurance was given in July. Within a month serious disturbances took place all over the country, which are described in Chapter VI.

Sir Herbert Samuel relinquished his appointment as High Commissioner on 30 June 1925, a year in which Jewish development had reached a higher point than ever before. The immigration figure had

[1] H.M.S.O. Command Paper 1989 (November 1923), p. 12.

reached a record peak of thirty-four thousand, and the Hebrew University had been declared open by Lord Balfour on Mount Scopus, before a distinguished gathering. As Sir Herbert himself said, the situation in Palestine during his years of office had been dominated by the Balfour Declaration. Many, if not most, of the difficulties encountered were inherent in the Mandate which had embodied the Declaration in its preamble. The policy set forth in the Declaration had two aspects. Two undertakings were given by the British Government. Firstly, to use their best endeavours to facilitate the establishment in Palestine of a National Home for the Jewish people, and secondly, to do so without prejudicing the civil and religious rights of existing non-Jewish communities in that country. To carry out both undertakings conscientiously and equitably could never be an easy task, and no High Commissioner found it so.

When he left Palestine the Jews gave Samuel an enthusiastic farewell, and the following tribute to his commissionership was paid in the Report of the Executive to the Fourteenth Zionist Congress. 'Sir Herbert has, by common consent, acquitted himself of his historic task with dignity and distinction, and carries with him in his retirement the enduring gratitude of the Zionist Organization and of the Jewish world at large. The contrast between the Palestine of 1920 and the Palestine of 1925 speaks for itself. Political unrest has subsided, a stable and efficient Administration has been built up, and there has been a marked and general quickening of economic life. Not only have the past five years brought Palestine peace, order and good government, but they have witnessed the successful completion of the first and most difficult step in the establishment of the Jewish National Home.'

Sir Herbert Samuel himself fully realized that much of the difficulty experienced in those first five years resulted from the doubt as to what was the meaning of that vital phrase, 'a National Home for the Jewish people'.

There were some among the Jews of the Diaspora who, after the Balfour Declaration had been made, were so filled with enthusiasm at the prospect of an immediate influx of large numbers of Jews into the Promised Land that they were inclined to discount the obstacles ahead and to forget the presence of more than half a million Arabs who owned most of the land. They hoped that the ancient prophecies would be fulfilled in the twinkling of an eye, although the leaders of the Zionist Organization gave no support to such visionary views.[1]

The Arabs, however, were naturally suspicious. They could not feel certain that the second undertaking given in the Balfour Declaration, guaranteeing their civil and religious rights, would be faithfully implemented. Supposing an overwhelming number of Jews were quickly brought into Palestine and the British withdrew. They, the Arabs, would be swamped.

These fears were, of course, groundless. Nevertheless they existed, and the necessity for dispelling them explains much of the Administration's acts of policy which disappointed the Jews without diminishing Arab hostility and suspicion.

Sir Herbert's greatest difficulty was, perhaps, and he had been one of the first to realize it, that he was a Jew and must therefore lean over backwards in order to be, and appear to be, a moderate Administrator, and always mindful of the second leg of the Balfour Declaration. It will be remembered that when Lloyd George first offered him the appointment, Samuel expressed doubts as to whether, from the political standpoint, he would be a good choice. He felt that measures which the non-Jewish population would accept from a British Christian governor might be objected to if introduced by a Jew. On the other hand, there was some advantage to be gained by appointing a Jew. 'The fulfilment of the Zionist programme,' he wrote, 'must be gradual . . . and Jewry in Palestine and throughout the world would be more likely to practise patience, without losing enthusiasm, if the pace were set by an Administrator who was known to be in sympathy with the ultimate aim, than if it were set by anyone else. . . .'

Let a Jew who served in the Samuel Administration as Attorney-General sum up his High Commissioner's five years' work. 'If he had not achieved in the five years all the promise that he set before himself when he came, yet he had made outstanding contributions to the fulfilment of the policy of the Mandate. He came to a country, seething with discontent and racial feeling, in which a considerable military force was still necessary to preserve the peace; he left the country appeased and tranquil, with the flames of racial conflict seemingly dying out, and

[1] See Report of the High Commissioner on the Administration of Palestine, 1920–1925, p. 25.

law and order adequately maintained with scarcely any military garrison. He came to a country in which the administrative services were ill-organized and the progressive functions of Government were hardly exercised at all. He left it in a state of economic and social progress, far ahead of that of any of the neighbouring lands.'[1]

[1] *England in Palestine* by Norman Bentwich.

CHAPTER V

Three Quiet Years

THE three years immediately following the departure of Sir Herbert Samuel were peaceful, but it was merely the calm before the storm. Nevertheless, during this period there were no organized protests against Jewish immigration, no demands for self-government, no meeting of the Palestine Arab Congress. But they were also years of economic depression. It was not part of the general world-wide financial crisis, which only began in 1929, and its causes are not accurately known. The collapse of the Polish Zloty, however, and the restrictions on Eastern European currency generally had seriously impoverished about half the total number of immigrants who came from Poland.

The Peel Commission, in its Report, attributed the Arab quiescence to 'the sharp decline in the fortunes of the National Home'. Others have attributed it to the steadying influence of Field-Marshal Lord Plumer's exemplary administration.

When he arrived many Jews regarded his appointment with suspicion. He was getting on in years and was a soldier. Would he understand their problems? Would he be too unbending, too conservative? Would he try to appease the Arabs? The Arabs on the other hand welcomed the arrival of a non-Jewish High Commissioner. Lord Plumer surely would understand the shortcomings of his predecessor's régime.

Both Arab and Jew soon had their answers. He would govern strictly and fairly in accordance with the clearly stated policy of H.M. Government. He told the Arabs, who presented him with a formidable list of demands and condemned the Samuel régime with extravagant vehemence, that he intended to follow, generally speaking, in the foot-steps of his predecessor and that he regarded agriculture as the primary industry of the country.

He also made it clear, beyond doubt, that he would not be perturbed by threats of civil unrest. On the occasion of the laying of the foundation stone of a new headquarters of the Bible Society, which Lord Plumer performed, some fanatical Moslems threw stones. Next day the Field Marshal called the Mufti to Government House and reprimanded him for the insult shown by his followers to the Christian faith. The Moslem disclaimed responsibility. 'Very well,' said the High Commissioner, 'but next time there is any stone throwing at a religious ceremony, there will be a new Mufti.' There was no more stone throwing. He proved to be a perfect, non-political governor.

A proposal to reduce the military forces and the British gendarmerie, made just before Sir Herbert Samuel's departure, had been postponed until the arrival of his successor so that the new High Commissioner could make the final decision after reviewing the situation. He decided to make considerable reductions. It became clear, however, after his departure that such reductions were premature, but full responsibility for the decision was taken by the new Colonial Secretary, Mr. Leo Amery, during the Palestine Debate in the House of Commons in 1930. The reductions were made, said Amery, because he had insisted on economies.

Lord Plumer's personality in the country, it has been said, was worth a battalion and it had not been appreciated, when he left in 1928, that an extra battalion was needed to make up for him.

Although a number of other factors, such as the reduction of Jewish immigration due to the economic crisis, undoubtedly helped him to maintain peace during his tenure of office, it must be acknowledged that the main cause was his firm touch, and the devotion which he gave to the practical need of the country for consolidation. He did much to improve the Arab peasants' standard of living and helped to ease the Jewish unemployment problem.

Lord Plumer's three years of office were not distinguished by any striking new policies, nor were they marred by any disturbances. The peace was kept throughout the whole territory without the use of any force, the policy of establishing a Jewish National Home was quietly and steadily pursued, agricultural development received every attention, local self-governing institutions received every encouragement, and, above all, national politics were avoided. These were anathema to the old soldier. 'Plumer remained with us,' wrote Dr. Weizmann in his autobiography, 'less than three years—all too short a period. He was succeeded by Sir John Chancellor, a man of much smaller calibre.'

CHAPTER VI

The 1929 Disturbances

THE first year of Sir John's term of office was quiet and uneventful. The economic crisis showed signs of passing and, as the situation improved, the immigration figures increased. The new High Commissioner, who had had previous experience of colonial government in Rhodesia and other places, soon showed that he was not disposed to let sleeping dogs lie, as had his predecessor, in the matter of setting up a parliamentary government. Shortly after his arrival he told an Arab delegation that he proposed to take up the question of the suspended Legislative Council with the Colonial Office when he visited England in a few months' time. He was, in fact, discussing possible constitutional changes in Palestine with the Colonial Secretary when the 1929 disturbances broke out.

As stated in a previous chapter, Sir John assured the Permanent Mandates Commission, when he appeared before it at its Sixteenth Session in July 1929, that the resources at the disposal of the Government of Palestine were sufficient to deal with any situation that was 'likely to arise', as the relations between the Arab and Jewish communities continued to improve.[1]

This proved to be an unfortunately inaccurate forecast, and as there had been a clear warning of possible impending trouble only three months before Sir John's arrival in Palestine, the reprimand administered by the Mandates Commission at its Seventeenth Session for the inexplicable failure to heed such a warning appears to have been fully justified.

The first sign of trouble brewing took place on the eve of the Jewish

[1] Permanent Mandates Commission: Minutes of the Sixteenth Session, pp. 79–80.

Day of Atonement, 24 September 1928, and is generally known as the Wailing Wall incident.

The Wailing (Western) Wall originally formed part of the western exterior of the ancient Jewish Temple. From time immemorial it has been the custom of Jews from all over the world to pray there, and it has been preserved and reverenced in Jewish memory as the last remaining visible reminder of that ancient Jewish shrine.

On the fast of Tisha b'Av, the day on which the end of the siege of Jerusalem is commemorated, hundreds of Jews, including many who are not religiously orthodox, visit the Wall to lament the destruction of their Temple by Titus.

This same Wall, however, is also part of the Haram esh-Sharif in which are enclosed the Dome of the Rock and the Mosque of El Aksa. It is an Islamic place of great sanctity, third only to Mecca and Medina as an object of veneration. It also has a legendary significance for Moslems, because within the thickness of the Wall itself there is a chamber where, according to ancient tradition, Mohammed's horse, Burak, was stabled when the prophet ascended to Heaven on the occasion of his celestial journey. Although, in law, the Wall is the property of the Moslem community, and the strip of pavement facing it, on which the Jews stand when saying their prayers, is owned by the Waqf, the Jews have, through the practice of centuries, established a right of access to the Wall.

In Article 14 of the Mandate it was provided that a special Commission be set up by the Mandatory Power to define and determine the rights and claims of the various religious communities in connexion with the Holy Places. An attempt had been made in 1922 by H.M. Government to reach a general agreement with regard to this special Commission, but without success. In the absence of any Commission there devolved on the Government the duty of giving rulings regarding such questions of rights and claims as arose. On all such occasions the guiding principle was, quite properly, considered to be the preservation of the *status quo*, and in his speech before the Council of the League of Nations in July 1922, Lord Balfour said that with regard to the Holy Places the British Government had no other desire than that of administering historic justice between the communities concerned.

In the absence of a Holy Places Commission which alone, under the terms of the Mandate, could finally determine rights and claims in connexion with the Wall, there were bound to be some disputes. These were, however, few in number. In 1925 a ruling was given to forbid the practice, which had grown up, of Jews bringing seats and benches to the Wall, even though they were only intended for the innocent purpose of providing a means of rest to worshippers who were aged or infirm.

The trouble in 1928 began, as already stated, on the Jewish Day of Atonement. On the evening of 23 September a complaint was made to the Deputy District Commissioner in Jerusalem by the Mutawali of the Abu Madian Waqf, in which the pavement and the whole area around the Wailing Wall is vested, to the effect that a screen had been fixed by bolts to the floor of the pavement adjoining the Wall to separate the sexes during worship in accordance with orthodox Jewish ritual. Some other innovations had also been introduced such as additional petrol lamps and a few mats, and the Ark was larger than usual.[1]

In order to investigate this complaint the Deputy District Commissioner visited the Wall during the evening service, decided that the screen would have to be removed before the service on the following day, and gave instructions to the beadle in charge to do so. A British police officer was instructed to remove the screen next morning if the beadle had failed to carry out the orders of the D.D.C.

On the following morning the police officer visited the Wall, and finding that the screen had not been removed asked some members of the congregation to take it away. They said that they could not do this because of the holiness of the day. The police, therefore, removed the screen themselves. This, not unnaturally, led to a mêlée in which a few Jews were slightly injured.

The Palestine Government issued a communiqué two days later in which they deeply deplored the shock that was caused to large numbers of religious people on a day so holy to Jews. They also regretted the fact that no Jewish police officer had been present at the Wall on the occasion in question, all Jewish officers in Jerusalem having been excused duty for the Day of Atonement. The Government considered it desirable that in future a responsible Jewish officer should be present on

---

[1] The Ark contains the Scrolls of the Mosaic Law.

solemn Jewish holy days. Nevertheless, the Government considered that the removal of the screen was necessary although they regretted all the circumstances which arose from the action taken.

The Jews, not only in Palestine but throughout the world, were horrified at what appeared to them interference with their religious rights and liberties which were supposed to be guaranteed by the Mandate. Protests were made by the Zionist Organization and the two Chief Rabbis of Palestine to the British Government and the League of Nations. The only replies that they received were expressions of regret that the incident had occurred. H.M. Government could hardly have withheld that, for the complaint made by the Arab Mutawali to the Deputy District Commissioner had not been handled with consummate skill. Even though the erection of a screen and the increase in dimensions of the Ark could properly be described as departures from the *status quo*, and it was 'the practice', as stated in the White Paper,[1] to take immediate action where it was established that the *status quo* had been infringed, it would yet seem reasonable to expect that an experienced member of the administration in Jerusalem would have realized that any action that was considered necessary should be carried out in such a way as to avoid any possible chance of offending the religious susceptibilities of the Jews on the most solemn day in their religious calendar.

The British Government excused the official responsible for this grave error of judgment by stating that he had no reason to suppose that the undertaking given by the beadle to remove the screen would not, in fact, be carried out. The possibility that the beadle might hesitate to remove the offence from religious motives was surely not so remote that it could be ignored and that, indeed, is what happened. But at least he reported his inaction to the Deputy District Commissioner and asked for a stay of execution which was refused. When a non-Jewish police officer was then ordered to secure the screen's removal, did it never occur to this British official that some trouble might ensue? Whatever responsibility history may attribute to the Deputy District Commissioner, who was doubtless trying to carry out his duties to the best of his ability, there can be no doubt about the serious after-effects of his decision. What had hitherto been possible and sincerely desired, namely

[1] H.M.S.O. Command Paper 3229 (November 1928), p. 5.

that there should be some mutual arrangement between the Jews and Moslems on this matter, was now, beyond doubt, unattainable, for, as was stated in the White Paper, public opinion in Palestine had definitely removed the dispute from the purely religious orbit and had made of it a political and racial question.

Ridiculous rumours spread all over Palestine and propaganda was circulating throughout the Moslem world that the Jews' intention was gradually to take possession of the Mosque of El Aksa on the pretence that it was the Temple, by starting with the Western (Wailing) Wall which is an inseparable part of the Mosque. Many organs of the Arabic Press dealt with the subject in their news columns in a way calculated to excite susceptible readers, and published several provocative articles.

The Zionist Organization repudiated these stories and rumours as utterly untrue and irresponsible, as indeed they were, and a public appeal was made to the Arabs in the following terms: 'We herewith declare emphatically and sincerely that no Jew has ever thought of encroaching upon the rights of Moslems over their own Holy Places, but our Arab brethren should also recognize the rights of Jews in regard to the places in Palestine which are holy to them. . . . We call upon our Arab brethren in general, and their responsible leaders in particular, to disperse the poisonous clouds of the false rumours which have recently been circulated, and to create possibilities for constructive co-operation for the benefit of the country and all its inhabitants, in the place of hostility and dispute.'

It was a pity that the Arab leaders did not accept this olive branch, but they were in no mood to co-operate. The General Moslem Conference, assembled under the presidency of the Mufti, demanded that Government action should at once be taken to prevent, once and for all, any 'seats, lamps, objects of worship or reading' being placed by Jews in the area of the Wailing Wall, and the Arabic Press in its columns continued to voice a growing feeling of resentment of the failure of the Palestine Government to give effect to the doctrine of the *status quo* contained in the White Paper.

During the whole of this time, and until 1 August 1929, no intemperate articles had appeared in the Hebrew newspapers, although Arab anti-Jewish propaganda had given the Jews considerable provocation. It was hardly to be expected that the Jewish leaders would be able to pacify their followers indefinitely, for public indignation was daily growing as a result of certain building operations undertaken by the Supreme Moslem Council, with the Government's approval, in the neighbourhood of the Wailing Wall, and the initiation of new religious ceremonies there which the Jews regarded as a patent infringement of the *status quo* and as certain to interfere with Jewish worship.

In an attempt to do so, however, an official of the Palestine Zionist Executive, who had been left in charge of the organization's affairs, telegraphed to the members of the Executive, who were in Zürich attending the Sixteenth Zionist Congress, asking for some statement to be made by the Executive regarding any action taken by them on the question of the Wailing Wall, as 'public agitation was growing'.

The reply was not encouraging, for it disclosed the fact that there appeared to be no prospect of reversing the Government's decision about the building, and urged that every effort should be made to 'damp down' agitation on the part of the Jewish people in Palestine. On receipt of this reply an appeal was made by the Zionist Executive's Palestine representative to representatives of the Hebrew Press which was, at last, beginning to grow restive. Meanwhile definite sign of the increase of tension had not been absent and two violent incidents occurred at the Wailing Wall during the first week of August, when three Jews were attacked and wounded by Arabs.

That serious trouble would eventually break out should have been obvious to anyone, and the British and Palestine Governments could never complain that they had not been forewarned. On 8 August two categorical warnings were given, one in London and one in Jerusalem. On that date Mr. Rutenberg, who was the Managing Director of the Palestine Electric Corporation, saw Mr. Luke who was acting for the High Commissioner whilst the latter was on leave. When both these gentlemen gave evidence there was a discrepancy regarding the exact terms of their conversation, but the evidence which is available today tends to confirm the accuracy of Mr. Rutenberg's memory rather than that of Mr. Luke. Mr. Rutenberg told the acting High Commissioner that Jewish feeling was 'getting worked up over the Wailing Wall', and they discussed the possibility of an organized body of Jews assembling at the Wall on the fast of Tisha b'Av, on 15 August, which might result in a large demonstration which could lead to serious trouble. The influx of Jews was expected to come from Haifa, and Luke asked Rutenberg to use his influence to prevent it. This Rutenberg did.

Simultaneously with this interview Colonel Kisch saw Sir John Chancellor and the Assistant Under-Secretary of State, Sir John Shuckburgh, at the Colonial Office. Kisch[1] produced all the reports recently received from the Zionist Executive's office in Jerusalem to the effect that the Mufti and his associates were stirring up religious incitement in connexion with the Wailing Wall. Kisch categorically warned Shuckburgh of the need for special precautions at the Wall on 15 August. Sir John appreciated the seriousness of the warning and telegraphed its substance to the Government in Palestine. The text of that telegram is not available, and it is noteworthy that neither the fact of its receipt nor its contents appear to have been communicated by the Palestine Government to the Shaw Commission which reported in March 1930 on the disturbances of the previous year.

Even though the acting High Commissioner took little or no preventive action on receipt of this information from the Colonial Office, and had not felt the preliminary rumblings which preceded the eruption on 23 August, his failure to withdraw his head from the sand after the Jewish demonstration on 15 August is difficult to understand. On that morning the Government most unwisely granted permission for a procession of two or three hundred Jewish youths to go to the Wall provided they did not march in military formation. After a resolution had been carried regretting the situation which had been allowed to develop in regard to the Wailing Wall dispute, the Zionist flag was unfurled, the 'Hatikvah'[2] sung, and a few excited youths in the crowd were heard shouting such slogans as 'The Wall is ours' and 'Shame on those who profane our Holy Places', but there was no violence. On the following morning the acting High Commissioner was informed by the Deputy Commissioner of the Jerusalem District that the Moslems intended to stage a counter-demonstration at the Wall immediately after midday prayer. The demonstrators, who numbered at least two thousand, arrived at the Wall in an excited state of mind. 'At the Wall

[1] Lt.-Col. Kisch had served with the Royal Engineers in Mesopotamia during the war, and joined the Palestine Zionist Executive on which he served as Director of the Political Department, in which appointment he was, for nearly nine years, the official spokesman of the Zionist Movement in Palestine.

[2] This is now Israel's national anthem.

an inflammatory speech was made by one of the Sheikhs of the Mosque of El Aksa, a table belonging to the Shammas or Jewish beadle was upset and broken, and petitions which had been placed in the crevices of the Wailing Wall by Jewish worshippers were taken out and burnt by the crowd, as were also some prayer books and prayer sheets. The Shammas, who is said to have been the only Jew present at the Wall, was hustled and his clothes torn.'[1] Still no effective precautionary action was taken by the Government, not even during the following week when a serious clash occurred at the funeral of a young Jew who had been stabbed by Arabs in a street in Jerusalem, and the crowd of Jewish mourners were treated with great violence by the police.

If the troops within the acting High Commissioner's jurisdiction, small in number though they were, had been held in readiness at some convenient place in Palestine, even as late as 21 August, the heavy casualties and widespread destruction of Jewish property would have been prevented. But the troops were not brought up in time. On the morning of 23 August the only British troops in Palestine were a section of an Armoured-Car Company and some Base Details, numbering in all six officers and seventy-nine men, stationed at Ramleh which is situated about twenty-five miles from Jerusalem on the Jaffa road. The remainder of the British military forces, numbering less than three hundred all told, and thirty-three officers and 551 other ranks of the Transjordan Frontier Force were all in Transjordan.

There was a strong police force consisting of about a hundred officers and 1,376 men, but of these only thirty-one officers and 142 other ranks were British. The native police, however, were useless and one of the witnesses who gave evidence before the Shaw Commission stated that 'though theoretically adequate in numbers and efficiency for their everyday duties, they collapsed under the stress of circumstances and became practically valueless'.

Even the members of the Shaw Commission who, with one exception,[2] appear to have leant backwards to avoid criticizing anyone, stated in their Report that when generous allowance was made for the trying circumstances in which they were placed, the local police in

---

[1] H.M.S.O. Command Paper 3530 (1930), p. 55. The Shaw Commission's Report.
[2] Mr. (afterwards Lord) Snell, a Member of Parliament who only signed the Report subject to certain reservations.

Palestine, regarded collectively, behaved during the riots in a manner which must have disappointed those who were responsible for their training and discipline.

Nor was the Intelligence System of the Palestine Police Force much better. It was generally admitted that it was inadequate and this may well have been, as it so often is, due to lack of funds. Through its incompetency, however, whatever the cause may have been, there is no doubt that the Government was not kept in touch with every form of subversive activity in Palestine, as it should have been.

The eve of the first outbreak of serious violence, 22 August, was a day of significant events. The Arab Press was full of provocative articles and announcements. A notice was delivered to the headman of a village near Nablus announcing the fact that fighting would take place next day between the Jews and the Moslems and calling on all who were of the Moslem religion to come to Jerusalem and help.[1] On the same morning the following appeared in the Arab newspaper, *Falastin*: 'In Jerusalem there is great excitement. The atmosphere is tense, and it is apprehended that tomorrow, when many fellahin assemble for prayers, a substantial answer will be given to these incidents.'[2]

An attempt made during a meeting that same evening between Arabs and Jews at the acting High Commissioner's house called, at the suggestion of one of the Jewish leaders, to agree on the issuing of a joint statement in order to calm public feeling, unfortunately proved abortive, for one of the Arabs refused to sign, saying that the time was not yet ripe for the signature of one document by prominent persons of the two races. The meeting adjourned until 26 August, but by then the riots were in full swing.

Early on the morning of 23 August it was noticed that many of the peasants from the neighbouring villages, who always came on Fridays into Jerusalem for the midday prayer, were carrying heavy sticks and clubs. The police officer in charge of the New City, Mr. Kingsley-Heath, had instructed his policemen to disarm these Arabs on the outskirts of the city, as they came in, and this was done. It would seem to have been a very wise and cautious move. Unfortunately an officer named Major Saunders decided to cancel Kingsley-Heath's order. Having cancelled the order, Major Saunders went to see the Mufti, and

[1] The Shaw Commission's Report, p. 75.   [2] I.e. at the Wailing Wall.

asked him if he knew why so many Moslems entering Jerusalem from the surrounding villages were carrying clubs. The Mufti said that it was due to their apprehension that owing to the strained relations between Arab and Jew at that time they might be attacked by the Jews during the midday prayer. It was rather credulous of Major Saunders to believe this story, having regard to the fact that up to that moment there had, so far, been no outbreaks of violence on the part of Jews against Arabs, but he did so and, furthermore, went away quite satisfied when the Mufti assured him that unless they were provoked the Moslems would not indulge in any violence.

It should have been obvious to anyone that there was more than a possibility of trouble, yet the police were not even armed lest, apparently, the sight of rifles should inflame the crowd, and a section of armoured-cars brought down from Amman as a reinforcement was, for some reasons never satisfactorily explained, kept at Ramleh thirty miles away.

After midday prayer the worshippers were addressed by the Mufti and left the Mosque quietly in two parties, still armed with sticks, knives and swords, one by the Damascus gate, the other towards the Jaffa road. Suddenly, catching sight of a Jew, the leaders of this second party rushed at him and hacked him to pieces. The crowd then broke into a number of savage bands to murder and loot. The English police, without their firearms, were unable to control them with their batons, and the Arab police were not dependable. One mob stopped a car containing a Jew, an English barrister resident in Jerusalem who was distinguished for his friendship with the Moslems and was devoting his life to bringing together the two branches of the Semitic race, and cut him and his two companions to pieces. . . . The news of violence, freely distorted, quickly spread. It was said that the Jews were attacking the Arabs and attempting to seize the mosques. Villagers and Bedouin flocked in, armed with various weapons, and fell upon the outlying Jewish quarters; others with rifles sniped from a distance at any person who ventured into the open.[1]

These murderous attacks on harmless Jews, who had offered no provocation whatsoever, went on most of the day. By 4.30 p.m. the Old

---

[1] This account is taken from *England in Palestine* by Norman Bentwich who, in 1929, was in Jerusalem where he held the appointment of Attorney-General.

City was quiet although there was desultory firing round the outskirts of the New City in the direction of the Jewish suburbs.

During the afternoon the acting High Commissioner had telegraphed to Malta for naval assistance, and had cabled to the Colonial Office for a battalion of British troops to be sent immediately. Early next morning he asked the High Commissioner for Egypt to send military assistance. The first contingent from Egypt did not take long to make the journey and a whole battalion had arrived by the following afternoon. Had those responsible for the security of Palestine only read the danger signals a little sooner many lives might have been saved.

Meanwhile, the police had told the Government that they were no longer able to accept responsibility for public security, and on the morning of 24 August a ferocious attack was made by Arabs on the Jewish ghetto in Hebron where more than sixty Jews—among them several women and children—were killed, and over fifty wounded. Destruction and looting were widespread, Jewish synagogues were desecrated and a Jewish hospital, which was open to all Palestinians irrespective of race or creed, was ransacked. Only the great personal courage of the sole British police officer in the town, Mr. Cafferata, prevented the attack from developing into a wholesale massacre of the Jews in Hebron. During that same day attacks were made on Jews in other Arab villages, and 'the horrors of Hebron were repeated on a smaller scale',[1] when the Arabs attacked several Jewish settlements.

The two days which followed the Hebron massacre were much quieter in Jerusalem, but several attacks were made by the Arabs on Jewish settlements some of which were burned to the ground. It was only after this that, not unnaturally, a few Jewish reprisals took place. Previously all the attacks had been made by Arabs on Jews.

With the arrival of more British troops on 27 August it was hoped that the situation would speedily be got under control, but one more serious incident took place before comparative quiet was restored. About 5.15 p.m. on the 29th Arab mobs attacked the Jewish ghetto in Safed, a picturesque old hill-town in upper Galilee. About forty-five Jews were killed or wounded in this attack, and several houses and shops were set on fire. The British officer in charge at Safed was Captain Faraday who was later criticized by the Jewish Press on the grounds

[1] The Shaw Commission's Report, p. 64.

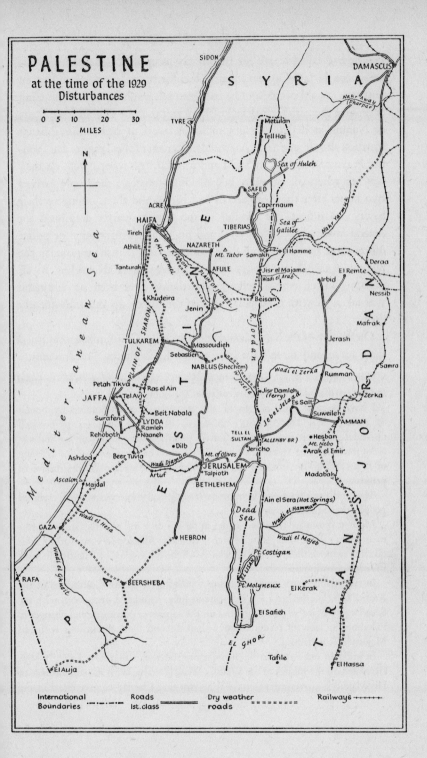

PALESTINE
at the time of the 1929 Disturbances

0 5 10   20   30
MILES

N

SYRIA

SIDON

DAMASCUS

TYRE

Nahr 'Awaj (Pharpar)

Metulla

Tell Hai

Sea of Huleh

SAFED

ACRE

Capernaum

HAIFA

Tireh

TIBERIAS

Sea of Galilee

Nahr Yarmuk

Athlit

NAZARETH

Mt. Carmel

Mt. Tabor

Samakh

El Hamme

Deraa

Tanturah

AFULE

Jisr el Majame

El Remte

R. Kishon

PLAIN OF JEZREEL

Wadi el Arab

Irbid

Nessib

Khudeira

Beisan

Jenin

R. Jordan

Mafrak

TULKAREM

Massoudieh

Jerash

Samra

Sebastien

Wadi el Zerka

Rumman

NABLUS (Shechem)

Petah Tikva

Ras el Ain

Zerka

JAFFA

Tel Aviv

Jisr Damieh (ferry)

Es Salt

Jebel Jelead

Suweileh

AMMAN

Beit Nabala

Surafend

LYDDA

Ramleh

Naaneh

Rehoboth

Dilb

TELL EL SULTAN

(ALLENBY BR.)

Hesban

Mt. Nebo

Arak el Emir

Ashdod

Beer Tuvia

Wadi Djamta

Jericho

Artuf

Mt. of Olives

JERUSALEM

Talpioth

Madabah

Ascalon

Majdal

BETHLEHEM

Ain el Sera (Hot Springs)

Dead Sea

Wadi el Hamman

GAZA

Wadi el Hesa

HEBRON

Wadi el Majeb

RAFA

Wadi el Ghuzil

BEERSHEBA

Pt. Costigan

El LISAN

Pt. Molyneux

El Kerak

El Safieh

P A L E S T I N E

T R A N S J O R D A N

EL GHOR

Tafile

El Hassa

El Auja

Mediterranean Sea

PLAIN OF SHARON

W. Farah

International Boundaries ---   Roads 1st.class ———   Dry weather roads ======   Railways ++++++

that he had failed to ask for British troops in time to prevent the disturbances. In fact Captain Faraday had for several days feared that an outbreak would occur, and he had been telegraphing and telephoning ever since the 24th for a detachment of troops to be sent up from Haifa or Nablus, as he had not got sufficient forces to deal with a difficult situation should one arise. A small detachment of the Transjordan Frontier Force had arrived in Safed and some British troops were on their way up when the massacre began. Unfortunately, they only arrived two hours after the Arab attack had begun and then, owing to their having no officer, the looting of the Jewish quarter continued for several hours after their arrival and no local administrative or police officer came forward to put their commander, a British sergeant, in the picture, or to help the troops distinguish between Arab and Jew. By an unhappy mischance the officer who should have been in command was taken ill with food poisoning on the march up and subsequently died.

On the day of the Safed disturbances the High Commissioner returned from leave, and three days later issued the following proclamation:

I have returned from the United Kingdom to find to my distress the country in a state of disorder and a prey to unlawful violence.

I have learned with horror of the atrocious acts committed by bodies of ruthless and blood-thirsty evil-doers, of savage murders perpetrated upon defenceless members of the Jewish population regardless of age and sex, accompanied, as at Hebron, by acts of unspeakable savagery, of the burning of farms and houses in town and country and of the looting and destruction of property.

These crimes have brought upon their authors the execration of all civilized peoples throughout the world.

My first duties are to restore order in the country and to inflict stern punishment upon those found guilty of acts of violence. All necessary measures will be taken to achieve these ends, and I charge all the inhabitants of Palestine to assist me in discharging these duties.

In accordance with an undertaking which I gave to the Committee of the Arab Executive, before I left Palestine in June, I initiated discussions with the Secretary of State when in England on the subject of constitutional changes in Palestine. In view of recent events I shall suspend those discussions with His Majesty's Government.

In order to put a stop to the mendacious statements that have recently been circulated on the subject of the Wailing Wall, I hereby, with the concurrence of His Majesty's Government, make it known that I intend to give effect to the principles laid down in the White Paper of the 19th of November 1928, after the methods of applying them have been determined.

This proclamation drew a violent protest from the Arab Executive who issued a statement making untrue and entirely irresponsible allegations against the Jews and accusing them of being responsible for the disturbances. The Shaw Commission, which nobody could accuse of being pro-Jewish, stated in its Report that in the course of its enquiry most of the statements contained in the Arab reply to Sir John's proclamation had been put to official witnesses and in almost every case had been found to be untrue.

The High Commissioner's proclamation, after the milk and water bulletins put out by Mr. Luke in Sir John's absence, had given the impression that the Palestine Government meant business and intended to deal with the aggressors with a strong hand. It was, therefore, most unfortunate that a second proclamation was later issued, largely counteracting the healthy effect of the first, in which it appeared that the High Commissioner was trying to water down the strong and well-founded words of condemnation which he had used immediately after his return.

The savage attacks made upon the Jews had been so outrageous and had caused such a stir throughout the civilized world, that the British Government had no alternative but to send out a Commission from England to investigate and report on the events which led up to the disturbances and to make recommendations as to the steps which should be taken to prevent any recurrence. The Commission, which arrived in Jerusalem on 24 October, was composed of Sir Walter Shaw, a former Colonial Chief Justice, and three Members of Parliament belonging to different political parties.

Lord Balfour, Mr. Lloyd George, and General Smuts apprehending, quite rightly, that the proceedings of the Commission would be used as an arena in which the Jews and Arabs could fight a propaganda battle, had written to the British Prime Minister, then Mr. Ramsay MacDonald, asking that questions of major policy should be investigated by some authoritative body from the Cabinet.

The Secretary of State for the Colonies, when he announced the Government's decision to appoint a Commission, emphasized the limitation of the scope of the investigation in these words: 'In view of the suggestions which have been made in certain quarters the Secretary of State desires to make it clear that His Majesty's Government have no idea of reconsidering the British tenure of the Mandate for Palestine, and that no inquiry is contemplated which might alter the position of this country in regard to the Mandate, or the policy laid down in the Balfour Declaration of 1917, and embodied in the Mandate, of establishing in Palestine a National Home for the Jews. The inquiry now initiated is, therefore, limited to the immediate emergency, and will not extend to considerations of major policy.'

The Report of the Commission, however, greatly exceeded this limitation. As the Mandatory Power was charged by the League of Nations with the duty of facilitating Jewish immigration under suitable conditions, and encouraging close settlement by Jews on the land, the two important questions of immigration and land settlement could hardly be said not to involve 'considerations of major policy'. Nevertheless, the Shaw Commission made recommendations to limit both of them. Nor was that all. The Commission proceeded to express views and to make proposals which affected the very constitutional basis of Palestine as laid down in the Mandate. The Report stated that there was no clear direction to assist either party (Arab or Jew) in the fulfilment of their aspirations and that there was an ambiguity in the Balfour Declaration and the Mandate. Finally, the Commission called upon H.M. Government to issue 'a clear definition of policy, backed by a statement that it was their firm intention to implement that policy in full'. That also was, surely, a 'consideration of major policy' and, in any event, a clear declaration that the policy under the Balfour Declaration and the Mandate was 'not susceptible of change' had already been made in the White Paper of 1922.

It was certainly no exaggeration to say, as the Peel Commission did in its Report, that 'as far as it went the Shaw Report was not unsatisfactory to the Arabs', and that it raised their hopes by expressing the opinion that Jewish immigration had been excessive in the past.[1]

There was one conclusion unfavourable to the Arabs, however, which the Commission could not avoid making, namely, that the outbreak in Jerusalem on 23 August was from the beginning an attack by Arabs on Jews for which there was no excuse; that the attacks were

[1] The Palestine Royal Commission's Report (July 1937), p. 71.

'vicious' and 'accompanied by wanton destruction of Jewish property', and that in the few instances in which Jews assaulted Arabs the attacks, 'though inexcusable', were mostly in the nature of reprisals.[1]

It was, perhaps, unfortunate that the Commission took on a legal character, and that all the interested parties, Arabs, Jews and the Palestine Administration were represented by counsel, for what might have been an open and straightforward enquiry became a forensic battle, and both Arabs and Jews made extravagant allegations against each other and delivered a two-pronged attack on the Palestine Government. The Government was, therefore, in the position of a defendant, and a great deal of the evidence given by the official witnesses was designed to clear themselves of charges of ineptitude and neglect. That the Government got off so lightly was perhaps due to the fact that the Jews overstated a good case, and made some accusations which could not be supported. This was unwise of them for, as the contemporary Attorney-General of Palestine has since written, 'The attitude of the Zionists in attacking the Palestine Administration had another regrettable consequence in estranging official and English sympathy, and driving the Administration to the side of the Arabs.'[2]

Having regard to the considerable criticisms made against the Shaw Commission's Report by the Permanent Mandates Commission and others, it is necessary to give a summary of its chief recommendations.

(1) The British Government should issue a clear statement of policy defining the meaning attached to the passage in the Mandate concerning the safeguarding of the rights of non-Jewish communities, and laying down more explicit directions as to the conduct of policy on such vital issues as land tenure and immigration.

(2) The Government should review the machinery for regulating Jewish immigration and non-Jewish interests should be consulted.

(3) The statement made in 1922, that the Zionist Organization's special position did not entitle it to share in the government of Palestine, should be reaffirmed. If possible Article 4 of the Palestine Mandate should be precisely defined.

[1] The Shaw Commission's Report, p. 158.
[2] *England in Palestine* by Norman Bentwich, p. 191. Bentwich as a Jew, was deemed to be precluded from taking part, and the Administration were represented by Mr. Kenelm Preedy and the Palestine Solicitor-General.

(4) Legislation should be introduced to make it a punishable offence to publish an article likely to cause a breach of the peace.

(5) The rights of both parties at the Wailing Wall should be determined by a Special Commission.

(6) H.M. Government should decide on the most suitable form of garrison for Palestine, and independent inquiries should be conducted into the Department of Police and the possibility of forming a reserve of special constables.

One member of the Commission, however, Mr. H. Snell, afterwards Lord Snell, although he signed the Report, stated in a 'Note of Reservations' that he was unable to agree with the general attitude of his colleagues towards the Palestine problem. Although, as he freely admitted, the policy of establishing the Jewish National Home in Palestine raised complicated racial and economic questions, he was convinced that they were neither unique nor insoluble, and believed that many of the immediate disturbances were due to fears and antipathies which, he was sure, the Moslem and Arab leaders awakened and fostered for political needs.

In particular, he attributed to the Mufti of Jerusalem a greater share in the responsibility for the riots than did the other members of the Commission, and considered that the Mufti must bear the blame of his failure to make any effort to control the character of an agitation conducted in the name of a religion of which, in Palestine, he was the head.[1] Nor was he prepared to accept the limitations, set by his colleagues, to the responsibility borne by the Arab Executive. The Report stated that the Commission had little doubt that some of the constituents who elected the Executive carried out, among the more ignorant Arabs, a campaign of propaganda calculated to incite them. Mr. Snell went further. He found it difficult to believe, and well he might, that the actions of individual members of the Executive were unknown to that body or indeed that they were acting in a purely personal capacity. There was every reason to take this view, and it was extremely naïve of the Commission to hold the contrary opinion, for there was ample evidence that the outbreaks of violence were the result of incitement, and yet there was none at all to associate the mass of the Arab population of Palestine

[1] Cf. the failure of Archbishop Makarios to condemn terrorism in Cyprus.

98

with those deplorable events. As Mr. Snell observed, the good relationship which in places existed between the two races was most strikingly
shown during the disturbances by some brave Arab workmen, who,
at great risk to themselves and their families, sheltered their Jewish
fellow-workers in their homes until the danger had passed, and then
conducted them, disguised in Arab clothing, in safety to their own
people.

It was still more naïve of the British Government, if indeed it was
not something worse, when dealing in its White Paper of May 1930[1]
with Mr. Snell's first reservation, to argue that whatever activities the
Mufti may have indulged in outside the knowledge of the Palestine
Government, in public he exerted his influence in the direction of promoting peace and restoring good order. On this point, according to the
Report, there was an absolute unanimity of opinion among the official
witnesses with whom the question of the Mufti's conduct was discussed.
The Mufti's subsequent record may raise some doubts as to whether
this consensus of opinion on the part of the officials of the Palestine
Administration had any sound basis.

Mr. Snell thought that too much importance had been attached in
the Report to the excited protests of Arab leaders on the one hand and
to the impatient criticisms and demands of Zionist leaders on the other.
'What is required in Palestine,' he wrote, 'is less a change of policy in
these matters[2] than a change of mind on the part of the Arab population, who have been encouraged to believe that they have suffered a
great wrong and that the immigrant Jew constitutes a permanent menace to their livelihood and future. I am convinced that these fears are
exaggerated and that on any long view of the situation the Arab people
stand to gain rather than to lose from Jewish enterprise . . . and in
spite of errors of judgment which may have resulted in hardship to
individual Arabs, Jewish activities have increased the prosperity of
Palestine, have raised the standard of life of the Arab worker, and
have laid the foundations on which may be based the future progress
of the two communities and their development into one state.'[3]

The Shaw Report was, naturally, received by the Arabs with great

[1] H.M.S.O. Command Paper 3582 (1930), p. 6. Palestine, Statement with Regard to
British Policy.
[2] He was referring to the problems of immigration and land settlement.
[3] The Shaw Commission's Report, p. 174.

joy. No one can have been surprised that it was greatly resented by the Jews, who described it in a Memorandum to the Permanent Mandates Commission of the League of Nations as 'one of the most unjust documents which our people have had to face in the course of 2,000 years of persecution'. Even if it did not deserve such strong condemnation as that, it cannot be denied that there was some just cause for complaint. It was not entirely extravagant to say, as the Jewish Agency did in its Memorandum of the Report, that it had found against the weight of the evidence in its denial that the disturbances were premeditated, and in its exoneration of the Mufti and the Arab Executive from responsibility. Nor can it be said that there was no foundation for the criticism that the Commission's judgments on Jewish immigration and land settlement were hasty, and that it had gone beyond its terms of reference in making tendentious interpretations of the Mandate and the Churchill Memorandum opposed to the policy of the Jewish National Home.[1]

But the Jews were not the only critics of the Report, for at a special session at Geneva in June 1930 the Permanent Mandates Commission of the League of Nations criticized both the Shaw Report and the British Government's execution of the task entrusted to them by the Mandate. Dr. Drummond Shiels and Mr. Luke, by then promoted to the post of Lieutenant-Governor of Malta, both appeared before the Commission and were subjected to a searching examination. The League of Nations Commission rejected the Shaw Commission's conclusion that the outbreak of violence was unpremeditated, and doubted whether the kindly judgment passed by the majority of the Commission upon the attitude of the political and religious Arab leaders was justified. Whether or not the disturbances were premeditated may be open to question, but there can be little doubt, if any, that there had been ample signs and warnings of impending trouble, and the Mandates Commission held that with a reasonable degree of foresight many of the incidents that caused the outbreak could have been avoided.

The Commission also made other criticisms, namely, that insufficient attention had been paid by the Mandatory Power to the 'social and economic adoption of the Arab population to the new conditions due

[1] Memorandum on the Report of the Commission on the Palestine Disturbances of August 1929. (The Jewish Agency for Palestine, London, May 1930).

to Jewish immigration', and that 'such inadequate forces had been maintained in the country as to jeopardize the security of persons and property'.

The British Colonial Office was not prepared to take these criticisms lying down, and published a reply pointing out that the Mandates Commission could scarcely appreciate the complexity of the problem as well as could the men on the spot.

Early in 1930 steps were taken to implement two of the Shaw Commission's recommendations. The Palestine Police Force was reorganized and Sir John Hope-Simpson, a former Indian Civil Servant, was sent to Palestine in order to examine there the problems of immigration and settlement. Meanwhile, pending the publication of Sir John's report, despite representations made personally to Lord Passfield, then Colonial Secretary, by Dr. Weizmann, the President of the Jewish Agency, immigration was suspended. Passfield had shown no sympathy towards the Jewish case and little understanding of it, and he was very reluctant to see Weizmann.[1] Nor would the Prime Minister consent to see him.

When, in October, Sir John's report was published it was seen that he took an extremely pessimistic view of the cultivable area of Palestine which has since been proved to have been an absurd underestimate. His survey of the country was made superficially from an aeroplane and the result was, in more senses than one, a bird's-eye view. He stated that, even if the land not occupied by Jews were divided equally among the Arab population, there would not be enough to support each Arab family at a decent standard of living, and that it was wrong to think that the Government was in possession of large areas of vacant land which could be made available for Jewish settlement. The rest of his report was designed to prove, from rather unreliable data, that there was not room for more than twenty thousand families to settle on the land.

Simultaneously with the publication of the Hope-Simpson report a Government statement was issued.[2] All the Jewish friends of the National Home, Zionist and non-Zionist alike, condemned it soundly,

---

[1] This was not the last time that the Jews in Palestine were to be disappointed at a Socialist's attitude to the Jewish National Home. However Weizmann was hardly prepared for Lady Passfield's (Beatrice Webb) light-hearted attitude to the repercussions of the 1929 disturbances. 'I can't understand,' she told him, 'why the Jews make such a fuss over a few dozen of their people killed in Palestine. As many are killed every week in London in traffic accidents, and no one pays any attention.'

[2] H.M.S.O. Command Paper 3686.

and Dr. Chaim Weizmann, who considered that it not only rendered but was intended to render the work of the Jewish Agency in Palestine impossible, resigned from the Presidency. Lord Melchett and another prominent Jew, Felix Warburg, also resigned from their respective positions as Chairman of the Agency's Council and member of its Administrative Committee. In his resignation statement Weizmann stated that he had taken such a drastic step as 'an emphatic protest against the one-sided and unjust criticism of our work' and because of his 'refusal to accept a policy which is in direct contradiction to the solemn promise of the British nation and the text of the Mandate'.

The Jews regarded the Command Paper as a disavowal of the Mandatory obligations sufficient to shake the confidence which they had so far shown in Great Britain as the Mandatory Power. It purported to reaffirm and clarify the Churchill White Paper, and repeated the assurance given to Parliament by the Prime Minister that there could be no question of receding from the international obligation conveyed by the terms of the Mandate, and that a double undertaking was, thereby, involved to the Jewish people on the one hand, and to the non-Jewish population of Palestine on the other. It went on to confirm the opinion of the Permanent Mandates Commission that these two obligations were of equal weight and in no sense irreconcilable, and expressed the 'firm resolve of His Majesty's Government to give effect, in equal measure, to both parts of the Declaration and to do equal justice to all sections of the population of Palestine'.[1]

Nevertheless, it went a step further than the Churchill Memorandum and, in the opinion of the Zionist leaders, it was a very far-reaching step. It appeared to them to detach the Jews of Palestine from World Jewry and to treat the Mandatory obligations as if they related only to the former, whereas the White Paper of 1922 consistently referred to the Jewish people as a whole and their rights in Palestine.

A few months before the publication of the 1930 Statement of Policy, Lord Cecil of Chelwood wrote an article on the essential character of the Palestine Mandate pointing out that it contained certain features which distinguished it from all other Mandates which owed their origin

---

[1] H.M.S.O. Command Paper 3582 (1930), p. 4. Palestine: Statement with regard to British Policy 1930.

to the provisions of Article 22 of the Covenant of the League of Nations. He described it as 'a deed of trust for the Jewish National Home'. The Arab rights were safeguarded effectively in a context which emphasized that they were subordinate, but not in any way antagonistic to the progressive fulfilment of the main purpose of the Mandate. 'To treat it', he wrote, 'as a set of directions for a kind of administrative tight-rope between the Scylla of injustice to the Arabs and the Charybdis of faith-breaking with the Jews would be to misinterpret it both in spirit and letter, and be the surest way to fall into both dangers and perpetuate the disquiet which has recently caused so deplorable a set-back.'

It was this very tight-rope that H.M. Government was trying to walk, and subsequent Governments continued the balancing trick with diminishing success until, in 1947, the British Foreign Secretary announced to Parliament and to the world that Great Britain had had enough and would leave its unwanted child on the doorstep of the United Nations.

The Jews were not, however, the only people to complain. Public criticism of the White Paper was widespread and there were many protests from eminent British statesmen, including the leaders of both the Conservative and Liberal Parties. Only the Socialists remained silent. Within ten days of its publication General Smuts cabled Ramsay MacDonald urging second thoughts. The South African Prime Minister's message was as follows:

As one of those responsible for the Balfour Declaration I feel deeply perturbed over the present reported Palestine policy, which makes a retreat from the Declaration. The Declaration was a definite promise to the Jewish world that the policy of the National Home would be actively prosecuted, and was intended to rally the powerful Jewish influence for the Allied cause at the darkest hour of the war. As such it was approved by the Government of the United States and the other Allies, and accepted by the Jews in good faith. It represents a debt of honour which must be discharged in full at all costs and in all circumstances. The original Declaration was far too solemn to permit of any wavering now. I would strongly urge that a Government statement be issued that the terms of the Balfour Declaration will be fully carried out in good faith, and that the Government's Palestine policy will be recast accordingly.

Three prominent members of the Conservative Party, Stanley

Baldwin, Austen Chamberlain and Leo Amery, in a letter to *The Times* on 30 October, wrote:

Without giving either the Jewish or Arab opinion an opportunity to express itself, or allowing the voice of Parliament to be heard, the Government have laid down a policy of so definitely negative a character that it appears to us to conflict, not only with the insistence of the Council of the League of Nations that it would be contrary to the intention of the Mandate if the Jewish National Home were crystallized at its present stage of development, but also with the whole spirit of the Balfour Declaration and of the statements made by successive Governments in the last twelve years.

Finally, on 3 November, Lord Hailsham, the former Conservative Lord Chancellor, and Sir John Simon, formerly Liberal Attorney-General and later to be, himself, Lord Chancellor, in a joint letter to *The Times*, attacked the Passfield White Paper on legal grounds. 'The Mandate,' they wrote, 'constitutes for the people of this country . . . a legal as well as a moral duty and breach of its terms by any British Government would lay this country open to a grave charge of breach of faith and disregard of its international obligations.' The letter then set out a number of paragraphs which appeared to Lord Hailsham and Sir John 'to involve a departure from the obligations of the Mandate'.

The British Prime Minister had probably expected an unfavourable reaction to the White Paper, though not such a violent storm of protest as, in fact, arose, for, two or three days before its publication, he had invited the Jewish Agency to appoint representatives to consult with a special committee of the Cabinet on Palestine policy. One of the members of the Cabinet Committee was the Prime Minister's son, Malcolm MacDonald, who was later in 1939 himself Colonial Secretary and the official Government sponsor of the Peel Commission's scheme of partition. The representatives of the Jewish Agency included Harry Sacher, Harold Laski, James de Rothschild, and Professors Brodetzky and Namier, and the meetings went on throughout the winter, and culminated in an agreement which Weizmann felt able to accept. The Prime Minister declined to issue a second White Paper, which would have involved a serious loss of face, but agreed to set out the results of the conference in a letter addressed personally to Weizmann which was made public in the House of Commons as an answer to a Parliamentary question.

In this letter the Prime Minister promised that the Mandate would be carried out, not only in accordance with the Articles but in conformity with the highly significant Preamble,[1] and recognized an undertaking to the Jewish people *as a whole*[2] and not merely to the Jews in Palestine. An attempt was made in the letter to correct a number of 'misconceptions and misunderstandings', particularly in respect of land settlement and immigration. It stated categorically that the Government 'did not propose to make any departure from the principles enunciated in the Churchill White Paper relative to immigration', and that in calculating the 'absorptive capacity', the policy of the Jewish Agency to employ Jewish labour in undertakings promoted by the Agency would be taken into account.

The letter was welcomed by public opinion in Great Britain which had received the Passfield White Paper unfavourably. Its acceptance by the Jews was not wholly enthusiastic, as some were disappointed that the Government's Statement of Policy had not been openly repudiated in an official document. Dr. Weizmann himself was bitterly attacked at the Zionist Congress later in the year, but this attitude on the part of certain Jews appears today to have been most ungrateful, for, as he wrote in his autobiography, whether he was right or wrong in accepting a letter in place of another White Paper, his decision should be judged by the results. 'It was,' as he wrote, 'under MacDonald's letter to me that the change came about in the Government's attitude and in the attitude of the Palestine administration which enabled us to make the magnificent gains of the ensuing years. It was under MacDonald's letter that the Jewish immigration into Palestine was permitted to reach figures like 40,000 for 1934 and 62,000 for 1930.'[3]

The measure of Weizmann's success on this occasion can be judged by the Arab reaction to what they called the 'black letter'. They were indignant at what they considered was a capitulation by the British Government to Jewish pressure. It was, they said, a breach of faith with the Arabs and a complete reversal of policy.

After the turbulent events of 1929 and their aftermath in 1930-1 there followed a period of comparative peace and quiet, but it proved to be only a temporary respite, for within five years the Arab rebellion had begun.

[1] See Appendix.   [2] The italics are mine.   [3] *Trial and Error*, p. 415.

CHAPTER VII

Palestine under Wauchope

IF they had done nothing else, the first ten years of British government in Palestine had revealed certain difficulties inherent in the Mandate, and the Administration had been rather like a see-saw, alternately tilting towards one side or the other as pressure was applied. As a result of the Arab attacks on Jews in 1929 the balance which the Mandatory Power had been trying to maintain between its two obligations had swung over to the Arab side. After publication of the Passfield Statement of Policy, in consequence of the pressure of world opinion, Jewish and non-Jewish, it swung the other way.

A National Government was elected to the British Parliament in October 1931 by a very large majority and Sir Philip Cunliffe-Lister, later Lord Swinton, became Colonial Secretary and continued as such until he became the Secretary of State for Air in 1935. He showed a keen interest in Palestine and an understanding of the problem of the Jewish National Home. At almost the same time Sir Arthur Wauchope was appointed High Commissioner and under him Palestine made its greatest progress. He was appointed by Ramsay MacDonald who had still remained at the head of the new Government although his own party had been disastrously defeated at the polls. The British Prime Minister realized that at such a critical time in the Mandate's history much depended on the choice of the right man. He was anxious to appoint a soldier, but told Weizmann that he wanted one who 'does it with his head, not his feet'. He could not have chosen better, for Sir Arthur was an able general, a distinguished administrator and a scholar. Despite the strong differences which developed between him and the Zionists towards the end of his commissionership they have always remembered him in Palestine as 'a friend, an intellectual, a soldier, an administrator, and a statesman'.[1]

The Jews will, also, always remember with gratitude that from the date on which he assumed responsibility for government in Palestine he kept the doors open, not only for capitalist refugees but for Jewish working men and women too, without whom the capital flowing into Palestine could not have been constructively applied to the development of the country, and during his term of office about 240,000 Jews entered Palestine as immigrants, compared with half that number during the combined tours of office of his three predecessors.

Sir Arthur was convinced that the 'double undertaking' involved in the Mandate, the simultaneous development of the Jewish National Home on the one hand, and self-governing institutions on the other, were not irreconcilable, and that real co-operation between Arab and Jew was not just a pipe-dream. He thought that one way of dispelling the Arab fears of increasing Jewish immigration was to raise the fellahin's standard of living. He never imagined that all this could be achieved by a wave of the wand, but he was convinced, as he told the Permanent Mandates Commission after a year in Palestine, 'that with the passage of time, Arabs and Jews would see that it was to their mutual advantage to work together'.[2]

Meanwhile, and not for the first time, a dissident faction within the Zionist movement began serious criticism of their leader, Chaim Weizmann. Within five years of the First Zionist Congress of 1897 in Basle the unfortunate Herzl who, as has been described in an earlier chapter, put Zionism on the map, was being attacked within the movement by a number of young men known as the Democratic Fraction, a leading member of which was the youthful Weizmann. This time he was the victim, and the attack was made by Jabotinsky, who led the Revisionists. The Revisionists would accept nothing short of a Jewish State on both sides of the Jordan, with all that it implied, and they regarded Weizmann's acceptance of the MacDonald letter, which gave something very much less than that, as political weakness, cowardice and betrayal. Weizmann became the object, as the Congress

---

[1] *Trial and Error*, p. 126.

[2] Permanent Mandates Commission: Minutes of the Twenty-Second Session, December 1932.

approached, of ever-increasing opposition and the butt of extremist propaganda, and during the Session a resolution of no-confidence in his policy was carried, and Sokolow was elected President in his place.

As Weizmann has himself stated, the conflict, which came to a head on this occasion, had been going on for years. 'It was,' he wrote, 'the conflict between those who believed that Palestine could be built up only the hard way, by meticulous attention to every object, who believed that in this slow and difficult struggle with the marshes and rocks of Palestine lies the great challenge to the creative forces of the Jewish people, its redemption from the abnormalities of exile, and those who yielded to those very abnormalities, seeking to live by a sort of continuous miracle, snatching at occasions as they presented themselves, and believing that these accidental smiles of fortune constitute a real way of life.'[1]

Opposition to his leadership had been growing in the United States, Germany and Poland amongst factions who, like Jabotinsky's Revisionists, wanted 'maximum' Zionism, and in Palestine a professor at the Hebrew University, who had previously been Weizmann's friend, published a virulent attack against him and accused him 'of degrading the Zionist movement through concessions and compromises on basic principles by joining with assimilationists . . . who were enemies of the national ideal'.[2] Weizmann, and he was surely right, felt that the political formulæ were of no use and might indeed even be harmful, so long as they were not the product of hard work put into the soil of Palestine. He believed in the path trodden by their own feet. His opponents wanted the easy road, paved with the promises of others. He told the Congress, 'The walls of Jericho fell to the sound of shouts and trumpets. I never heard of walls being raised by that means.'[3]

It was not only a theoretical political opposition which Dr. Weizmann had come up against, but a group organized by a Dr. Goldmann who called themselves Radical Unionists. Their policy was aggressive, and they did not believe in cautious compromise. 'It emphasized the role of private capital and middle-class immigration into Palestine and

---

[1] *Trial and Error*, p. 418.
[2] *Palestine*, Vol. II, p. 743 (Esco Foundation for Palestine).
[3] *Trial and Error*, p. 419.

urged the floating of an international loan for the expansion of economic work in Palestine on a large scale.'[1] Weizmann considered this unrealistic.

The election of Sokolow in Weizmann's place was a great blow for Jabotinsky, not merely because he had expected to succeed the man whose leadership he had so bitterly attacked but because the new President had worked hand in hand with the old ever since 1916, and the new leadership did not mean that there would be any fundamental change in Zionist policy in respect of collaboration with the Mandatory Government or the desire for co-operation with the Arabs. The new Executive merely continued the policy of the former President, and four years later Weizmann returned to office as President of both the World Zionist Organization and the Jewish Agency.

$$* \quad * \quad * \quad * \quad *$$

During the first two years of Wauchope's tenure of office the fortunes of the National Home had been steadily improving. Although at first there had been a slight decrease in the immigration figures, the unfavourable balance had been redressed by a reduction of emigration. By 1932, however, the immigration figure had risen to over nine thousand and there were less than four hundred emigrants. But there was another factor which had also enlarged the total strength of the Jewish community. For some years a large number of Jews had been coming to Palestine and illegally remaining in the country by entering with tourists' passports and staying beyond the permitted time. Many others smuggled themselves in by land and sea. In 1931 the Government decided to allow about six thousand, who admitted their illegal presence, to be registered as immigrants.

As had happened before, though they were always loath to admit it, whenever more Jewish immigrants and capital came into the country, the Arabs' economic position improved. Wages rose, and agricultural produce fetched higher prices, communications improved, and many more schools were opened. It would not have seemed unnatural if this increased prosperity had had a conciliatory effect on the Palestinian Arabs, but many incidents occurred which clearly showed that there was only a lull in the battle. Several Jews were murdered during those

---

[1] *Palestine*, Vol. II, p. 743 (Esco Foundation for Palestine).

two years by unknown Arab assassins, Jewish orange trees were destroyed and cattle maimed. In 1931 the rifles, which had for some years been stored in sealed armouries in the more isolated Jewish settlements, were replaced by shot guns. This could hardly be regarded as in any way provocative. The shot guns were more efficient for defence, but useless for attack, and the fact that they replaced rifles was, surely, a clear indication that the members of those settlements harboured no aggressive intentions.

It was just at this time, when the fires of Arab antagonism were smouldering beneath the surface, that a new complication began to make itself felt.

In January 1933 the appointment of Hitler as Chancellor by the aged Marshal von Hindenburg ushered in the Nazi régime and the beginning of a twelve years' reign of terror for the Jews of Germany. It was not long before a series of laws was passed which, in effect, removed Jews from every department of public life, from the Civil Service, from the professions, from education, and from the Services, and a steady stream of refugees began to pour out of Germany. Simultaneously the conditions for Jews in Poland and Roumania were consistently deteriorating. The Report of the Palestine Royal Commission, which was written while this new Exodus was still going on, described the situation in these words: 'It was the blackest crisis which the Jewish people has had to face in modern times, blacker because more widespread, and in some respects more painful, than the crisis of the Russian pogroms before the war.' Had the Report been written eight years later this paragraph would have been worded differently.

Many of those who had to flee their homes in order to save their lives naturally turned their eyes to the 'Land of their Fathers'. In Germany the Jews were now regarded as foreigners and had no rights of citizenship. Had not the Churchill Memorandum of 1922 declared that the Jewish people were in Palestine 'as of right and not on sufferance'? The immigration figures rose sharply in that first year of National Socialism to more than thirty thousand. With the increase in the number of immigrants the economic position of the country made great strides, rising from over two and a half to more than three and a half million pounds in the same year.

The Arab Executive's reaction to this boom in the Jewish National

Home was immediate and typical. A manifesto was addressed to the Arab Nation declaring that 'the general tendency of Jews to take possession of the lands of this holy country and their streaming into it by hundreds and thousands through legal and illegal means has terrified the country'.

The fact that this development of the National Home brought prosperity to Arab and Jew alike meant nothing to the Arab leaders. There seemed for the first time a possibility that the Jews could become a majority in Palestine within measurable time. The manifesto hinted at this danger, and falsely stated that it was the Government's policy to 'drive the nation away from its homeland for foreigners to supersede it'. It called upon the nation's sons 'for action and sacrifice in these hard times'.

The propaganda in the Arab Press became so inflammatory that an Ordinance was enacted which enabled the authorities to suspend any journal which published any matter 'likely to endanger the public peace'. Flagrantly untrue charges were openly made against the Government which was accused of 'deliberately flooding the country with Jews with the object of displacing Arabs from the land and depriving them of their employment'.

The situation was not improved when the Zionist Congress, assembled at Prague in view of events in Germany, demanded in a resolution that the Jewish National Home should be developed with the least possible delay and 'on the largest scale'. The stage was set clear for more trouble and the first sign of it was manifested in October 1933. A general strike was announced to take place on 13 October simultaneously with a demonstration outside the Government offices in Jerusalem. The crowd which took part in the demonstration was only dispersed after several baton charges by the police. A fortnight later there was a serious disturbance at Jaffa where it was found necessary to fire on the Arab mob who got out of hand. For the next two days the rioting continued and spread to Nablus and Haifa. Altogether one policeman was killed and fifty-six injured; twenty-six rioters or bystanders were killed and 187 wounded.

Nevertheless, the disturbances were never as serious as those in 1929, and they differed from the previous outbreaks of violence in one other particular. It was the first time that Arab ill-feeling had been publicly manifested against the Government. Hitherto it had only been against the Jews. There was, therefore, no commission of investigation after the 1933 riots to enquire into the causes of unrest and violence. It was at last realized that the attempted Arab rising in 1933 had been a 'challenge to Great Britain's position in Palestine'.[1]

During the next two years, as the National Home grew, the Arab hatred and apprehension of it increased. There were over forty thousand lawful immigrants in 1934, and over sixty thousand in 1935. Even when the Government cut down by half, as it did in 1934, the 'absorptive capacity' figure, and took effective steps to stop illegal immigration, it did nothing to pacify the Arabs. Every effort was made to prevent Arabs selling their land to Jews. To do so was to risk public denunciation in the mosque, as well as in the Press. The Arab Executive protested to the High Commissioner about immigration and land purchase claiming that the provisions in the Mandate to safeguard the rights of the non-Jewish communities in Palestine were being violated. Sir Arthur retorted by saying that immigration was still within the absorptive capacity of the country and he was doing everything in his power to protect Arab farmers and increase the yield of the land; but it made no difference to the Arab Executive's attitude which continued to be wholly uncompromising, perhaps because during the last two years the extreme Arab nationalists had been strengthening their grip on the Arab population, principally through the various youth organizations which had been gradually permeated with a dangerous form of aggressive nationalism. This strengthened the Executive's hand and made it more intransigent than ever.

The appointment of Haj Amin el-Husseini as Grand Mufti of Jerusalem was, at last, realized to have been what many thought at the time, a mistake, for under his leadership the Moslem religious organization of Palestine was dedicated to the dissemination of anti-Jewish propaganda and had become a kind of Resistance Movement to the 'occupying' Mandatory Power.

On 25 November 1935 the five Arab parties, in which the cleavage which became apparent in 1937 had not yet shown itself, presented a memorandum to the High Commissioner making the following demands:

[1] *Rebellion in Palestine* by John Marlowe, p. 133.

(1) The establishment of democratic government.

(2) The prohibition by law of the transfer of Arab land to Jews.

(3) The immediate cessation of Jewish immigration, and the formation of a committee to assess and determine the absorptive capacity of the country.

Three months later the Arab leaders received a reply, prepared by the Colonial Office, but communicated to them by Sir Arthur. A definite step towards democratic government had been taken in December, the Arabs were told, when the proposition was made to set up a Legislative Council with a large unofficial majority. Action would be taken to prevent the Jewish purchase of land except in cases where the Arab owner still retained an adequate acreage to subsist himself and his family. The rate of immigration, the High Commissioner said, was already carefully gauged according to the country's capacity, but a new statistical bureau was to be set up to assess this in the future.

It was in connexion with this proposal for a Legislative Council that the differences of opinion, already mentioned, between the High Commissioner and the Jewish Agency arose.

It had been suggested as long ago as 1922 in the Churchill White Paper, raised again in the White Paper of 1930, and included in the instructions given by the British Prime Minister to the new High Commissioner shortly after his appointment in November 1931.

Although there was at all times considerable opposition to it in Zionist circles, it was not until after the Nineteenth Zionist Congress in 1935 that the opposition became general.

Dr. Weizmann was frequently consulted on the subject by Sir Arthur during the time that Weizmann held no official position in the Jewish Agency. Weizmann tried his best to dissuade the High Commissioner from pressing on with the idea, but with no success. The Legislative Council proposal was to consist of fourteen Arabs, seven Jews, two business men of unspecified race, and five British officials. Of this total of twenty-eight, twelve were to be elected and sixteen appointed.

The main Jewish objection to the proposal was stated by David Ben Gurion in these words: 'Any attempt to transfer legislative power, formally or actually, to those elements who do not recognize the obligations of the Mandate and the rights of the Jewish nation to its land;

any attempt which will reduce the hopes of attaining a sincere and trust-worthy Arab-Jewish understanding, any such attempt will meet the strongest and most determined opposition from the Jewish people.'[1] This put into words what was a widespread feeling amongst Zionists, namely, that to establish a Legislative Council with an Arab majority, which had already rejected the basic principle of the Jewish National Home and the Mandate, would not lead to mutual co-operation and would most likely be used as a forum for anti-Jewish propaganda.

Whether or not this was a reasonable objection is open to argument. The Council was to be so constructed that the number of Arabs would be counter-balanced by the combined voting strength of the Jews, the British officials and the two unspecified business members. Furthermore, the Council would not be competent to grant immigration certificates. This was to be reserved for the High Commissioner. Unfortunately the Jewish leaders felt, from previous experience of British officials in Palestine, unable to trust them to uphold the principles of the Mandate and they suspected, rightly or wrongly, that when the Legis-lative Council had come into existence, it would not be long before it was given greater powers than was originally intended. Although this suspicion was, perhaps, not fully justified it would not be fair to say that it was without some foundation.

The effect on public opinion in general of the refusal of the Jews to accept the British Government's proposal for a Legislative Council was unfortunate. 'The Jews refused to agree to a Legislative Council. They were not, then, in favour of democratic rule.' Thus the public reasoned. Weizmann, who realized the danger of this only too well, was prepared to discuss the possibility of creating a Legislative Council on which there was equality of representation. It would, at least, ensure regular contacts between the two peoples, and in that way it was not impossible that the fears which kept Arab and Jew apart might be dispelled by patience and fair dealing.[2]

For his reasonable approach to this very thorny problem Weizmann was subjected to a torrent of abuse from the followers of Jabotinsky and other extremists in the Movement who were not content with merely calling him an appeaser, but even accused him of being a British agent.

[1] The Nineteenth Zionist Conference, 1935, XXXIV, p. 52.
[2] *Trial and Error*, p. 468.

The Jews, however, were not the only opponents of the British Government's Legislative Council scheme. There was considerable opposition in the British Parliament and debates were held in both Houses. Lord Snell, who had been a member of the Shaw Commission, Winston Churchill and Leopold Amery, who had both been Colonial Secretaries since the Mandate, all opposed it, as did Josiah Wedgwood, always a staunch supporter of the Balfour Declaration. The British Labour Party also attacked the scheme which they thought would be more likely to increase the power of the Arab ruling classes over the illiterate masses than to lead to fruitful co-operation between Arab and Jew. Lastly, the proposal was criticized by the Permanent Mandates Commission at its Twenty-Ninth Session in June 1936, and Lord Lugard, one of its members, who was a former Colonial administrator of great experience, considered that it was 'extremely inadvisable', and was likely to be 'a futile source of friction', for in the Council the majority would be unable to enforce a majority decision.

The Arabs in Palestine, although few of their leaders had embraced the scheme in its entirety, were gravely disturbed at the widespread opposition to it in London and elsewhere, and it was not long before their feelings were translated into action. The rejection of the Legislative Council scheme has frequently been blamed as the cause of the serious disturbances which began in April. The Royal Commission on Palestine, however, which was appointed on 7 August to ascertain the underlying cause of those disturbances, stated categorically that the rejection of the proposal was not the cause of the trouble although it helped to bring it to a head. Outside influences also had their effect, and the events in Syria and Egypt that gained both those countries their national independence, and the newly won sovereignty of the Lebanon all stimulated nationalist agitation in Palestine.

The first incident occurred on the Tulkarm–Nablus road on the night of 15 April, when ten motor-cars were held up by Arabs, the passengers robbed, and two of them, who were Jews, murdered. On the following night two Arabs were found murdered near the town of Petah Tiqva, and it was presumed that they had been killed as a reprisal for the murders on the previous evening. The funeral of one of these victims in Jaffa led to serious rioting in the Tel-Aviv district on 17 April.

A much more serious disturbance occurred two days later, on

19 April, when more attacks were made by Arabs on Jews, three of whom were killed. The official communiqué issued by the Palestine Government stated that 'owing to false rumours, which were at once contradicted, that Arabs had been killed, crowds assembled at eleven o'clock in the Manshia quarter of Jaffa, and disturbances arose, in the course of which several attacks were made upon Jews'.

Next day the Arab National Committee decided to call a general strike, and five days later a newly formed high-powered committee, afterwards known as the Arab Higher Committee and presided over, as usual, by the Mufti, adopted a resolution to continue the strike until such time as the British Government changed its Palestine policy particularly in regard to the vexed question of immigration.

This strike, which began in Nablus on 22 April, very quickly spread to Jaffa and Jerusalem where the shops were first affected, and before the end of the following week it had reached the port of Haifa. By 20 May it was country-wide. Groups of fellahin organized attacks on the troops, the police and, of course, on many Jewish settlements. Bands of guerrillas swept down from the hills to carry out lightning raids on isolated Jewish farms. Once again the Administration had not seen the danger signals, and did not have adequate forces available to deal with a situation which looked like getting out of hand. A request had to be sent to the Commander-in-Chief British Troops in Egypt for reinforcements, and on 11 May an infantry battalion arrived in Palestine, the advance guard of many more troops from Egypt and Malta which came in during the next three months, so that by the middle of September the total number was twenty thousand.

During the months of May and June violence and sabotage increased and although the Government extended the curfew, imposed collective fines, and interned some of the worst Arab agitators, the disorders continued. Jewish settlements were under constant sniping fire, railway trains were derailed, bridges blown up, roads mined, and telephone communications cut.

The worst trouble, however, came from the hills where the bands of guerrillas, already mentioned, were gradually organized into a large rebel army which was estimated to have reached by the autumn of 1936 a total strength of some five thousand men, well trained, well armed, and well clothed. They were not all Palestinians, for many

Syrians, Iraqis, and Transjordanian Arabs had drifted over the frontier into Palestine ready for a fight and eager for plunder. It was, in fact, a Syrian, Fauzi ed Din el Kauwakji, who commanded this rebel force. During the war he had fought with the Turkish Army and later, after the French occupation of Syria, was awarded the Légion d'Honneur whilst serving with the French Forces in the Deuxième Bureau of the General Staff. When the Druses started an insurrection in 1925 he joined them, and was sentenced to death, but managed to escape to the Hedjaz, where he became Military Adviser to King Ibn Saud. Finally he became an officer in the Iraqi Army, and it was after he resigned his commission there in 1936, that this soldier of fortune came to Palestine. When he assumed command of the rebel forces, with the self-imposed title of 'Generalissimo', the activities of Arab terrorist gangs greatly increased, many Jews were murdered, and sabotage was widespread causing serious damage and loss of life.

The restraint and self-discipline exercised by the Jewish population in the face of great and incessant provocation was such that public acknowledgment was made of it by the Palestine Government. Moreover, practical steps were taken by the Administration to help the Jews defend life and property. Nearly three thousand Jews were enrolled as supernumerary constables, and a number of licences were issued for rifles over and above the arms which the Jewish settlements were allowed to maintain in their sealed armouries.

In exercising such commendable forbearance the Jews were following a two-point policy under the guidance of the Jewish Agency and other official organizations. They were determined to defend their settlements against enemy attack, and as the British Administration was unable to guarantee them protection, they were entirely justified in so doing; but they would not, however great the provocation, carry out indiscriminate reprisals.[1] This self-restraint was maintained throughout the whole of the summer except for a few reprisals in August which were not repeated.

It was a long time before the British Government fully realized the serious nature of the disturbances and the determination of the Arabs to continue them. On 18 May, however, the Colonial Secretary, Mr. J. H.

[1] The two concepts of this policy were 'haganah' (self-defence) and 'havlagah' (self-restraint). *Palestine*, Vol. II, p. 795 (Esco Foundation for Palestine).

Thomas, announced that H.M. Government would send out a Royal Commission to Palestine, as soon as order was restored but not before, to investigate the causes of the unrest and the alleged grievances of Arabs and of Jews. It would not, however, be within the competence of the Royal Commission to question the terms of the Mandate. This undertaking did not greatly impress the Arab leaders who pointed out that H.M. Government had already appointed no less than six commissions of inquiry with very little result, and the outrages continued unabated.

The Commission's full terms of reference were not announced until the third week in July, but although they authorized the Commission to 'ascertain whether, upon a proper construction of the terms of the Mandate, either the Arabs or the Jews have any legitimate grievance on account of the way in which the Mandate has been, or is being, implemented', and to make recommendations for their removal if the Commission considered them well founded, the announcement had no soothing effect on the Arabs, and the Jews were, not unnaturally, fearful of the results of what they regarded as truckling to violence.

The danger that the conflagration might spread to other parts of the Moslem world led to efforts being made by various Arab rulers to mediate and bring the disturbances to an end. The Emir Abdullah of Transjordan had two meetings with the members of the Arab Higher Committee in June and August to persuade them to call off the strike and accept the Royal Commission, but he was unsuccessful. Later, at the suggestion of King Ibn Saud and the Imam of the Yemen, the King of Iraq intervened and it was thought, for a time, that Nuri es-Said, the Iraqi Foreign Minister, would succeed in obtaining some concession from the British Government in respect of immigration. Before the negotiations had proceeded very far, however, the situation changed and H.M. Government took up a firmer attitude. Mr. Ormsby-Gore, in a reply to a letter from Dr. Weizmann, who had sent him a cutting from the *Palestine Post* announcing the formula for immigration supposed to have been agreed between Nuri Pasha and the British Colonial Secretary, stated that Nuri had never been authorized to give any assurances to the Arabs about the reduction or suspension of Jewish immigration, and that his terms had never been accepted by the British Government.

Two or three days later, on 8 September, the Colonial Office issued a Statement of Policy. It stated that reinforcements had had to be sent out from England because the disturbances had reached a point at which they were 'a direct challenge to the authority of the British Government in Palestine'. Furthermore, the decision of the Arab leaders not to call off the strike until immigration was suspended was responsible for 'all efforts to introduce a reasonable spirit of accommodation' having so far failed. The Statement ended by declaring that the Government was determined to put an end to the disturbances without delay, that the 1st Division would shortly leave England for Palestine, and that Lieutenant-General J. G. Dill, later Field-Marshal Sir John Dill, would take over command of all the armed forces there.

The reinforcements duly arrived, and with them sterner measures were initiated. With not less than twenty thousand troops in the country it became possible to mount offensive operations against the considerable guerrilla forces of Fauzi ed Din el Kauwakji and an Order-in-Council was made authorizing the High Commissioner or the G.O.C. Palestine Forces to proclaim martial law.

The end of the disturbances was now drawing near. With such a large regular armed force against them it could only be a question of weeks before the Arab irregulars could no longer put up any effective resistance, and they were, in fact, allowed to disband before October was out.

The ordinary Arab, who took no active interest in politics, had long been weary of the general strike, and all wanted to get back to work. The oranges were just ready for picking, and the 1936 season was likely to be a record one, for civil war was raging in Spain which was Palestine's chief competitor. All that was needed was an opportunity of ending the strike without losing face. This was, fortunately for the Arab Higher Committee which would soon have found it difficult to regiment its followers, supplied by the Heads of the four leading Arab States, Iraq, Saudi Arabia, Transjordan and the Yemen, each of whom addressed an identical appeal to the President of the Arab Higher Committee and their 'sons, the Arabs of Palestine'.

We have been deeply pained by the present state of affairs in Palestine. For this reason we have agreed with our brothers the Kings and the Emir to call upon you to resolve for peace in order to save further shedding of blood. In doing this, we rely on the good intentions of our friend Great Britain, who has declared that she will do justice. You must be confident that we will continue our efforts to assist you.[1]

On 11 October the Arab Higher Committee, when publishing the text of these appeals, announced that they had decided 'to respond to the appeal of Their Majesties and Highnesses, the Arab Kings and Emirs, and to call upon the noble Arab nation in Palestine to resort to quietness and to put an end to the strike disorders'. So comparative peace reigned after six months of terrorism. Although there were still a few isolated incidents all organized violence was over.

It had been a costly six months. Many lives were lost and much property destroyed. Although there are no accurate records of the Arab casualties, the official list gave 195 killed or died of wounds, and 804 wounded. These figures include only those whose deaths were verified or who were treated in hospital for their wounds. It is thought that at least one thousand Arabs were killed, nearly all of them in fighting, for there were very few murdered by the Jews.

The Jewish official lists, however, were probably accurate. The figures given by the Jewish Agency were eighty-two murdered and 369 wounded, all in attacks by Arabs. Damage to Jewish property was reliably estimated at about £250,000 including the destruction of eighty thousand citrus trees, sixty-two thousand other fruit trees, sixty-four thousand forest trees, and more than sixteen thousand dunams of growing crops. The casualties of the Palestine Police Force and the Transjordan Frontier Force were one officer and fifteen other ranks killed or died of wounds, and fifteen officers and eighty-seven other ranks wounded. The British armed forces lost two officers and nineteen other ranks, and seventeen officers and eighty-seven other ranks wounded. The loss suffered by the Arab and Jewish communities through loss of business, interruption of employment and other causes, cannot be estimated but it is thought to have amounted to several million pounds.

In its Report after the 1929 disturbances, the Shaw Committee categorically expressed the opinion which, it said, was supported by the evidence of practically every witness who was questioned on the spot, that the outbreak of violence in August 1929 neither was nor was

[1] Palestine Royal Commission's Report (July 1937), chap. IV, para. 17, p. 101.

intended to be a revolt against British authority. That could not be said of the riots of 1933, nor to an even greater degree to the disturbances of 1936. Although they were Jewish lives that were taken, and it was Jewish property that was destroyed, the outbreak was directly aimed at the Administration. 'It was', as the Peel Commission stated in its Report, 'an open rebellion of the Palestinian Arabs, assisted by fellow Arabs from other countries, against British Mandatory Rule.'[1] Throughout the strike the Arab Press carried on a wild and irresponsible campaign of calumny against the British Government, and even went so far as to accuse the military authorities of causing poisoned sweets to be dropped in the vicinity of Arab villages by planes of the R.A.F.

The main 'underlying causes'[2] were found by the Royal Commission to be:

(1) The desire of the Arabs for national independence.
(2) Their hatred and fear of the establishment of the Jewish National Home.

These were and, it seemed, always would be the *underlying*[3] causes. They were permanent, they were inseparable and, many people thought, they were inherent in the Balfour Declaration and the Mandate. They had been the causes behind former disturbances and would, in all probability, lead to further trouble in the future.

[1] Palestine Royal Commission's Report (July 1937), p. 104.
[2] To ascertain these was one of the tasks of the Commission as set out in Royal Commission of 7 August 1936.
[3] The italics are mine.

CHAPTER VIII

The Peel Commission

THE necessary conditions having been fulfilled, namely that order should be restored, the Royal Commission was able to leave for Palestine where it arrived on 11 November. Its Chairman was Lord Peel, and its members were men of distinction.[1] It was welcomed by most of the Jewish leaders in a spirit of hope and confidence, for many of them not only recognized it as an extremely competent body, but believed that it would prove to be thorough and impartial, and that its findings would go a long way towards solving their problems.

On the day on which the Commission sailed from England the Colonial Secretary had announced in Parliament that H.M. Government considered that a suspension of Jewish immigration prior to the Commission's findings would not be justifiable. On hearing of this announcement the Arab Higher Committee decided to boycott the Commission, but this was called off on 6 January 1937, and evidence was heard from the Mufti and other Arab representatives. Once again it was only the intervention of the Kings of Iraq and Saudi Arabia which enabled the Higher Committee to change their decision without losing too much face.

The members of the Commission when they reached Palestine found the atmosphere charged with tension and pessimism. It was Armistice Day and they attended the usual ceremony at the British War Cemetery on Mount Scopus which overlooks Jerusalem and is the site of the original buildings of the Hebrew University, since 1948 in 'no-man's-

[1] The composition of the Commission was as follows: The Rt. Hon. Earl Peel, G.C.S.I., G.B.E., The Rt. Hon. Sir Horace Rumbold, Bt., G.C.B., G.C.M.G., M.V.O., Sir Laurie Hammond, K.C.S.I., C.B.E., Sir Morris Carter, C.B.E., Sir Harold Morris, M.B.E., K.C., Professor Reginald Coupland, C.I.E.

land', and they could not help reflecting 'that the Peace which followed the Armistice of 1918 was an even less real peace in Palestine than in Europe'. What they saw and heard during the next few days convinced them that the armistice in Palestine was just a temporary cessation of hostilities and not a prelude to peace. Nevertheless, as the Commission stated in the Report, they 'tried to prevent their judgment being unduly darkened by the circumstances of the moment . . . and to discount all such factors in the problem as might fairly be regarded as the transient outcome of the recent disorders'.[1]

In this dark and sombre picture there was one bright spot. Twelve years ago, the Report stated, the 'National Home was an experiment: today it is a going concern'. The process of agricultural colonization had advanced by leaps and bounds, but the Commission were even more impressed by the rapid growth of urban development; Tel-Aviv, by then the largest town, a few years earlier had been a suburb of Jaffa. There was the same contrast in Jerusalem where, alongside the Old City, a modern New City of lovely stone buildings had sprung up, and in Haifa where, in the new harbour, European ships were discharging cargoes for Arab and Jew alike. And, in the National Home, the Commission found that the Jews were happy and imbued with a sense of 'mission'. Released, in many cases, from an anti-Jewish environment, and 'restored' to Palestine, they had a new confidence and a new zest of living because of the knowledge that they were engaged in building up a great future. The Arabs, however, although they had shared in large measure in the material benefits which Jewish immigration had brought to Palestine, felt balked of their national independence and frightened of an eventual Jewish domination.

It was with this contrasting picture in their minds of light and darkness, of hope and fear, that the Commission set about their difficult and responsible task. As the Arabs had not yet withdrawn their boycott the Jews were the first to present their case, the main plank of which was that the interests of Arabs and Jews were not irreconcilable. The Jewish memorandum insisted that there could be co-existence between the two peoples. The Jews still stood by the Churchill White Paper of 1922. The principal Jewish witness was Weizmann, who has written of the tremendous responsibility which he felt rested on his shoulders when

[1] Palestine Royal Commission's Report (July 1937), chap. V, para. 1, p. 113.

giving evidence, for he was speaking not only for the Jews in Palestine, but 'of countless others in other lands . . . and for generations long since dead, for those who lay buried in the ancient and thickly populated cemeteries on Mount Scopus and those whose last resting places were scattered all over the world'.[1]

He spoke to the Commission of the six million Jews 'pent up in places where they are not wanted, and for whom the world is divided into places where they cannot live and places which they may not enter'. For such people an immigration certificate for Palestine meant an end of racial discrimination, the satisfying of all their longings, the answer to all their prayers. It was not enough in seeking to explain to the members of the Commission how the Jews had reached such a condition, to tell them the history of Jewish persecution in Central Europe, and in order to reveal the deeper and more enduring causes behind the longing of many a Jew to return to the land of his fathers, Weizmann used these very striking words: 'When one speaks of the Jewish people one speaks of a people which is a minority everywhere, a majority nowhere, which is to some extent identified with the races among which it lives, but still not quite identical. It is a disembodied ghost of a race, and it inspires suspicion, and suspicion breeds hatred. There should be one place in the world, in God's wide world, where we could live and express ourselves in accordance with our character, and make our contribution to civilization in our own way, and through our own channels.' Weizmann reminded the Commission that the official Jewish organization had, since the Mandate was put into operation, pursued a moderate policy and had done their best to co-operate with the British Government and the Palestine Administration. The Jews respected the rights of the Arabs as much as they valued their own. They did not wish to dominate or be dominated, and they were even prepared to accept parity on the Legislative Council whatever 'the future ratio between the Arab and Jewish population might become'.[2]

Nevertheless, apart from this concession, the Jews insisted that there must be no restriction placed on immigration other than the 'economic absorptive capacity', and there must be no new measures to restrict the sale of Arab land to Jews, and nothing done to prevent the Jewish popu-

[1] *Trial and Error*, p. 471.
[2] Palestine Royal Commission's Report (July 1937), p. 143.

lation from becoming, in due course, in the majority. The Commission did not attempt to blame the Jewish leaders for putting forward what the Report called 'maximal' demands when stating the official case, indeed they considered it quite normal for them to do so.

The extremists under Jabotinsky, who gave evidence before the Commission at a special session held in London after their return there, wanted much more. The Transjordan was to be included in the National Home and many millions more immigrants were to be allowed to enter Palestine without delay.

The Arab attitude to the problem, was entirely unreasonable. Nothing but the immediate granting of national independence could possibly pave the way to peace in Palestine. The Arab Higher Committee assured the Commission that the welfare of the Jewish minority would be guaranteed, but two answers given by the Mufti to questions put to him by a member of the Commission did not seem consistent with such a promise:

Q. Does His Eminence think that this country can assimilate and digest the 400,000 Jews in it?
A. No.
Q. Some of them would have to be removed by a process kindly or painful as the case may be?
A. We must leave all this to the future.

The Commission, while not questioning the sincerity or the humanity of the Mufti's intentions, could not but be reminded of the fate which befell the Assyrian minority in Iraq despite similar assurances.

The Arab representatives were not even prepared to admit that Jewish money and Jewish immigration had conferred any benefits on their own people, and went so far as to contrast the years spent under Turkish rule favourably with what they were experiencing under the Mandate.

Some of the Arab witnesses, moreover, disclosed pronounced anti-Jewish feelings unconnected with the rate of immigration but prompted solely by an unreasoning racialism. 'In Germany 70,000,000 Germans, who are cultured and civilized and have all the necessary means of government, cannot bear 600,000 Jews.' Before seven years had passed German culture and civilization had liquidated about five million Jews in Europe, and the Arabs of today are waiting to continue what Hitler left unfinished.

Although neither Arab nor Jew had a good word to say for the Palestine Government its position was hardly enviable. The Commission thought it only fair to point this out in their Report. It was poised, the Report stated, above two irreconcilable communities, compelled to follow a path between them which was ill-defined by a vague legal instrument, critically watched at every step by both the rival parties in Palestine, and from outside by the Permanent Mandates Commission of the League of Nations and Jews throughout the world.

It seemed to the Commission that the Government's task would have been much easier had Palestine been a British territory, in which event it would have had a free hand to devise measures for bringing the two peoples together and inculcate in them a sense of common citizenship. This was impossible because of the Mandatory character of the government and, above all, by the specific provisions in the Mandate which required the maintenance of the existing rights of the Arabs side by side with the establishment of a Jewish National Home.

These requirements appeared to the Commission to make the Mandatory Power's task almost insuperable, and the fact that the Mandate was framed mainly to realize the nationalist ideals of Zionism could scarcely have been better calculated than it was to keep the races apart. There were three official languages, and each community could maintain its own schools in order to educate its own children in their mother tongue. There was a Jewish Agency to advise and co-operate with the Government on matters connected with the National Home, and the Supreme Moslem Council, later superseded by the Arab Executive, to ensure that the Arabs' rights were safeguarded. There were three national flags flown, the Union Jack, the Arab flag and the banner of Zionism. The only reason why there were not three national anthems played was that there was no Arabian equivalent of 'God Save the King' or the 'Hatikva'.

All these factors tended to keep Arab and Jew apart rather than draw them together. Had the Mandate been drafted otherwise, the hope and expectation of many a Jew and Gentile might have been realized, and Palestine eventually have become a self-governing State within the British Commonwealth, where Arab and Jew could have lived side by side as fellow citizens of a great world-wide civilization in complete individual freedom yet with a common loyalty.

It was, because of the above considerations, therefore, that the Commission felt that there could never be a possibility of a lasting settlement of the problems except through an entirely new approach. It was their view that the conflict between Arab and Jew was inherent in the situation from the outset. Neither conciliation nor firmness would solve the problem. The Government's handling of the 1936 outbreak had carried the policy of conciliation to its farthest possible limit. The Commission considered that had the Government adopted a more rigorous and consistent policy it might have repressed the conflict for some time, but it would not have resolved it; for it was as much about the future as the present. Who in the end would govern Palestine? The answer to that, the Commission thought, must surely be 'Neither'. The problem, they decided, could not be solved by giving either the Arabs or the Jews all they wanted. They thought that half a loaf was better than no bread, and recommended partition as the only solution. Neither side would get all it wanted, but both sides would get freedom and security.

Partition would bestow certain advantages on each of the parties and give one great boon to both. To Arab and Jew, the Commission contended, partition, and nothing but partition, offered the prospect of peace. The advantages to the Arabs were many. They would gain their national independence; they would no longer fear being 'swamped' by the Jews and, perhaps, ultimately coming under Jewish rule; the anxiety, completely unjustified though it was, that the Holy Places should ever come under Jewish control would be forever removed; lastly, the new Arab State would receive financial assistance on a substantial scale both from H.M. Government and from the Jewish State.

The Jews would get their National Home, and would never become subject to Arab domination; the National Home would be more than just a name, it would be converted into a Jewish State and the rate of immigration would be theirs alone to determine.

Finally, the Report stated, numberless men and women all over the world would feel a sense of deep relief if an end were made to strife and bloodshed in a thrice hallowed land.

★ ★ ★ ★ ★

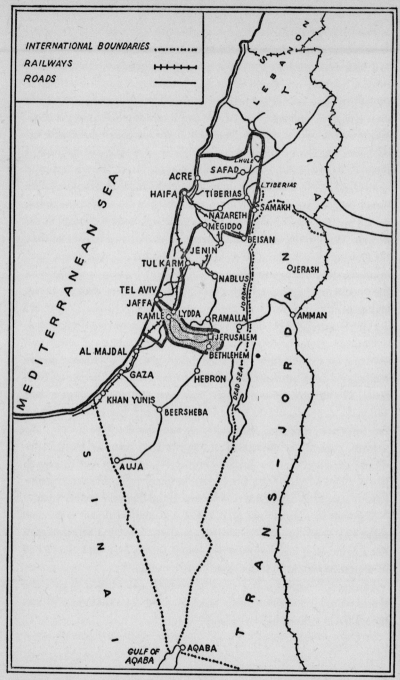

PROVISIONAL SCHEME OF PARTITION AS PROPOSED BY THE
PALESTINE ROYAL COMMISSION, 1937

The partition proposal got a very mixed reception from the Jews. Those who opposed the scheme did so for various reasons. The extremists opposed it because they were 'Maximalists'. The non-Zionists were against it because they were opposed to a Jewish State on principle, believing that the reconstitution of the Jews as a nationality would prejudice their rights as citizens of other countries. The more reasonable Zionists, however, welcomed the idea without reserve, because for the first time there appeared to be a definite possibility of forming a Jewish State, an opportunity not to be lightly cast aside.

The subject of partition was first put to Dr. Weizmann by the Commission at a session held *in camera* on 8 January 1937. He was asked what he thought of the idea but it was, of course, impossible for him to give an official answer without consulting his colleagues, although his first personal reaction was that the suggestion had great possibilities, although it was obvious that the territory to be given to the Jews would not be large and would include the southern triangle of the Negev.

Weizmann believed that even a small Jewish State, well organized and living at peace with its neighbours, was better than none, and could make a great contribution to civilization. He saw, in the idea of partition, a real possibility of coming to terms with the Arabs, for a Jewish State, with definite boundaries internationally guaranteed, would banish the ever-haunting fear that the Jews would absorb the whole of Palestine.

There would be no danger of the Jews overrunning such boundaries, for that would amount to an act of war and would turn world opinion against them. Nor was that all. There was one other great advantage. The Jews would be a majority in their own State, not a minority in an Arab Palestine.

Weizmann's hopes and vision were not shared by all his co-Zionists, and there was considerable and violent opposition from a strong American group, which included Hadassah, the orthodox party and some of the Revisionists. It was no coincidence that the chief opponent of partition was Ussishkin for it was he who had led the opposition against Herzl at the time of the Uganda offer.[1]

Nevertheless, the resolution carried by the delegates by a two-to-one

[1] See page 20.

majority did not completely reject the idea of partition, although it
declared that the scheme suggested by the Royal Commission was
unacceptable. The Executive was empowered to enter into negotiations
with H.M. Government to ascertain the precise terms for the proposed
establishment of a Jewish State and to report on such proposals to a
newly elected Congress for a decision.

The proposal that Palestine should be partitioned met with uncompromising hostility from the Arab community in Palestine, and was
also condemned by a Pan-Arab Congress held at Bludan in Syria which
was attended by five hundred delegates from Syria and neighbouring
Arab countries.

World reaction to the Commission's scheme was, also, generally
unfavourable, and there was little enthusiasm for any plan which entailed
dividing the Holy Land. The Permanent Mandates Commission of the
League of Nations, while agreeing that the British Government should
be empowered to explore the possibility of what they called 'a new
territorial solution', considered that it would be unwise to establish two
independent States without a further period of Mandatory supervision.
They put forward that in the event of the Peel Commission's
recommendations being implemented, the Jewish and Arab States
should remain under a transitional Mandatory régime, either
under separate Mandates or in some form of provisional federation, until they had given sufficient proof of their ability to govern
themselves.

H.M. Government came to the conclusion that the Royal Commission's scheme for partition represented 'the best and most hopeful
solution of the deadlock'[1] between Arab and Jew, and issued a White
Paper on the subject. It stated that pending the completion of the details
of the proposed partition scheme steps should be taken to prevent Jewish
land purchases in all projected Arab territories, and that a 'political
high level' for Jewish immigration should be fixed.

Pending the implementation of the partition plan the Government
had no intention of surrendering their responsibility for peace, order
and good government in Palestine, and if serious disorders were, once
again, to break out and military intervention became necessary, the

[1] H.M.S.O. Command Paper 5513 (July 1937). Palestine: Statement of Policy by H.M.
Government in the United Kingdom.

High Commissioner would delegate powers in respect of the whole country to the General Officer Commanding the military forces.

★ ★ ★ ★ ★

During the first eight months of 1937, after the Peel Commission had returned to England and its report was in preparation, there was comparative quiet in Palestine. However, after the murder in Nazareth on 26 September of the acting District Commissioner for Galilee, Mr. Andrews, who was killed in an ambush with his police escort, a new reign of terror began which continued with but little abatement until the outbreak of World War II. During the year 1938 alone the casualties reached a total of 3,717, including sixty-nine British, ninety-two Jewish and 486 Arab civilians, besides 1,138 rebels killed. Before the rebellion was got under control the British military forces had reached a strength of nearly twenty thousand.

In the spring of 1938 the Palestine Partition Commission, commonly known as the Woodhead Commission, was appointed by the Colonial Secretary.[1] It was some weeks before it arrived in the country, having been delayed on account of the disturbances. When it duly reported in October to the new Secretary of State, Mr. Malcolm MacDonald, the Commission found itself unable to recommend any practical plan for partition which would fulfil its terms of reference. Nevertheless, it examined, in addition to the Peel plan, two other schemes, without coming to any definite conclusions on either of them. The first of these was a revised version of the Peel scheme, excluding Galilee from the Jewish State, the second reduced the size of the State still further and the Commission stated, though with little enthusiasm, that *if any plan were to be chosen* it regarded this last as the least objectionable.[2]

By the following month, November, partition was dead. In a new White Paper, the second in sixteen months, the British Government made a complete reversal of policy. The partition scheme so strongly espoused in July 1937 was rejected. 'The political, administrative and financial difficulties involved in the proposal to create independent Arab and Jewish States in Palestine are so great that this solution of the problem is impracticable.'[3]

[1] Rt. Hon. W. G. A. Ormsby-Gore, M.P.
[2] The italics are mine.   [3] H.M.S.O. Command Paper 5893 (1938), para. 4.

The Government would, therefore, continue to be responsible for governing the whole of Palestine, and would have to find other means of meeting the needs of the difficult situation consistent with their dual obligation to the Arabs and the Jews. In order to promote an understanding between the two communities the Government proposed, without delay, to invite representatives of the Palestinian Arabs, of neighbouring States and of the Jewish Agency to come to London and confer with it regarding future policy and in particular the question of Jewish immigration. The Government reserved the right to refuse to receive those leaders whom it regarded as responsible for the campaign of assassination and violence.

Thus, in seven short paragraphs, the only positive results of the Peel Commission, made after months of patient and painstaking enquiry, were brought to naught, and further inroads made upon the Jewish National Home.

CHAPTER IX

The Twilight Deepens

IN accordance with the intention expressed in the 1938 White Paper the British Government sent invitations to attend the Round Table Conference in London to the Palestinian Arabs, the neighbouring States of Egypt, Iraq, Saudi Arabia, the Yemen and Transjordan on the one hand and to the Jewish Agency on the other.

It will be remembered that in the case of the Palestinian Arabs the Government had declared that it would not accept as representatives any leader regarded as responsible for the campaign of assassination and violence in Palestine. The Mufti was excluded from the Conference on that ground but other members of the Arab Higher Committee, who were being detained as exiles in the Seychelles, were immediately freed and allowed to attend as delegates and remain, throughout the Conference, in consultation with the Mufti, although their return to Palestine was not permitted.

There was much discussion between the Mufti and the Palestinian leaders as to who should be chosen as delegates, and still more wrangling took place between the Mufti's followers and those of the Nashashibi group.[1] Two rival delegations arrived in London and it was left to the Colonial Office to reconcile the two parties before the Conference assembled.

The Jewish delegation was a strong one and widely representative. It was composed of the official delegates from the Jewish Agency, many distinguished Jews, Zionist and non-Zionist, from the British Commonwealth and Empire and foreign countries.

---

[1] This group was composed of the followers of Fakhri Bey Nashashibi whose cousin Raghib, former Arab Mayor of Jerusalem, was leader of the Palestine Arab Defence Party.

The Conference, however, got off to a bad start on 7 February 1939 when the Arabs refused to recognize the Jewish Agency or even to sit at the same table as the Jews. The British Prime Minister, Mr. Neville Chamberlain, had, therefore, to go through the ridiculous performance of pronouncing two addresses of welcome, to the Arabs at 10.30 a.m. and to the Jews at noon.

The two separate halves of the Conference continued to cold-shoulder each other for two weeks until 23 February when the first joint meeting of Jewish and Arab representatives was held. Not only did it achieve no positive results, but at the end of it the two differing points of view were still poles apart. After one more similarly fruitless meeting it was realized that no useful purpose would be served by a continuance of the joint sessions, and the Conference reverted to the original procedure and resumed separate sittings until it rose on 17 March, having accomplished nothing. The Zionist leaders may be forgiven for wondering, as they did, whether the British Government called the Tripartite Conference together merely to pave the way for a predetermined course of action for which no conference was necessary.

It was some weeks before the British Government's Statement of Policy was issued as a White Paper[1] during which time Europe had been moving ever nearer to war. In March one of the natural consequences of Munich had come about, the annexation by Hitler of the remainder of Czechoslovakia, and during the next two months large numbers of Jews fleeing from the coming destruction were trying to reach the shores of Palestine to find sanctuary in their National Home. Already, in anticipation of the White Paper, restrictions on Jewish immigration were in force and many 'coffin' boats, as they were aptly called, 'crowded and unseaworthy vessels roamed the Mediterranean in the hope of being able ultimately to discharge their unhappy cargoes of men, women and children in Palestine. Some sank in the Mediterranean or the Black Sea. Some reached Palestine either to be turned back or to have their passengers taken off and interned or transhipped to Mauritius.'[2] 'Why', said Chamberlain when Hitler occupied Prague, 'should England risk war for the sake of a far-away country of which we know very little and whose language we don't understand?' When they heard those words spoken about the Czech Republic, the country

[1] H.M.S.O. Command Paper 6019 (1939).   [2] *Trial and Error*, p. 495.

of the Masaryks and Beneš, the Jews in Palestine, still waiting for the publication of the White Paper, must have reflected that if Czechoslovakia were spoken of like that their prospects were not very rosy.

They had not long to wait, for the document which was shortly to become a White Paper was disclosed to Dr. Weizmann just before the Tripartite Conference ended and within a day or two of the Nazi occupation of the Czech capital. One morning he received a letter from the Colonial Office which had obviously been addressed to him in error, for it was clear from the contents that it was intended only for members of the Arab delegation. It contained the outline of what afterwards appeared in the White Paper as the Government's policy and was submitted for Arab approval. An Arab State of Palestine in five years, a limited Jewish immigration during those five years, and none thereafter without Arab consent. Weizmann could scarcely believe his eyes although he has since said that after what had happened to Austria and Czechoslovakia nothing should have surprised him.

When, at last, on 17 May the White Paper was issued the Zionist leader's worst fears were realized. As the St. James's Palace Conference had proved abortive the Government considered itself free to formulate its own policy, and was convinced that in the interests of the peace and well-being of the whole people of Palestine a clear definition of policy and objectives was essential. As partition had been found to be impracticable it had become necessary to devise an alternative policy which would, consistently with British obligations to both Arabs and Jews, meet the needs of the situation. The first statement to be made, therefore, in accordance with this decision was an unequivocal declaration by H.M. Government that it was not part of British policy that Palestine should become a Jewish State.

The Government did propose, however, to establish within ten years an independent Palestine State in treaty relations with the United Kingdom. There would, of course, first have to be consultation with the Council of the League of Nations regarding the termination of the Mandate.

During a transitional period, during which Britain would remain responsible for governing the country, the people of Palestine would be given an increasing say in the government, by the appointment of Arab and Jewish representatives as heads of Departments approximately in proportion to their respective populations.

Five years after the restoration of peace and order an appropriate body, representative of the people of Palestine and the British Government, would be set up to consider and make recommendations regarding the proposed new constitution. Adequate provisions would, of course, have to be made for the protection of the different communities in Palestine and the special position of the Jewish National Home. If, at the end of ten years, it appeared to the British Government that the establishment of the independent State should be postponed there would have to be consultations with the representatives of the people of Palestine, the Council of the League of Nations, and the neighbouring Arab States before deciding on such a postponement.

The Government further proposed in the White Paper that the total number of Jews to be admitted in Palestine as immigrants during the five years commencing 1939 should be seventy-five thousand, subject to the country's economic absorptive capacity, and that thereafter no further immigration would be permitted unless the Arabs of Palestine were prepared to acquiesce in it. The Government was determined to check illegal immigration but, as a contribution towards the solution of the Jewish refugee problem, twenty-five thousand refugees would be allowed to enter Palestine as soon as the High Commissioner was satisfied that adequate provision for their maintenance was ensured.

Finally, while acknowledging that the administration of Palestine was required under Article 6 of the Mandate to encourage close settlement by Jews on the land, subject to the rights and position of other sections of the population not being prejudiced, the High Commissioner would be given general powers to prohibit and regulate transfers of land with effect from the publication date of the White Paper, and would retain such powers during the transitional period.

The reaction to this extremely partisan document, which ended with a rather unctuous prayer for peace in a country revered by many millions of Moslems, Jews and Christians throughout the world, was vigorous and almost entirely unfavourable, if not condemnatory. As the White Paper was almost a complete victory for the Arab delegation it was reasonable to expect that it would have been welcomed by them. The Palestine Higher Committee rejected it, and demanded a full

acceptance of all their demands without any qualifications. 'The ultimate decision', the Committee declared, 'as to the fate of a virile people
depends on its own will, not on White or Black Papers. Palestine will
be independent within the Arab union and will remain Arab forever.'
A small minority of the Arab political leaders, however, considered
that the British policy 'furnished an acceptable basis for the furtherance
of Arab aspirations'.

It is hardly surprising that the White Paper shocked the Jewish community in Palestine and that demonstrations were held throughout the
country on 18 May, and the document denounced in all the synagogues
and at public meetings as a breach of faith. A statement was issued by
the Jewish Agency to the same effect. The Jewish people, according to
this document, regarded the new British policy as a breach of faith and
a surrender to Arab terrorism. The Jewish people had no quarrel with
the Arabs, and Jewish work in Palestine had not had an adverse effect
upon the life and progress of the Arab people who were not, as were
the Jews, landless or homeless. The Jewish people had shown the desire
for peace even during the years of disturbances when they practised
great restraint and had seldom retaliated to Arab violence. It was in the
darkest hour of Jewish history that the British Government proposed to
deprive the Jews of their last hope and to close the road back to their
Homeland. 'The historic bond between the people and the land of
Israel cannot be broken,' the statement ended, 'and the Jews will never
accept the closing to them of the gates of Palestine, nor let their national
home be converted into a ghetto.'

The official Zionist view was expressed in a letter which Dr. Weizmann sent to the High Commissioner on 31 May. He made the point,
so often made before, that the very essence of the Jewish National
Home was the possibility of Jews entering into Palestine 'as of right and
not on sufferance', which had been specifically acknowledged by
Winston Churchill in his 1922 Memorandum when he was Colonial
Secretary. 'A National Home for Jewish people', wrote Weizmann,
'loses its meaning the moment that the entry of Jews is forbidden save
with the permission of the Arabs. The test of the Jewish National Home
must, therefore, be the effective possibility for any Jew who is able to
settle in it, without causing injury to others, to do so as a matter of right.
The emphasis placed by the White Paper of 1922 on the fact that the

Jews are in Palestine "as of right" obviously extends to their right of entry. This is fully recognized by the insistence in that White Paper that "for fulfilment of this policy it is necessary that the Jewish community in Palestine should be able to increase its numbers by immigration". But the present Statement of Policy, while apparently admitting that the present Jews of Palestine are there as of right, proceeds to deny the right of entry to Jews who are not yet there. It thereby undermines the basis of the right of the existing Jewish population, and shatters the whole conception of the Jewish National Home.'

The practical reason given by the British Government for trying to get rid of its Mandatory obligations was that to continue honouring them would mean 'rule by force'. The Government, however, appeared to have overlooked the fact that the new policy was nothing more nor less than a triumph of force. Looking back on the history of the three previous years the Government's *volte-face* must have appeared to the Arab terrorists as a handsome dividend on their campaign of violence, and to the Jews as a penalty for their restraint and moderation. Weizmann reminded the Government that as continued British rule in Palestine was still being challenged by the Arab leaders, that too would involve the use of force.

The reception given to the White Paper by Press and Parliament was little better, and those who opposed it in the House of Commons did not do so merely for political reasons. The Prime Minister was Neville Chamberlain, and it was perhaps not unnatural that the entire Labour and Liberal parties criticized the new Palestine policy. But it was also attacked by some leading members of the Prime Minister's own party, particularly those who had been closely connected with originating the Jewish National Home policy and considered the White Paper to be a violation of the pledge given to the Jews in both the Balfour Declaration and the Mandate.

One of these was Leo Amery who had previously been Secretary of State for the Colonies. He had no doubt whatsoever that the Government's new policy was a direct negation of the principles upon which the British administration in Palestine had been based, and a repudiation of the pledges on the strength of which Great Britain had been entrusted with the Mandate. It was a confession of failure and an act of appeasement. 'The Jews, fortunately, were not like the Jews in

Germany, a hopeless minority; they were a formidable body of people and they would not wait passively', Amery said, 'until in due course they and the land they had created were handed over to the terrorist control of the Mufti.'

If it was ever intended by the authors of the Balfour Declaration that the Jews should remain a permanent minority in Palestine, why, it might well be asked, were those very specific safeguards introduced for the non-Jewish population? The very fact of their introduction was, surely, proof positive that the future possibility of a Jewish majority existed. If the Jews could go to Palestine 'as of right and not on suffer-ance' how could it be suggested that the Government had no further obligation to facilitate immigration? The Peel Commission had said that the Jews understood that if the experiment succeeded the National Home would develop in course of time into a Jewish State. Why did the Jews understand that to be the case? Was it not because from 1918 to 1920 they had been told so by President Wilson, by Lloyd George, by Lord Balfour, by several successive Colonial Secretaries and many other eminent British statesmen? All these and many other questions were asked by various Members of Parliament during the 1939 White Paper Debate in May 1939, and to none of them could a satisfactory answer be given.

Many other speakers in the Debate described the policy as a 'cynical breach of pledges given to the Jews'. What made it even worse was that it came at a time when tragedy was staring thousands of European Jews in the face. In Germany the anti-Jewish laws and decrees were driving thousands of Jews away, and many of them wanted and tried to get to the land of their fathers, to Palestine. When they arrived there they were turned away as 'illegal immigrants' or, if they succeeded in land-ing, as like as not they were sent off to Mauritius and detained there.

Winston Churchill delivered against the White Paper one of the great speeches of his long and distinguished Parliamentary career. He reminded the House of his Memorandum of 1922 and was surprised, as well he might be, that the Colonial Secretary, Mr. Malcolm MacDonald, should have sought to found his argument in support of the White Paper upon it. The Memorandum had begun by stating that H.M. Government had no intention of repudiating the obligations into which they had entered towards the Jewish people. He stood by every word that had been quoted from the Memorandum, and he would not alter a sentence of it, even after a lapse of over sixteen years.

The decision to stop immigration after five years' time and make its continuation subject to Arab acquiescence, Churchill categorically branded as a breach and repudiation of the Balfour Declaration. He understood perfectly the distinction between making a Jewish National Home in Palestine and making Palestine a Jewish National Home. In fact he was one of the first to draw that distinction, but what sort of National Home, he asked, 'is offered to the Jews of the world when we are asked to declare that in five years' time the door of that home is to be shut and barred in their faces'?

He finished his speech thus:

I end upon the land of Palestine. It is strange indeed that we should turn away from our task in Palestine at the moment when, as the Secretary of State told us yesterday, the local disorders have been largely mastered. It is stranger still that we should turn away when the great experiment and bright dream, the historic dream has proved its power to succeed. Yesterday the Minister responsible descanted eloquently in glowing passages upon the magnificent work which the Jewish colonists have done. They have made the desert bloom. They have started a score of thriving industries, he said. They have founded a great city on the barren shore. They have harnessed the Jordan and spread its electricity throughout the land. So far from being persecuted, the Arabs had crowded into the country and multiplied till their population has increased more than even all world Jewry could lift up the Jewish population. Now we are asked to decree that all this is stopped, and all this is come to an end.

We are asked to submit—and this is what rankles most with me—to an agitation which is fed with foreign money, and ceaselessly inflamed by Nazi and by Fascist propaganda.[1]

The Government's win by a majority of only eighty-nine was, virtually, a defeat, for when the Whips were on, as they were on that occasion, its usual voting strength was 413. Included in those who voted against the White Paper were about thirty-five Government supporters, and 110 abstained.

Many speakers, including Churchill and Amery, urged that the views of the Permanent Mandates Commission should be ascertained and taken into consideration before Parliament voted on the Government's proposals. This suggestion was not followed, it may well be because the

[1] House of Commons Official Report, 23 May 1939.

British Government had little doubt what those views would be. When the Commission met in June and considered the policy for Palestine, as laid down in the 1939 White Paper, it, too, did not think much of it. Although Malcolm MacDonald was himself present to explain and defend the new policy he met with no success. He argued that it was not out of step with the terms of the Mandate nor inconsistent with previous policy. To base his argument on juridical rather than political grounds proved, in the end, a great mistake, for many members of the Commission considered that it would have been better in every way if the Colonial Secretary had simply relied on the hard inescapable facts.

The Commission's Chairman, Monsieur Orts of Belgium, said that he and all the members had listened with attention to Mr. MacDonald's preliminary statement and to his answers to their questions. As the session proceeded, however, the soundness of the Colonial Secretary's argument that the new policy did not depart from the terms of the Mandate, seemed to him, the Chairman, less certain. If this argument had failed to convince certain members of the Commission, was not the explanation simply that, on this occasion, the Mandatory Government had asked the League to follow it on ground which was, by its very nature, unfavourable? If, as it had done in 1937, the Mandatory Government had implicitly admitted that the Mandate had proved in practice to be incapable of application, perhaps the Commission would have followed it, just as they had done in 1937. If the British Government had taken its stand purely on political grounds, it might perhaps have over-persuaded the Commission. By taking up the position it had done, it had cut itself off from any possibility of convincing the Mandates Commission.

Nor could the Commission understand why, at the end of the ten years' transitional period, if circumstances required the postponement of the proposed independent State, the British Government thought it necessary to consult the neighbouring Arab States. That it should consult the representatives of the people of Palestine seemed right and proper, to do so with the Council of the League of Nations, surely, went without saying. To consult the Arab States, however, was to admit that they were to be asked their opinion regarding the advisability of a certain policy being pursued by the Mandatory Power. That assumed that they had a right of intervention in the matter. Whence had they derived such a right? Was not consent to the establishment of a Jewish National Home in Palestine the very moderate price which the Arabs had agreed to pay for the liberation of lands extending from the Red Sea to the borders of Cilicia on the one hand, and Iran and the Mediterranean on the other, for the independence they were then winning, or had already won, and which they would never have gained by their own efforts, and for all of which they had to thank the Allied Powers and, particularly, the British forces in the Near East?[1]

When, at the end of the session, the Commission reported to the Council of the League of Nations it declared that the policy set out in the White Paper was not in accordance with the interpretation which, in agreement with the Mandatory Power and the Council, the Commission had placed upon the Palestine Mandate. A minority of three members, however, which included the British representative, thought that the existing circumstances would justify the policy, provided the Council did not oppose it.

What action would have been taken when the Permanent Mandates Commission's Report, together with the British Government comments thereon, came to be considered in due course by the Council of the League can only be a matter for guesswork, for the outbreak of war on 3 September prevented the Council meeting as arranged. It is very doubtful, however, whether the League would have approved of the policy contained in the White Paper, having regard to the fact that practically no one had so far said a good word for it.

*   *   *   *   *

Six weeks before war came, the Twenty-First Zionist Congress had opened in Geneva, and its Chairman, Dr. Weizmann, has said that it took place in an 'atmosphere of unreality and irrelevance', for the delegates met under the shadow of the White Paper, which menaced the National Home, and under the shadow of a war which bid fair to spread death and destruction over Europe and perhaps further. The White Paper was, of course, unanimously rejected, but many opposing

---

[1] For a full account of the proceedings see Minutes of the Thirty-Sixth Session of the Permanent Mandates Commission of the League of Nations, Geneva, June 1939.

views were heard, during the debate, on what attitude should now be adopted by the movement and the Jewish community in Palestine, particularly towards the Mandatory Power.

The different approaches were as follows:

(1) A small group, known as the Jewish State Party, led by Meir Grossman favoured complete non-co-operation with the British Government and advocated civil disobedience.

(2) A larger group, led by David Ben Gurion, proposed a departure from the Weizmann policy which had always meant co-operation with Great Britain. He took the view that the only way in which the Jews could prevent the British Government from appeasing the Arabs was by causing the Palestine Administration the greatest trouble and inconvenience, if and when they tried to implement the new policy. He considered that, as the Mandates Commission had condemned the White Paper as a violation of the Mandate, the Jews would be morally justified in adopting a policy of non-co-operation towards the Mandatory Power. The White Paper, he said, had created a vacuum which must be filled by the Jews themselves. The Jews should act as though they were the State in Palestine and continue to do so until there was one there.

(3) What might be called the 'official' view, that was always held by Dr. Weizmann himself and still adhered to despite many disappointments, was that as a relationship with some great Power was necessary in order to attain the aims of Zionism, the devil you knew was better than the one you did not. Furthermore, as the Jews could not do other than side with the British in the forthcoming war against Hitler, it would be highly inconsistent to support the British Commonwealth against Germany and, at the same time, bedevil the situation in Palestine. This eminently sound view was strongly supported by the noted American Zionist and delegate to the Congress, Rabbi Abba Hillel Silver. He regarded the White Paper as a temporary document which would later be replaced. While they should refuse to accept it, and should oppose it with all their might, no extreme measures should be taken and no force should be used. He disagreed profoundly with Ben Gurion. He thought it dangerous for the Jews to act as though they were, in fact, a State when they were not. It might put weapons into the hands of their enemies.

(4) The fourth party in the discussions, led by the leader of the Jewish Labour Party, took a middle line between the old policy of conciliation and self-restraint, and the aggressive policy of non-co-operation and active resistance.[1]

When the Congress rose all knew that war was just round the corner. As they parted and said good-bye many knew that it would be for ever. For most of the Polish delegates it was their last Congress. With more than a million and a half other Polish Jews they died or were gassed in the concentration camps, or perished in the rising of the Warsaw ghetto.

[1] *Survey of International Affairs*, Vol. I (1938).

CHAPTER X

World War II

THAT the Jews inevitably had no choice other than to work for the victory of Great Britain and her Allies does not detract from the value of what they did to help attain that end. Some Jews, like Dr. Weizmann, whose home had been in Britain for so many years and who had rendered her signal service during World War I, found more than a touch of irony in the failure of certain British circles to appreciate this inevitability.

On the outbreak of war he had written, as President of the Jewish Agency, to the Prime Minister assuring him of the loyalty of the Jewish community and their resolve to support Britain and fight on the side of the Allies.

In this hour of supreme crisis, the consciousness that the Jews have a contribution to make to the defence of sacred values impels me to write this letter. I wish to confirm, in the most implicit manner, the declarations which I and my colleagues have made during the last months, and especially in the last week: that the Jews 'stand by Great Britain and will fight on the side of the democracies'.

Our urgent desire is to give effect to these declarations. We wish to do so in a way entirely consonant with the general scheme of British action, and therefore would place ourselves, in matters big and small, under the co-ordinating direction of His Majesty's Government. The Jewish Agency is ready to enter into immediate arrangements for utilizing Jewish man-power, technical ability, resources, etc.

The Jewish Agency has recently had differences in the political field with the Mandatory Power. We would like these differences to give way before the greater and more pressing necessities of the time. We ask you to accept this declaration in the spirit in which it is made.

It was not generally expected in Zionist circles, after the White Paper had been so widely criticized in Parliament, where almost every statesman of note had described it as a breach of faith, and had also been condemned by the Mandates Commission, that any of its provisions would be implemented. This expectation was not realized, for in February 1940 the British Government brought out a set of Land Regulations under which Jews were debarred from acquiring land in the greater part of Palestine and acquisition was restricted in other areas.[1] The whole country was divided into three zones. In Zone A, which comprised over four million acres, or more than sixty-three per cent of the total acreage, no Jew could buy land. In Zone B, consisting of over two million acres, or more than thirty-one per cent of the total, the purchase of land by Jews could only be authorized in special circumstances. It was only in Zone C, which consisted of not more than 332,000 acres, that the Jewish purchase of land was not subject to any administrative restrictions.

Ever since the outbreak of war, and until the publication of these Regulations, there had been peace and quiet and a return of neighbourly relations between Arab and Jewish villagers. The Regulations soon put an end to that. There were numerous Jewish public demonstrations against them early in March in all the large cities, and these led to some violence. Two soldiers and two policemen were injured and, as usual, there were heavy casualties amongst the Jews, four hundred being wounded, of whom two subsequently died. Many Arabs also did not like the Regulations, and were extremely annoyed at not being able to sell their land when and to whom they pleased.

Once again the Government's action was almost universally criticized and condemned, particularly in Parliament where many members of all three political parties supported a vote of censure moved, on behalf of the Labour Party, by Mr. Philip Noel-Baker, although it was eventually defeated. The motion regretted that 'disregarding the express opinion of the Permanent Mandates Commission that the policy contained in the White Paper on Palestine was inconsistent with the Mandate, and without the authority of the Council of the League of Nations, His Majesty's Government have authorized the issue of the Regulations controlling the transfer of land which discriminate unjustly against one section of the inhabitants of Palestine'.[2]

[1] Palestine Land Transfer Regulations, 28 February 1940.
[2] Parliamentary Debates, House of Commons, Vol. 357.

Lloyd George and Winston Churchill

Lord Robert Cecil

Sir Mark Sykes

The Grand Mufti of Jerusalem

Speaking in the House of Commons on the vote of censure against the Government the Colonial Secretary, still Mr. MacDonald, said that if these Regulations were not put into force he feared that the whole mood of the Arab people might change as there was already an increasing undercurrent of unrest amongst them. Nearly everyone else in the know was convinced that the converse was nearer the truth.

But the gravest objection to the implementation of Part III of the White Paper was upon moral grounds, because of its timing. This was urged very strongly by Mr. Philip Noel-Baker, who moved the vote of censure.

He reminded the House of Churchill's words regarding the Balfour Declaration spoken two years earlier. Churchill had said that the decision to issue the Balfour Declaration had been taken by H.M. Government 'in the dire need of the war, with the object of promoting the general victory of the Allies, for which they expected and received valuable and important assistance'. 'Today,' Mr. Noel-Baker said, 'the Jews are a weak and hunted race. Tens of thousands, perhaps hundreds of thousands of them have already perished, their property has been stolen and destroyed, and it is because, in the general holocaust of civilized standards, their influence has gone that we dare to do this shameful act, that we try and repudiate the moral contract which we made with them during the last Great War.'

It seemed a strange moment, as Sir Archibald Sinclair pointed out, to inflict yet another wrong on the tortured, humiliated, suffering Jewish people, who were exerting themselves to help the Allies in the war, were rendering great services, were willing to fight in defence of Palestine, if need be, and eager to send troops to fight in France for the sake of Britain.

The prohibition and restriction of land purchase, however, was not the only wrong which the British Government were prepared to inflict upon the Jews. As the Nazi persecution of the Jews in Central Europe intensified it had been hoped that there would be, perhaps, a relaxation of the severe quota regulations on immigration. Hundreds of thousands of Jews from Poland and other countries turned their eyes towards their Homeland, but they could not enter except as illegal immigrants. Measures had been taken by the Palestine Government to punish illegal immigrants by sending them to prison prior to deportation. Sometimes when immigrant ships, which had now been justly named 'coffin' ships, were apprehended, they were put back to sea without the passengers being allowed to land; sometimes the immigrants were transferred to some other ship and sent to Mauritius for internment; and sometimes, in cases where the refugee passengers had already succeeded in landing, the ships were impounded until the end of the war.

Many heart-rending incidents took place. Large numbers of Jews found themselves stranded in south-eastern Europe between the Scylla of the advancing Nazis and the Charybdis of the British Government's strict immigration policy. Many of these unfortunate people committed suicide rather than return home and end their lives in a gas chamber.

Those who were deported to Mauritius escaped Himmler and the Gestapo, but many died from disease caused by the inadequate conditions of their captivity. The island was most unhealthy and, shortly after about sixteen hundred had arrived there from Austria, Czechoslovakia and Poland, an epidemic of typhus was followed by an outbreak of malaria. Answering a question put to him in the House of Commons, the Colonial Secretary stated that ninety-three internees had died.

The Palestine Government was completely relentless, and the following is a typical official announcement regarding illegal immigration which was made on 20 November 1940, to be followed by many others in a similar strain:

H.M. Government are not lacking in sympathy for refugees from territories under German control. But they are responsible for the administration of Palestine and are bound to see to it that the laws of the country are not openly flouted. Moreover, they can only regard a revival of illegal Jewish immigration at the present juncture as likely to affect the local situation most adversely, and to prove a serious menace to British interests in the Middle East.

It is difficult to imagine how the entry into Palestine of another twenty thousand Jews a year would have constituted 'a serious menace to British interests in the Middle East', but it would have saved the lives of another eighty thousand Jews.

Mr. Churchill certainly did not share this alarmist view, for on 1 March 1941 he wrote thus to the Secretary of State for the Colonies, Lord Moyne:

General Wavell, like most British Military Officers, is strongly pro-Arab. At the time of the licences to the shipwrecked illegal immigrants being permitted he sent a telegram not less strong than this, predicting widespread disaster in the Arab world together with the loss of the Basra-Baghdad-Haifa route. The telegram should be looked up, and also my answer, in which I overruled the General and explained to him the reasons for the Cabinet decision. All went well and not a dog barked. . . .

Nevertheless, despite their knowledge that they would have to be smuggled ashore on arrival in Palestine, provided they were able to get that far and evade the patrol boats which kept a look-out up and down the coast, thousands of Jews sailed from various European ports in unseaworthy leaky ships crammed full to the gunwales.

During the first month of the war a ship named *Tigerhill*, packed with Jewish refugees fleeing from certain death in Poland, was fired on by a naval patrol. Three refugees were killed and the others were refused permission to land. A protest was made by a number of British Members of Parliament, but the Colonial Secretary justified the action taken on the grounds that 'to authorize the indiscriminate landing of refugees in Palestine would worsen rather than improve the security position there'.[1]

Many other illegal immigrant ships were intercepted during the next two years, but probably the worst tragedy of all occurred in February 1942. The *Struma*, a small cattle boat of some two hundred tons, with 769 Jewish refugees on board, had left the port of Constanza in October 1941. After a long and difficult voyage she steamed into Istanbul harbour on 26 December in very poor shape. She remained at Istanbul for a little over two months while repairs were carried out. During this period negotiations went on between the Turks and the British authorities in Palestine as to the ultimate destination of the ship's passengers. The details of the negotiations are unimportant, but the final outcome was that as the Palestine Government, then headed by Sir Harold McMichael, who had relieved Sir Arthur Wauchope as High Commissioner in 1937, had refused to allow the passengers to enter Palestine, the Turkish authorities sent the ship back to sea, short of food and water. On 24 February news was received that the vessel had blown up and sunk near the Bosphorus with the loss of all on board including seventy children.

[1] Parliamentary Debates, House of Commons, Vol. 351.

This news brought protests from all over the world which were not assuaged by the non-committal statement which was made by the Colonial Secretary in the House of Commons when the matter was raised there. 'His Majesty's Government,' said Mr. Harold Macmillan, 'earnestly hope that such a tragedy will not occur again. It does not lie in their power, however, amid the dangers and uncertainties of war, to give any guarantee, nor can they be party to any measures which would undermine the existing policy regarding illegal immigration into Palestine in view of the wider issues involved.' As the British Government was not prepared to relax the restrictions on immigration to let these wretched refugees into Palestine it would have sounded less hypocritical had the Colonial Secretary not expressed the pious hope that no similar incident would happen in the future.

A few days after the sinking of the *Struma* the following poster appeared all over Palestine in English and Hebrew:

MURDER

Sir Harold McMichael, known as High Commissioner for Palestine, wanted for murder by drowning 800 refugees on board the *Struma*.

For years the Jewish organizations in Palestine had managed to restrain even their extremists, and had so far, since the war began, observed a political truce. From now on the Jewish Agency was no longer in complete control, and a campaign of terrorism began. It was regrettable, and some dreadful things were done which the Hebrew Press and the Jewish leaders, on more than one occasion, publicly condemned, but it cannot be denied that the Jews had held their hand for a long time despite tremendous provocation.

*   *   *   *   *

Dr. Weizmann was determined to follow up the promise of help which he had given Mr. Chamberlain on the outbreak of hostilities and to translate it into reality. In August 1940 he had written to ask Winston Churchill for an interview and suggested that the Jews in Palestine should be allowed to bear arms. If it so happened that the British forces had temporarily to withdraw from Palestine the Jews would all be massacred, men, women and children by the Arabs, encouraged and directed by the Nazis. Palestinian Jewry could raise a force of fifty thousand men which might, in that eventuality, be a godsend.

In September Churchill and Weizmann discussed the suggestion further. The Jewish leader had worked out a skeleton scheme which he put to the Prime Minister and subsequently, on his instructions, submitted to the Chief of the Imperial General Staff, then General Sir John Dill, who had previously been in command of the First Corps in the British Expeditionary Force. The scheme envisaged large-scale recruitment of Jews in Palestine for the fighting services and the formation of Jewish battalions and, possibly, brigades and divisions. A cadre of officers, sufficient for a Jewish division to begin with, was to be selected at once from Jews in Palestine, and trained in Egypt. It was also suggested that a Jewish desert unit might usefully be formed and that foreign Jews resident in England might also be enlisted.

Although the Prime Minister was, according to Dr. Weizmann, unreservedly co-operative and in favour of the scheme, it was exactly four years before a Jewish Brigade was formed. Mr. Churchill had, in fact, already been trying to raise Jewish units in Palestine so that some of the twenty-three British and Australian infantry battalions and Yeomanry regiments in that country could be released to fight elsewhere. In the second volume of his book *The Second World War* he has written of the difficulties encountered. 'In bringing home the troops from Palestine I had difficulties with both my old friends, the Secretary of State for India, Mr. Amery, and the Secretary of State for the Colonies, Lord Lloyd, who was a convinced anti-Zionist and pro-Arab. I wished to arm the Jewish colonists.'

On 28 June 1940 Mr. Churchill wrote the following minute to Lord Lloyd:

Prime Minister to Secretary of State for the Colonies
The failure of the policy which you favour is proved by the very large numbers of sorely-needed troops we have to keep in Palestine.

> 6 battalions of infantry,
> 9 regiments of Yeomanry,
> 8 battalions of Australian infantry,

the whole probably more than twenty thousand men.

This is the price we have to pay for the anti-Jewish policy which has been persisted in for some years.

Should the war go heavily in Egypt, all these troops will have to be with-

drawn, and the position of the Jewish colonists will be one of the greatest danger. Indeed I am sure that we shall be told we cannot withdraw these troops,
though they include some of our best, and are vitally needed elsewhere. If the
Jews were properly armed, our forces would become available, and there would
be no danger of the Jews attacking the Arabs because they are entirely depen-
dent on us and upon our command of the seas. I think it is little less than a scandal
that at a time when we are fighting for our lives these very large forces should
be immobilized in support of a policy which commends itself only to a section
of the Conservative Party. I had hoped that you would take a broad view of the
Palestine situation, and would make it an earnest objective to set the British
garrison free. I would certainly not associate myself with such an answer as you
have drawn up for me.[1] I do not at all admit that Arab feeling in the Near East
and India would be prejudiced in the manner you suggest. Now that we have
the Turks in such a friendly relationship the position is much more secure.

Again on 12 August the Prime Minister for a third time returned to
the attack and wrote to General Ismay, for General Wavell:

I do not consider that proper use is being made of the large forces in Palestine.
The essence of the situation depends on arming the Jewish colonists sufficiently
to enable them to undertake their own defence, so that if necessary for a short
time the whole of Palestine can be left to a very small British force.

When, at last, in July 1944 the formation of the Jewish Brigade was
really being discussed in detail Churchill had this to say:

Prime Minister to Secretary of State for War
1. I am in general agreement with your proposals for a Jewish fighting force,
but I think the brigade should be formed and sent to Italy as soon as
convenient. . . .
2. I like the idea of the Jews trying to get at the murderers of their fellow
countrymen in Central Europe, and I think it would give a great deal of satisfaction in the United States.

Regarding a proposal that the Brigade should be allowed its own
flag Churchill wrote, 'I will consult the King about this. I cannot con-
ceive why this martyred race, scattered about the world and suffering
as no other race has done at this juncture, should be denied the satisfaction of having its flag. However, not only the King but the Cabinet
may have views on this.'[2]

[1] It has not been possible to obtain from official or unofficial sources a copy of this
document.
[2] On 31 October 1944 it was announced by the Jewish Agency that a special flag had
been approved by the British Government for the Jewish Brigade—horizontal blue stripes
on a white background, with a blue Shield of David in the centre. A blue and white
shoulder flash with a Shield of David in gold had also been authorized.

But it had been a hard fight all the way to bring this about, as there had been Colonial Office and War Office opposition at almost every stage, and the discussion referred to above only took place because of the firm action which had been taken by the Prime Minister sixteen days earlier. On 10 July he had written thus to Sir Edward Bridges:

In your report [about the War Cabinet meeting on forming a Jewish fighting force] you said that it was decided that a brigade group should be carefully examined. I certainly understood, and hold very strongly the view that a brigade group should be made.

When the War Office say they will carefully examine a thing they mean they will do it in.

The matter must, therefore, be set down for an early meeting of the War Cabinet meeting this week, and the Secretary of State for War should be warned of my objection. A copy of the further letter from Dr. Weizmann may also be forwarded to the War Office.

Finally, in September 1944 the War Office made this announcement: 'His Majesty's Government have decided to accede to the request of the Jewish Agency for Palestine that a Jewish Brigade Group be formed to take part in active operations.' In his review of the war situation given by Churchill in the House of Commons on 29 September he referred to the War Office announcement and said, 'I know there is a vast number of Jews serving with our forces and the American forces throughout all the armies, but it seems to me indeed appropriate that a special Jewish unit of that race, which has suffered indescribable torment from the Nazis, should be represented as a distinct formation among the forces gathered for their final overthrow.'

*   *   *   *   *

As long as things were not going too well for the Allies the Jews in Palestine exercised restraint, and the end of the political truce did not come until after the victory at El Alamein which removed any immediate danger of a German–Italian invasion of Palestine. The slogan which best summed up this policy was, 'We shall fight the White Paper as if there were no war, and we shall fight the war is if there were no White Paper.'

Nevertheless, Jewish terrorist activity which, as has already been mentioned, began in a small way in 1942 shortly after the *Struma* incident as a result of anger and resentment at the obstinate maintenance of immigration restrictions, had, by the end of 1943, greatly increased. Although an announcement had been made regarding the continuation of immigration after May 1944 still, of course, on a reduced scale, the situation had been progressively deteriorating throughout the year during which an attempt was made on the life of the High Commissioner, and Lord Moyne was assassinated in Cairo. Government offices were damaged by incendiary bombs and two British police officers were shot during an encounter in the Jewish quarter of Haifa. The National Council of Jews in Palestine issued a statement calling on the Jewish population to condemn these outrages and do everything in their power to circumvent the terrorists and saboteurs, but the only answer was a further crop of outrages in which two police cars were wrecked and several British police inspectors narrowly escaped injury. Week after week, further shooting of British police officers followed, until on 23 March explosions occurred in the police stations of Jerusalem and Jaffa, and six British policemen were shot in Tel-Aviv in broad daylight.

The two chief organizations responsible for these outrages were the Irgun Zvai Leumi and the Stern Group. The former body was formed in 1935 from dissident members of the Hagana. The Hagana and its associated force, the Palmach, was an illegal and well armed military organization, under a central command with subsidiary territorial commands.

It consisted of:

(1) A static force composed of settlers and town-dwellers, with an estimated strength of forty thousand.

(2) A field army, based on the Jewish Settlement Police and trained in more mobile operations. The estimated strength of this force was sixteen thousand.

(3) A full time force (the Palmach), permanently mobilized and provided with transport, with an estimated peace establishment of two thousand and a war establishment of about six thousand.

The Irgun Zvai Leumi, or National Military Organization, was an underground movement with an estimated strength of between three and five thousand. The members of the Irgun did not regard themselves as terrorists and disliked being so called. They liked to think of themselves as a legitimate underground resistance movement like the French Maquis during the German occupation. In this case Great Britain was the occupying power. It was a comparison which did little credit to their intelligence. They had a military organization and issued official communiqués in military style.

Irgun's operations were conducted almost exclusively against the Administration, and they bombed and set on fire Government buildings, army installations and police stations. Although they carried arms, they boasted that these were never used except in self-defence when they were attacked, and they consistently denied any complicity in the shooting of British policemen.

The Stern Group originated as a dissident splinter-group of extremists from the Irgun, when the latter decided in 1939 temporarily to suspend offensive operations on the outbreak of war. Generally known as the Stern Gang, it was composed of some three hundred or more dangerous fanatics. It got its name from a Pole named Abraham Stern who had been in Italy during Mussolini's régime before it became anti-Semitic. During that time Stern became an anglophobe, and when he came to Palestine he found a ready-made outlet for his fanatical hatred of the British. It was nothing more nor less than a secret terrorist society composed mostly of young Polish Jews and other recent arrivals from Central Europe, though there were a few Sabras[1] amongst them. There were few of them who had not had a dose of Nazi occupation and all that it entailed. They were embittered, savage and ruthless, but that was not their fault. They were not able to distinguish between the old enemy and the new, for to them the Mandatory Power was the enemy. In their tortured minds Great Britain 'was holding down by force and fraud a country which she had invaded and in which she had no rights. She was denying to Jews and Arabs alike freedom and independence. Her authority was without legal or moral warrant, and the duty of every good citizen was to take up arms against her in a holy war. In waging that war they were not "terrorists", they were an army entitled to use all the devices and arts of warfare, and entitled to be treated as belligerents.'[2] Although most of this was utter nonsense, and

[1] Sabra: prickly pear. The colloquial name for a Palestine-born Jew.
[2] *Israel, the Establishment of a State* by Harry Sacher.

in no way excuses the crimes they committed, it makes them more understandable and less unforgivable.

The activities of these misguided young men were condemned from the first by the Jewish Agency as the acts of 'a gang of lunatics endeavouring to establish a reign of terror'. On 7 August an attempt was made to assassinate Sir Harold McMichael who was due to be relieved two months later. The attempt was unsuccessful, but he and two of his escort were wounded. This attack was vehemently condemned by all the Jewish organizations and Press as a 'dastardly act'.

Almost three months later to the day, Lord Moyne, the British Resident Minister in Egypt, was murdered in Cairo. Both these crimes were the work of the Stern Gang. On hearing the news, Dr. Weizmann wrote to the Prime Minister to express his 'deep moral indignation and horror', which would be shared by Jews throughout the world. He assured Mr. Churchill that Palestine Jewry would, as its representative bodies had already declared, go to the utmost limit of its power to cut out, root and branch, this evil from its midst. As anyone but these crazy youths would have realized, had they stopped to think, the attempted assassination did the cause of the National Home considerable harm and estranged some of its truest friends. Churchill, in a statement in the House of Commons said: 'This shameful crime has shocked the world and has affected none more strongly than those like myself who, in the past, have been consistent friends of the Jews and constant architects of their future. If our dreams for Zionism are to end in the smoke of an assassin's pistol, and the labours for its future produce a new set of gangsters worthy of Nazi Germany, many like myself will have to reconsider the position we have maintained so consistently and so long in the past.'

Although some of the more leftish organs of the British Press seem to have regarded Mr. Churchill's words as 'unnecessarily harsh and threatening', no one had more right to speak frankly as a friend than he had, and the *Palestine Post*, in a leading article, spoke for the majority. 'There is no one from whom the bitter words could have come with better grace and greater sincerity, or been received with greater understanding.'[1]

The relief of Sir Harold McMichael by Lord Gort brought about a

[1] *Palestine Post*, 19 November 1944.

lull in terrorist activities which continued until his much regretted
retirement because of ill-health a year later.

*   *   *   *   *

In July 1945 a general election had taken place in Great Britain and
Mr. Churchill's Coalition Government, to the surprise of many people,
was no more. A Socialist administration under Mr. Attlee had taken its
place and, having regard to the Labour Party's promises when in
opposition, hope for the future rose to new heights in the Jewish
National Home. In 1935 Mr. Attlee had said that the British Labour
Party recalled with pride that in the dark days of the Great War they
associated themselves with the ideal of a National Home in Palestine for
the Jewish people, and that ever since then successive Party Conferences
had repeatedly affirmed their enthusiastic support of the effort towards
its realization. The Party had never faltered, and would never falter, in
their active and sympathetic co-operation with the work of political
and economic reconstruction now going forward in Palestine.

Mr. Herbert Morrison, criticizing the 1939 White Paper in the House
of Commons as a leading member of the Opposition, had said: 'I think
it ought to be known by the House that this breach of faith, which we
regret, this breach of British honour, with its policy with which we
have no sympathy, is such that the least that can be said is that the
Government must not expect that this is going to be automatically
binding on their successors.'

At the Party's Conference in 1944, the official view on Jewish immigration had been expressed in the following terms: 'There is surely
neither hope nor meaning in a "Jewish National Home" unless we are
prepared to let the Jews, if they wish, enter this tiny land in such numbers as to become a majority. There was a strong case for this before the
war, there is an irresistible case now, after the unspeakable atrocities of
the cold and calculated German Nazi plan to kill all the Jews in Europe.'

Finally, at the 1945 conference which was held in Blackpool only two
months before the general election, Mr. Dalton, soon to be a Cabinet
Minister, said this: 'This Party has laid it down and repeated it so
recently as last April . . . that this time, having regard to the unspeakable
horrors that have been perpetrated upon the Jews in Germany and other
occupied countries in Europe, it is morally wrong and politically

157

indefensible to impose obstacles to the entry into Palestine now of Jews who desire to go there. We consider that Jewish immigration into Palestine should be permitted without the present limitations.'

Fine words indeed, and calculated to lead anyone, unmindful of the broken vows and promises of politicians, to believe that if and when the British electors were sensible enough to put a Socialist Government into power, the Jewish dream of centuries would at last become a reality. Disillusionment was not far off.

CHAPTER XI

The Anglo-American Committee and After

MR. Attlee's Government had not been long in power before a statement on its Palestine Policy was made. The new Foreign Secretary, Mr. Ernest Bevin, announced it in the House of Commons on 13 November 1945 and, on the same day, President Truman stated in Washington that the United States Government had agreed to the formation of an Anglo-American Committee of Enquiry to study and report on the problems of European Jewry and Palestine.

Less than three months previously the World Zionist Conference had met in London and endorsed the petition submitted to the British Government by the Jewish Agency in the previous May. In this the following requests were made:

(1) That an immediate decision be announced to establish a Jewish State.

(2) That the Jewish Agency be invested with all necessary authority to bring to Palestine as many Jews as it might be found necessary and possible to settle, and to develop, fully and speedily, all the resources of the country, especially land and power resources.

(3) That an international loan and other help be given for the transfer of the first million of Jews to Palestine and for the economic development of the country.

(4) That reparations in kind from Germany be granted to the Jewish people for the rebuilding of Palestine, and—as a first instalment—that all German property in Palestine be used for the resettlement of Jews from Europe.

(5) That international facilities be provided for the exit and transit of all Jews who wish to settle in Palestine.[1]

The World Zionist Organization also stressed the need for urgent action, for there could not be any solution to the 'inseparable twin problems of the Jewish people in Palestine except by constituting Palestine undivided and undiminished as a Jewish State in accordance with the purpose of the Balfour Declaration. Any delay in the solution of the problem, any attempt at half measures, any decision which, however favourable, remains on paper and is not faithfully and speedily implemented, would not meet the tragedy of the hour and might only increase suffering among the Jewish people and tension in Palestine.'

The Bevin statement was a great blow to Zionism for it belied all the Labour Party's promises which had been stated and restated on so many occasions. The Party had repeatedly promised almost unlimited immigration and now there was what Dr. Weizmann has called 'a trickle of fifteen hundred refugees a month'. Instead of acknowledging once more, as other Governments had done before, the original purpose of the Balfour Declaration it reverted, to use Dr. Weizmann's words once again, 'to the old shifty double emphasis on the obligation towards the Arabs of Palestine as being of equal weight with the promise of the Homeland to the Jews'. The Zionist Organization of America also protested that the pre-election pledges of the Labour Party had been violated, and accused H.M. Government of attempting to reduce Jewish Palestine 'to another ghetto'.

When the American President announced the U.S. Government's agreement to the setting-up of the Anglo-American Committee, he also disclosed that in August he had asked Mr. Attlee to allow a hundred thousand displaced Jews from Germany and Austria to enter Palestine, and that the British Prime Minister had declined to do so. Nevertheless, he was still in favour of the creation of a 'democratic State in Palestine', not based, however, on 'religion, race or creed'.

In his speech in the House of Commons announcing the Government's proposals, Mr. Bevin mentioned that there had recently been demands made for large-scale immigration into Palestine. The problem

[1] Royal Institute of International Affairs, Information Paper No. 20, 'Great Britain and Palestine 1915–1945'.

of Palestine, however, was very difficult, he said, for the Mandate required Great Britain to facilitate Jewish immigration and to ensure close settlement by Jews on the land, at the same time safeguarding the rights and position of other sections of the population. There was, therefore, a dual obligation, and it was just this which had been the main cause of trouble during the past twenty-six years.

Pending receipt and consideration of the interim recommendations of the joint committee, H.M. Government would consult with the Arabs with a view to coming to some arrangement which would ensure that there was no interruption of immigration at the monthly rate then prevailing. After the Government had considered the interim recommendations it would explore the possibilities of devising other temporary arrangements for dealing with the Palestine problem until a permanent solution could be reached, and would submit a plan to U.N.O. for such a solution, if possible an agreed one.

Once again it was a case of ifs, buts and peradventures. It was one more effort to gain time and do nothing. It was the same old recipe with the same old ingredients. There was, however, one new departure. The United Nations Organization had just been brought into existence: might it not be a good idea to 'pass the baby' on to it?

* * * * *

The Anglo-American Committee was duly appointed and given the following terms of reference which were agreed by both the Governments concerned:[1]

(1) To examine political, economic and social conditions in Palestine as they bear upon the problem of Jewish immigration and settlement therein, and the well-being of the peoples now living therein.

(2) To examine the position of the Jews in those countries in Europe where they have been the victims of Nazi and Fascist persecution, and the practical measures taken or contemplated to be taken in those countries to enable them to live free from discrimination and oppression, and to make estimates of those who wish or will be impelled by

---

[1] See H.M.S.O. Command Paper 6822. Exchange of Notes regarding the Constitution of a Joint Anglo-American Committee of Enquiry into the Problems of European Jewry and Palestine.

their conditions to migrate to Palestine or other countries outside Europe.

(3) To hear the views of competent witnesses and to consult representative Arabs and Jews on the problems of Palestine as such problems are affected by conditions subject to examination under paragraph (1) and paragraph (2) above and by other relevant facts and circumstances, and to make recommendations to His Majesty's Government and the Government of the United States for *ad interim* handling of these problems as well as for their permanent solution.

(4) To make such other recommendations to His Majesty's Government and the Government of the United States as may be necessary to meet the immediate needs arising from conditions subject to examination under paragraph (2) above, by remedial action in the European countries in question or by the provision of facilities for emigration to and settlement in countries outside Europe.

The urgent need for a speedy investigation was impressed on the Committee by both Governments who asked for a Report within a hundred and twenty days from the first session. It would not have been possible for the full committee to visit all the countries concerned within so short a time, and only sub-committees visited Germany, Poland, Czechoslovakia, Italy and Greece as well as the capitals of Syria, Iraq, Saudi-Arabia and Transjordan to hear the views of the Arab Governments. The members sat in full committee, however, at Washington, London, Vienna, Cairo and in Palestine, and concluded their deliberations at Lausanne.

When the sub-committees visited Germany, Austria and Italy they found about ninety-eight thousand Jewish displaced persons.[1] In the American and British Zones of Germany and Austria the majority were living in camps where accommodation and maintenance were provided by the occupation authorities. There were other Jews living in the camps who were not D.P.s. In those early days after the cessation of hostilities the conditions in the camps were not always very satisfactory, although everything possible was being done for the physical needs of the inmates. Little could be done, however, for their morale which was

---

[1] Displaced persons, commonly known as D.P.s. The name was given to persons outside their national boundaries by reason of war.

Chaim Weizmann
First President of the State of Israel
(*Portrait by Oswald Bisley*)

David Ben Gurion reading the proclamation establishing the State of Israel
(A portrait of Herzl is hanging on the wall)

non-existent owing to the horrors of Nazi persecution. It did not improve their mental outlook to have to live in Germany where they saw around them, to use the Committee's own words, 'Germans living a family life in their own homes and outwardly little affected by the war', whilst they, the scattered survivors of Central European Jewry, were, perforce, still living under some form of restriction.

When the Committee recommended, as it did, that a hundred thousand certificates should immediately be authorized for the admission into Palestine of Jews who had been the victims of Nazi and Fascist persecution, and the relaxation of immigration laws generally, it was done as an 'emergency and humanitarian measure'. The Committee felt that it would do something to relieve the feelings of urgency with which the Jews were looking beyond Europe, and that if it did not encourage some of those who were left behind to resettle themselves in Europe, it would at least help them to wait patiently for their chance of emigration to come.

The members of the Committee would have been less than human had they not understood and sympathized with the longing of the Jewish survivors of Nazi persecution to leave the scene of such dreadful memories and put the horrors of the past behind them. Three members of the Committee, however, had visited the Warsaw Ghetto which left an impression on their minds, which, according to the Report, would forever remain. 'Areas of that city on which formerly stood large buildings are now a mass of brick rubble, covering the bodies of numberless unknown Jews. Adjoining the ghetto there still stands an old barracks used as a place for killing Jews. Viewing this in the cold grey light of a February day one could imagine the depths of suffering there endured. In the courtyards of the barracks were pits containing human ash and human bones. The effect of that place on Jews who came searching, so often in vain, for any trace of their dear ones, can be left to the imagination.'

Was it any wonder that the Committee found that in Poland, Hungary and Roumania the chief desire of the Jewish survivors was to get away? Was it unnatural that the vast majority of the Jewish D.P.s and migrants believed that the only place which offered a new life of happiness, peace and security was Palestine?

'We know of no country,' the Report declared, 'to which the great majority can go in the immediate future other than Palestine. Furthermore, that is where almost all of them want to go. There they are sure they will receive a welcome denied them elsewhere. There they hope to enjoy peace and rebuild their lives. We believe it is essential that they should be given the opportunity to do so at the earliest possible time. Furthermore, we have the assurances of the leaders of the Jewish Agency that they will be supported and cared for.'

The Committee, however, went further than that, and commented on the provision of the 1939 White Paper that after the lapse of five years Jewish immigration should be subject to Arab acquiescence, a view which could result in Arab dominating Jew.

The Committee's second recommendation for immediate action was about the Land Policy. They recommended that the Land Transfer Regulations of 1940 should be rescinded and replaced by other regulations based on a policy of freedom in the sale, lease or use of land, irrespective of race, community or creed and, providing adequate protection for the interests of small owners and tenant cultivators.

These two recommendations on immigration and land purchase alone constituted a reversal of the pre-war Government's 1939 White Paper Policy and vindicated Jewish opposition to it.

In its comment on this recommendation the Committee showed up the Regulations in their true colour. Their avowed object had been, as described in greater detail elsewhere, to protect Arab tenants and small owners by prohibiting the sale of land to a Palestinian Jew in one zone, by restricting it in another, and allowing free and unrestricted sales in a third. Its effect had been to segregate Arab and Jew and discriminate against the Jew. What was needed was to bring the two people closer together. The Regulations had, moreover, pleased neither of them.

The Committee was entirely opposed to any legislation or restrictions which discriminated against Arab or Jew, and it did not believe that the desired protection for the Arab could be provided only by confining the Jew to particular portions of Palestine in accordance with some kind of apartheid doctrine. That might well be consistent with a policy of partition, such as the Peel Commission had recommended, but that had been knocked on the head long ago, and the Anglo-American Committee's suggestion was the exact opposite, namely that there should be no question of Arab dominating Jew or vice versa, but that

Palestine must be established as a country in which the legitimate national aspirations of both Jews and Arabs could be reconciled without either side fearing the ascendancy of the other.

The Committee's final suggestion would, very likely, not have needed implementing had their other main recommendation been adopted. This was that it should be made clear to both sides that any attempt by threats of violence, by terrorism or the organization of illegal armies to prevent the recommendations being implemented would be resolutely suppressed, and that the Jewish Agency should at once resume active co-operation with the Palestine Government in the suppression of terrorism and illegal immigration.

There is little doubt that if the hundred thousand certificates had been given, the old policy of immigration reintroduced, and the universally disliked and senseless Land Regulations repealed, the reign of terror would have quickly come to an end. In any event it would gradually have faded away from lack of the support of Jewish public opinion.

But this was not to be. The British Prime Minister and his Cabinet colleagues were no more moved by the sorry plight of the survivors of Hitler's 'Final Solution of the Jewish Question' than they were influenced by the unanimity of the Joint Committee's Report. Mr. Attlee announced in the House of Commons that the admission of a hundred thousand Jewish immigrants into Palestine, whose immediate entry had been recommended by the Committee, would not be allowed 'unless and until the illegal armies maintained in Palestine have been disbanded and their arms surrendered'. Nor was that all. The Prime Minister also made it clear that his Government was not prepared to make any decision upon the Committee's recommendations concerning immigration in advance of their general decision on the Report, which must be considered 'as a whole in all its implications'.

This vague announcement came as a great shock to the Jews though it did not deceive anyone. It was generally expected that if the Committee presented a unanimous report, Mr. Bevin would carry out its recommendations; many had certainly gained that impression from what he had said at the time of its appointment. It may well be that he and others in the Government never imagined that the Committee could do it in the time or that they would agree. It was, however, as punctual as it was brief. It is impossible to resist the conclusion that the

Government had already decided on their policy, and that the Committee's recommendations, being what they were, proved to be an acute embarrassment.

In any event Mr. Attlee dealt the Report a mortal blow with these words: 'His Majesty's Government wish to be satisfied that they will not be called upon to implement a policy which would involve them single-handed in such commitments, and in the course of joint examination they will wish to ascertain to what extent the Government of the United States would be prepared to share in the resulting additional *military* and financial responsibilities.'[1] Surely no one could really have expected that the United States Government would undertake military responsibilities in Palestine under the Mandate now that the war was over.

The Prime Minister's statement also shook to its foundations what little faith the Jews still had in the Mandatory Power, slender though it was, and it confirmed the well-founded suspicion that, not for the first time, the appointment of the Anglo-American Committee had only been done to gain time.

Two other events in 1946, which took place shortly after the Prime Minister's announcement, also had an unfortunate effect on Jewish opinion, added to the resentment at the Government's attitude, and increased the general feeling of tension.

The first was the news that the ex-Mufti of Jerusalem had escaped from France, where he had been interned after his arrest in Germany, and had been given political asylum in Egypt. Haj Amin el-Husseini had done enough in Palestine between the two wars to convince anyone of ordinary intelligence that he was no friend of the British, yet a succession of colonial administrators and at least two Royal Commissions appear to have been ignorant of the fact. By the time the war had ended, however, the matter was beyond all doubt. After the assassination of the District Commissioner of Galilee in 1937 the Mufti had escaped to Beirut whence he continued to direct the Arab campaign of terrorism in Palestine. From there, in 1941, he went to Baghdad and took a leading part in Rashid Ali's pro-Nazi revolt in Iraq. After this rising had been put down by the British forces, the Mufti fled to

---

[1] The italics are mine.

Germany where he directed anti-British and anti-Semitic activities until the end of the war. He conducted pro-Axis propaganda amongst Arab prisoners of war, helped to organize an SS Division of Bosnian Moslems, and worked hand in hand with those who were helping Hitler to carry out his plans for the extermination of European Jewry.[1]

The second was an extremely distasteful speech made by Mr. Bevin in Bournemouth on 12 June during the Labour Party's Conference. He cannot in retrospect have been very proud of it and it was, doubtless, attributable to the heady atmosphere of these annual political rallies. Mr. Bevin told the Conference that if a hundred thousand certificates were to be issued forthwith for Jewish immigrants to Palestine, it would entail sending another division of troops there. He went on to make the astounding statement, which did little credit to the intelligence of his audience, that in order to finance the transfer and resettlement of these immigrants the Chancellor of the Exchequer would have to find £200,000,000. No one knew better than he that the British taxpayer had never been called upon to pay a farthing for Jewish immigration and settlement.

But the supreme gaffe was yet to come. On the day of the publication of the Anglo-American Committee's Report, the President of the United States, Mr. Truman, speaking in Washington, had expressed satisfaction that his earlier request for the immediate admission of a hundred thousand Jews into Palestine had been endorsed by the Committee, and urged that the 'transference of these unfortunate people should now be accomplished with the greatest dispatch'. Apropos the President's remarks, Mr. Bevin told his audience of Socialist delegates, in the worst of bad taste, that the reason why Americans were so concerned for the immigration of Jews into Palestine was that they did not want to 'have too many of them in New York'.

It was hardly likely that Mr. Attlee's statement and these other minor irritants would improve the situation, and on the night of 16–17 June a new series of attacks was made on rail and road communications throughout Palestine. More illegal immigrants landed, trains were blown up and, as the tide of violence mounted, repressive measures had to be taken. Many Jewish settlements were searched, hundreds of

[1] Statement Presented by the Jewish Agency to the United Nations Special Committee on Palestine.

Jewish settlers detained, and three Jews were sentenced to death. As a reprisal for this, five British officers were kidnapped by Irgun and held as hostages for the three sentenced men. This reprisal was condemned by the Jewish Agency. The five officers eventually escaped or were released, and the death sentences were commuted.

*   *   *   *   *

Meanwhile, in London, the Committee's Report was still being examined at a joint meeting of British and American officials throughout June and July. Their object was to formulate a detailed plan for the implementation of the Anglo-American Committee's recommendations. The product of these discussions had very little in common with the Committee's proposals although it purported to be based on them. Indeed, during a debate in the House of Commons its origin was disclosed by a previous Colonial Secretary, Mr. Oliver Stanley, who stated that it had been drawn up in outline in the Colonial Office long before the Anglo-American Committee had even been appointed.

Although it was never published in full, it was explained to the House of Commons by Mr. Herbert Morrison on 31 July, during the absence of the Foreign Secretary, and has since come to be known as the Morrison Plan, its official name, however, being the Provincial Autonomy Plan.

Besides dealing with the broader aspects of the refugee and displaced persons problem, the plan also included what Mr. Morrison called 'a new policy for Palestine', based on the conclusion, arrived at by the so-called experts at the series of meetings in London, that the political aspirations of the two communities in Palestine were irreconcilable, and that the only chance of peace and of an immediate advance towards self-government lay in so framing the constitution of the country as to give to each community a chance of managing its own affairs.

The scheme was, that Palestine should be divided into four areas, an Arab Province, a Jewish Province, a District of Jerusalem, and a District of Negev. The Jewish Province would include the great bulk of the land on which Jews had already settled and a large area between and around these settlements. The Jerusalem and Negev Districts would both be administered by the Central Government and would consist respectively of Jerusalem and Bethlehem with their immediate surroundings, and the uninhabited triangle of waste-land in the south of Palestine beyond the limits of cultivation existing at the time. The Arab Province would include the remainder of Palestine and was, in fact, about forty per cent of the total area. The Arab and Jewish Provinces would enjoy a certain measure of self-government, but the Central Government, administered by a British High Commissioner, assisted by a nominated Executive Council, reserved all authority over defence, foreign relations, and customs and excise.

This plan for provincial autonomy, according to Mr. Morrison, would greatly simplify the problems of Jewish immigration into Palestine. The Arab Province would have full power to exclude Jewish immigrants, and the Jewish Province would be able, subject to the Central Government's authorization, to admit immigrants within the economic absorptive capacity.

The Morrison scheme was no more popular than its predecessors, and was rejected, once again, by both Arab and Jew. The World Zionist Congress, held in Basle in December 1946, described it as 'a travesty of Britain's obligations under the Mandate, designed to divide Palestine into Arab, Jewish and British Provinces all of which would be under the unfettered control of the British Administration'. The Congress appealed to the United Nations to support the Jewish people 'in its claim for statehood in Palestine and a place in the family of Nations'. The Arabs, in their turn, rejected the plan because it maintained the rule of Britain while they wanted independence.

But there was still more difficult opposition for Mr. Bevin to overcome, for the scheme met with severe criticism from the President of the United States of America. This rejection of the plan by Mr. Truman was as unwelcome as it was unexpected. The British Government had expected that he would give it his blessing forthwith, but he recalled the six American negotiators, and invited the American members of the Anglo-American Committee to pronounce judgment on these proposals which purported to implement their recommendations. In rejecting the scheme he used these words:

The British Government presented to the Conference the so-called Morrison Plan for provincial autonomy and stated that the Conference was open to other proposals. Meanwhile the Jewish Agency proposed a solution of the Palestine problem by means of the creation of a viable Jewish State, in control of its own immigration and economic policies, in an adequate area of Palestine instead of in the whole of Palestine. It proposed further the immediate issuance of certificates for a hundred thousand Jewish immigrants. This proposal received widespread attention in the United States, both in the Press and in public forums. From the discussion which has ensued it is my belief that a solution along these lines would command the support of public opinion in the United States.

I cannot believe that the gap between the proposals which have been put forward is too great to be bridged by men of reason and goodwill.

* * * * *

Meanwhile serious action had been taken by the British Government against the Jewish Agency and the Jewish community in Palestine. On 29 June British troops, acting under the orders of the Commander-in-Chief Middle East, suddenly descended upon the headquarters of the Jewish Agency, which they occupied, and arrested four members of the Executive in their homes, Rabbi Fishman, the acting Chairman, Moshe Shertok,[1] Head of the Political Department, Isaac Gruenbaum, Head of the Labour Department, and Bernard Joseph the Legal Adviser. Although it was the Sabbath, Rabbi Fishman was forcibly put into an army truck and taken to Latrun. When he protested against his arrest he was maltreated.

Simultaneously a number of Jewish settlements were subjected to searches by troops. Several thousand Jews, mostly from the agricultural settlements, were taken into custody. During these operations five Jews were killed and a large number injured, great damage was done to property, and hundreds of Jews were interned in a new detention camp at Rafa.

While this operation was being carried out the High Commissioner broadcast a statement that it was not the Government's intention to proscribe or close the Jewish Agency, and that it was undertaken not against the Jewish community as a whole but against one section only.

On 1 July the British Prime Minister made a statement in the House of Commons explaining why this action had been taken, and a few days later, the Government issued a White Paper[2] giving information regarding the acts of violence which had impelled it to take active steps against the persons and the organizations whom it considered had made

[1] Later, as Moshe Sharett, Foreign Minister of Israel.

[2] H.M.S.O. Command Paper 6873. Palestine, Statement of Information relating to Acts of Violence.

themselves responsible for the planning and carrying out of these outrages listed in the White Paper.

These attacks had been going on ever since October 1945 and they
came to a climax on 18 June 1946 with the kidnapping of six British
officers. The information in the Government's possession regarding
these incidents, some of which was published in the White Paper, led
them to draw the following conclusions:

(1) That the Hagana and its associated force, the Palmach, working
under the political control of some of the leading members of the
Jewish Agency, had been carrying on an organized campaign of
sabotage and violence as the 'Jewish Resistance Movement'.

(2) That since October 1945 both Irgun Zvai Leumi and the Stern
Group had been working in co-operation with the Hagana High
Command in connexion with some of these operations.

(3) That the broadcasting station of Kol Israel, which claimed to be
the 'Voice of the Resistance', was supporting both those terrorist
organizations and working under the general direction of the Jewish
Agency.

(4) Although a distinction had fairly to be drawn between Hagana
and the terrorists, there was definite evidence, which the Jewish Agency
never made any serious effort to refute, of a close connexion between
the Agency and Hagana. The evidence upon which these conclusions
were based came from three main sources:

(a) A number of telegrams sent from London to Jerusalem and
vice versa between September 1945 and May 1946.

(b) Broadcasts by Kol Israel about certain specific acts of violence
between 23 September 1945 and 23 June 1946.

(c) Information published in three journals connected with the
Stern Group, I.Z.L.,[1] and the 'Jewish Resistance Movement'.
These were named respectively *Hamaas*, *Herut* and *Eshnav*. All
these three bodies of irregulars took part in the widespread
operations in October 1945, February 1946, and June of the same
year which not only resulted in serious damage and destruction
but caused serious loss of life.

Seven of these telegrams referred to a series of attacks made on the

---

[1] I.Z.L.—Irgun Zvai Leumi.

Palestinian railway system, a number of police launches at Haifa and Jaffa, and an attempt to blow up the Haifa oil refinery. All this took place during the night of 31 October–1 November 1945. The attacks on the railway permanent way were made by the Palmach, and the line was blown up in 153 places, completely disrupting all traffic. Simultaneously the I.Z.L. attacked the station and yards at Lydda, damaging three locomotives, wrecking a signal box, and burning an engine shed. There were several casualties including one British soldier.

It is beyond all doubt that these widespread attacks were the result of careful joint planning and that their object was to warn H.M. Government of what might follow if it did not change its Palestine Policy. The following exchange of telegrams is clear proof of this.

To London from Sneh[1] in Jerusalem—23 September 1945:

It is suggested that we do not wait for the official announcement [i.e. Mr. Bevin's awaited statement of policy] but call upon all Jewry to warn the authorities and to raise the morale of the Yishuv. . . .[2] It has also been suggested that we cause one serious incident. We would then publish a declaration to the effect that it is only a warning and an indication of much more serious incidents that would threaten the safety of all British interests in the country should the Government decide against us. Wire your views with reference as before but referring to statistical material about immigration during the war years. The Stern Group have expressed their willingness to join us completely on the basis of our programme of activity. This time the intention seems serious. . . . Wire your views on the question of the union. . . . Sneh.

The following extracts from subsequent telegrams which passed between London and Jerusalem clearly prove that the Jewish Agency's Executive agreed to the proposed operations.

To London from Bernard Joseph[3] in Jerusalem—10 October 1945:

It is essential that we should know at once whether such actions are likely to be useful or detrimental to your struggle. Should you be opposed to any action whatever wire that we should wait for the arrival of Wlsly. Should you agree to isolated actions wire that you agree to sending a deputation to the dominions. If Hymin meant us only to avoid a general conflict not isolated cases send greetings to Chill for the birth of his daughter.

[1] Sneh was Security Member of the Jewish Agency Executive.
[2] Yishuv: the Jewish Community in Palestine.
[3] Bernard Joseph was the Jewish Agency's legal adviser and a member of the Executive, and was at that time acting as Head of the Political Department in the absence of Moshe Shertok in London.

From Moshe Shertok in London to Bernard Joseph in Jerusalem—12 October 1945:
David will not leave before a fortnight. . . . David himself favoured delegate dominions. Please congratulate Chill on birth of daughter. Signed Shertok.

The allusions to 'delegate dominions' and the congratulations sent to Chill were, of course, in accordance with the code suggested in Joseph's telegram of 10 October, intended to indicate that the Executive members in London, while wishing to avoid a general conflict, were prepared to sanction the proposed isolated operation.

Not only, therefore, did H.M. Government have proof positive that the outrages of 31 October–1 November had the blessing of the Jewish Agency's Executive but also that their completion and results were duly reported to London on 1 November in another telegram.

The next major operation was carried out between 20–25 February 1946. On the 20th the Palmach attacked the R.A.F. Radar Station at Haifa, blowing it up and causing six R.A.F. casualties. Two days later, according to the British communiqué, co-ordinated attacks were made by members of the same organization on camps of the Palestine Mobile Force at three separate places. At one of them serious damage was caused, one police officer wounded and three women and one child suffered from shock. On 25 February the I.Z.L. and the Stern Group attacked three airfields, including Lydda. They succeeded in destroying seven aircraft and damaging eight others.

It will be remembered that the widespread attacks on the railway system on 31 October–1 November 1945 were stated in the telegram sent by Sneh to London on 23 September as intended as a 'warning and an indication of more serious incidents'. *Eshnav*, the official organ of the 'Jewish Resistance Movement' had this to say of this second series of operations, in its issue of 4 March 1946: 'The first warning, on 1 November 1945, by the Jewish Resistance was disregarded, and the whole Yishuv was compelled to carry out a second warning during the last fortnight expressed in the attacks on the Palestine Mobile Force Stations and Airfields.'

The incidents were described in a Kol Israel broadcast on 3 March in the following terms: 'This last fortnight has seen a renewed intensity in the struggle of the Jewish people against the forces which aim to throttle them and their natural aspirations for normal nationhood in their National Home.' The speaker then described the operations and continued: 'Those three attacks are symptomatic of our struggle. In all cases the onslaught was made against the White Paper in its despicable battle to repudiate its undertaking to the Jewish people and the world, and not against the men who use this weapon. It is not our object to cause the loss of life of any Briton in this country; we have nothing against them because we realize that they are the instruments of a policy, and in many cases unwilling instruments.' The terrorist movement was clearly getting a little out of hand, but there was much worse to come.

During the evening of 16 June 1946, Hagana carried out a series of attacks on road and rail bridges along the frontiers of Palestine inflicting damage which was reliably estimated at £250,000. One officer in the Royal Engineers was killed. Next evening the Stern Group attacked the Haifa Railway Workshops. Finally, on 18 June five British officers were kidnapped while lunching at an Officers Club in Tel-Aviv, and a sixth was kidnapped in a main street of Jerusalem.

There had been some warning of these events, for on 12 May the following broadcast had been made by Kol Israel, at Moshe Shertok's request:[1] 'The Jewish Resistance Movement thinks it desirable to publish the warning it intends to lay before His Majesty's Government. Present British policy is executing a dangerous manœuvre and is based on an erroneous assumption. Britain, in evacuating Syria, Lebanon and Egypt, intends to concentrate her military bases in Palestine and is therefore concerned to strengthen her hold over the Mandate, and is using her responsibility to the Jewish people merely as a means to that end. . . . We therefore warn H.M. Government that if it does not fulfil its responsibilities under the Mandate—above all with regard to the question of immigration—the Jewish people will feel obliged to lay before the nations of the world the request that the British leave Palestine. The Jewish Resistance Movement will make every effort to hinder the transfer of British bases to Palestine and to prevent their establishment in this country.'

Announcing the success of the operations on 18 June, the speaker on Kol Israel said that their object was 'to disturb British bases and

---

[1] That this broadcast was made at Moshe Shertok's request is proved by the following telegram sent to 'Daniel' in London from Sneh in Jerusalem on 12 May: 'Please pass on to Ben Gurion the text of the broadcast of Kol Israel sent herewith; with a note that the broadcast was made at the request of Shertok.'

communications, to prevent the Arabs of the neighbouring countries who talked so much about coming to fight the Jews in Palestine, and to mark the closing up of these frontiers before British immigrants'. 'This is the voice of Israel, the voice of Jewish Resistance', the announcer said five days later. 'Last week we had to destroy the bridges—these bridges are just as much use to us as to the authorities, but they had to be destroyed to show our feelings.'

The three major operations listed above were by no means the only incidents of violence and sabotage which took place during those eight months. During the first six months of 1946 alone nearly fifty separate incidents took place involving violence and loss of life. Much damage was done to railway installations, R.A.F. and police stations, and to coastguard stations. Roads were mined and vehicles blown up.

The kidnapping of six British officers, however, was the last straw and the Government came to the conclusion, not without regret, that it could no longer remain impassive to such aggression. To do nothing would be to abandon all hope of re-establishing law and order, and it was not prepared to yield to threats of violence.

On 9 July 1946, after a meeting of the Inner Zionist Council, a statement was issued by Dr. Weizmann, on behalf of the Executive Council of the Jewish Agency. In it he summarized the action taken by the British troops since 29 June. The excuse offered by the Government for these offensive measures against the Jews in Palestine and the Jewish Agency was what he stigmatized as 'those deplorable and tragic acts of violence in which Jews and non-Jews have lost their lives'. They were acts which had sprung from despair of ever securing justice for the Jewish people by peaceful means. Dr. Weizmann complained that H.M. Government had persistently delayed every action which could have brought relief to the victims of Nazism and criticized it, not only for failing to carry out the urgent recommendations of the Anglo-American Committee, but for even refusing to accept them in principle.

He laid the blame fairly and squarely upon Great Britain as the Mandatory Power for being responsible for the present dangerous situation and the disastrous consequences that might ensue. He urged the British Government, in the name of the Jewish Agency, to change its calamitous course, to respond to the demands of international justice and enable the Yishuv to embark upon a new phase of fruitful effort in serving their brethren and reclaiming the land of Palestine. Finally, he appealed to the conscience of the world and to the innate justice of the British people, confident that they would never allow one of the great constructive endeavours of modern times, and no one could gainsay that, to be imperilled by a policy of repression carried out in their name.

Nevertheless, although he realized that this new and violent mood of Zionism arose in part 'from the bitter frustration of legitimate hopes', he did not approve of it. Writing in his autobiography he condemned what he called 'negative features; a relaxation of the old traditional Zionist purity of ethics, a touch of militarization and a weakness for its trappings; here and there, something worse, the tragic futile, un-Jewish resort to terrorism, a perversion of the purely defensive function of Hagana; and worst of all, in certain circles, a readiness to compound with the evil, to play politics with it, to condemn and not to condemn it, to treat it not as the thing it was, namely an unmitigated curse to the National Home, but as a phenomenon which might have its advantages'.

★　　★　　★　　★　　★

Dr. Weizmann's appeal to the British people's sense of fair play and to the conscience of the world does not appear to have fallen completely on deaf ears, for H.M. Government's policy of repression was almost immediately relaxed. The searching of settlements stopped, the Agency headquarters was handed back, and Rabbi Fishman was released, together with over six hundred detainees.

The Government's action against the Agency and the Yishuv, however, had not dismayed the terrorists. On the contrary it and encouraged them to further efforts, and on 22 July they blew up the Government offices and military headquarters in the King David Hotel in Jerusalem. About ninety-one persons, British, Arabs and Jews, were killed by the explosion. Most of them worked in the building, but a few were casual visitors.

This senseless act was almost universally condemned both in Palestine and abroad. Protest meetings were held, and the horror and disgust of the large majority of the Jewish community in Palestine was expressed in many of the leading newspapers. In *Davar*, the Labour daily, the following appeared: 'The entire Yishuv has been shocked to the core by the criminal and abhorrent distortion given yesterday to the struggle of the Jewish people by a gang of dissidents. This criminal massacre has no reason and no atonement. . . . It is a crime committed not only against the many dead and wounded, but against the Jewish community and its future.' And the editor of *Haaretz*, a middle-class newspaper asked this question. 'Even if murder could get us a State—which is more than doubtful—what would such a State be worth?'

The British counter to this latest act of terrorism came quickly. A curfew was imposed and many suspects arrested. On 25 July all Jewish places of entertainment, restaurants, shops and private dwellings were put out of bounds to all British troops. The following letter was circulated to all formation commanders and commanding officers by General Sir Evelyn Barker, General Officer Commanding Palestine:

The Jewish community of Palestine cannot be absolved from responsibility for the long series of outrages culminating in the blowing up of a large part of the Government offices in the King David Hotel causing grievous loss of life. Without support, actual or passive, of the general Jewish public the terrorists gangs who actually carried out these criminal acts would soon be unearthed, and in this measure the Jews in this country are accomplices and bear a share of guilt.

I am determined that they shall suffer punishment and be made aware of the contempt and loathing with which we regard their conduct. We must not allow ourselves to be deceived by the hypocritical sympathy, shown by their leaders and representative bodies, or by their protests that they are in no way responsible for these acts as they are unable to control the terrorists. I repeat that if the Jewish public really wanted to stop these crimes, they could do so by acting in co-operation with us.

Consequently I have decided that with effect from receipt of this letter you will put out of bounds to all ranks all Jewish establishments, cafés, restaurants, shops and private dwellings. No British soldier is to have social intercourse with any Jew, and any intercourse in the way of duty should be as brief as possible and kept strictly to the business in hand.

I appreciate that these measures will inflict some hardship on the troops, yet I am certain that if my reasons are fully explained to them they will understand their propriety and will be punishing the Jews in a way the race dislikes as much as any, by striking at their pockets and showing our contempt.

The Jews, of course, considered these arbitrary measures unfair and uncalled for, as they did not feel blameworthy for the terrorist campaign, though there is, undoubtedly, another side to the story, and the Zionist leaders could possibly have exercised a better control over their more undisciplined followers, had they not been somewhat divided on this issue, and acted with more firmness much earlier.

General Barker's cheap and vulgar strictures about Jews in general, however, which were contained in the last paragraph of his circular letter, were quite inexcusable and caused justifiable resentment both in Palestine and abroad. In the House of Commons six days later Mr. Herbert Morrison, speaking in the absence of the Foreign Secretary upon a motion for the adjournment, referred to the circular letter in the following terms. 'Although the Government are satisfied that the instructions given by the Commander were justified in the present disturbed state of the country, at the same time, making allowances for the provocation to which our Forces are exposed, and recognizing that the letter was written shortly after the outrage at the King David Hotel, the Government feel that they must dissociate themselves from the actual terms in which the letter is couched. The Chief of the Imperial General Staff is dealing with this aspect of the matter, and I am sure that it can be safely left in Field-Marshal Montgomery's competent hands.'

Nevertheless, the blowing up of the King David Hotel had aroused the British, as nothing had done before, to a fuller understanding of the 'evil thing' which had to be fought. The curse of Hitler, Mr. Morrison said, had not yet fully been removed. Some of his victims, fleeing from the ravaged ghettoes of Europe, had carried with them the germs of those very plagues from which they had sought to escape—intolerance, racial pride, intimidation, terrorism and the worship of force.

Zionism was the expression of a profound and splendid impulse in the soul of the Jewish people, he continued, and Zionists should beware lest this modern perversion of their faith should bring ruin on them and it. Sane and healthy nationalism has inspired many of the finest achievements of mankind, its perversion spells only degradation and depravity. . . . The leaders of the Jewish community in Palestine had failed to preserve their movement from the contagion of such false ideals.

There was one Zionist leader, however, Dr. Weizmann, the greatest of them all, who recognized terrorism as an 'evil thing' and never ceased to condemn it as completely foreign to the ideal of Zionism. When he appeared before the United Nations Special Committee on Palestine he said that the White Paper had released certain phenomena in Jewish life which were un-Jewish and contrary to Jewish ethics and Jewish tradition. 'Thou shalt not kill' had been ingrained in the Jews ever since Mount Sinai, and it was inconceivable ten years ago that the Jews should break that commandment. Unfortunately they were breaking it while the Committee was sitting and the vast majority of Jews deplored it. 'I hang my head in shame when I have to speak of this fact before you.'

Dr. Weizmann considered that the terrorist groups in Palestine represented a grave danger to the whole future of the Jewish State and that it was next door to anarchy. He not only condemned it as wrong in itself, he also deplored its natural effects. The Jews had many hostages all over the world, and although Palestine was the primary consideration, it had no right to endanger the situation of Jews outside Palestine and, in any event, the Jews within it should remember that the building up of Palestine itself would depend to a large extent upon the goodwill of their brothers elsewhere.

Jewish terrorism in Palestine was, indeed, an unpleasant business, and led to much unnecessary bitterness and anti-Jewish feeling amongst the British troops stationed there, which their G.O.C.'s regrettable words did nothing to lessen. But what had brought it into being?

The disturbances of 1936-9 had set a bad example to the Jews in Palestine. During those years hundreds of them had been killed and many thousands of pounds' worth of their property had been damaged or destroyed. During the whole of that time, although they had arms, neither the Yishuv nor Hagana had carried out any reprisals. Both had exercised considerable restraint in the face of great provocation. There had, it is true, been some isolated attacks by Jews on Arabs, but they had been remarkably few and far between and universally condemned by all the Jewish organizations and the community alike. Then came the 1939 White Paper, which could only be regarded by the Jews as a complete vindication of the Mufti's policy of violence and sabotage. If violence could meet with such success, what was the point of exercising self-restraint?

When war broke out the terrorism almost ceased, and over thirty thousand Jews volunteered for service in the armed forces. As the news of Hitler's attempt to exterminate European Jewry reached Palestine, however, a sense of impotent rage swept over the Yishuv as they looked on helplessly while the gates of the National Home were bolted and barred by the British Administration against the Jewish refugees from Central Europe many of whom were their own kith and kin.

When, eventually, the war was over, many thought that at last the restrictions on immigration would be considerably relaxed, but they were not. A mere trickle of fifteen hundred a month was allowed to enter when even the American President had asked for an immediate hundred thousand. It was then that a Resistance Movement really began to develop. In its early stages its activities were mostly of the Scarlet Pimpernel variety, its main objective being to facilitate the landing of 'illegal' immigrants and frustrate the efforts of the British military forces to intercept them. This received a great measure of support from the Jewish community as a whole. It was only much later that the tempo quickened, and the savage killing of soldiers and civilians and the wanton destruction of property began. The Jewish Agency and the great moderate majority realized that widespread acts of terrorism would damage their cause rather than assist it, but the extremists were now quite out of control and, as the months passed by, the toll of death and destruction steadily mounted.

★　★　★　★　★

On the very same day as General Barker's unfortunate letter was circulated, invitations to a conference in London were issued to the Governments of the States belonging to the Arab League, to the Jewish Agency, and to the Palestine Arab Higher Executive.

The decision to call this meeting, which came to be known as the London Conference of 1946–7, arose in this way. The States who were members of the Arab League had been asked to give their views on the Report of the Anglo-American Committee, and had met at Bludan in Syria. They agreed, after discussion, to invite the British Government to negotiate 'for the conclusion of an agreement which will put an end to the present situation in Palestine and transform it into one, in conformity with the provisions of the Charter and agreeable with its aims'.

It had always been the declared intention of H.M. Government to consult all interested parties before reaching a final decision on their Palestine policy, and it was for this reason that the Anglo-American Conference of officials, held just before the announcement of the

'Provincial Autonomy Plan', had recommended that if their proposals were adopted by the two Governments, they 'should be presented to Arab and Jewish representatives as a basis for negotiations at a conference to be convened by the United Kingdom Government'. When the Conference assembled the British delegation put forward the Morrison Plan as a basis for discussion, but it was rejected unanimously by the Arab delegates who were then invited to submit alternative suggestions. They put forward the following constitutional proposals: the first step was to be the establishment of a Provisional Government consisting of seven Arab and three Jewish ministers of Palestinian nationality to whom all legislative and executive powers would be transferred, subject to the High Commissioner's power to veto during the transitional period. When an electoral register had been prepared, elections were to be held for a Constituent Assembly of sixty members.

The Provisional Government, meanwhile, was to prepare a draft constitution for Palestine in which the following principles were to be embodied:

(1) Palestine should be a unitary state.

(2) It should have a democratic constitution with an elected legislature.

(3) The constitution should provide guarantees for the sanctity of the Holy Places, covering inviolability, maintenance, freedom of access and worship in accordance with the *status quo*.

(4) Freedom of religious practice, subject to suitable safeguards, should be guaranteed, including the maintenance of separate religious courts for matters of personal status.[1]

(5) The law of naturalization should provide, amongst other conditions, that the applicant should be a legal resident of Palestine for a continuous period of ten years before his application.

The Arabs also proposed that, unless and until legislation provided otherwise, Jewish immigration into Palestine should be entirely prohibited, and that the Land Transfer Regulations of 1940 should remain in force unchanged. To make it virtually impossible that there should

---

[1] In this connexion it is worthy of notice that in Israel today the Moslem Sharia Courts are maintained by the Israeli Government as the domestic courts for the Israeli Arabs. They deal with all matters of personal status.

ever be any change, the new constitution was to provide that any altera-
tion in the immigration and land regulations could only be effected by
legislation requiring the consent of Arabs in Palestine as expressed by a
majority of the Arab members of the Legislative Assembly.

These proposals regarding Jewish immigration and land transfer
restrictions were a classic example of 'heads I win, tails you lose'. It was
only *Jewish* immigration which was to be entirely prohibited, and it
required a majority of *Arab* members to sanction it. There was, however, no similar provision requiring the consent of a majority of Jewish
members to allow non-Jewish immigration. A simple majority in the
Legislative Assembly, which the Arabs could always command, would
suffice. This was the kind of democracy in the minds of the Arabs when
they spoke of Palestine having 'a democratic constitution'.

When this new constitution had been adopted, a Legislative
Assembly would be elected, and the first Head of the independent
Palestine State would then be appointed. To him the High Commissioner would then transfer his authority, and a treaty would be
concluded defining the future relations between H.M. Government and
the Government of Palestine.

Early in October the Conference had to adjourn in order that some of
the delegates could attend the United Nations General Assembly and
the Council of Foreign Ministers. It remained adjourned for nearly four
months.

It was during this recess that the Zionist Congress met in Basle and
denounced the Morrison Plan as 'a travesty of Britain's obligations
under the Mandate'.[1] The Congress then proceeded to reaffirm its
political aims in the following terms:

(1) Palestine to be established as a Jewish Commonwealth integrated
in the structure of the democratic world.

(2) The gates of Palestine to be opened to Jewish immigration.

(3) The Jewish Agency to be vested with the control of immigration
and given the necessary authority to develop the country.

When the Conference reassembled on 27 January 1947, the representatives of the Jewish Agency made three suggestions. Firstly, that
Palestine should become a Jewish State. Secondly, that if no decision

[1] See p. 168 above.

could yet be made about Palestine's ultimate status, Jewish immigration should be permitted up to the full extent of the country's economic absorptive capacity, and that there should be no closed areas for Jewish land purchase or settlement. In other words, that the Mandate should be administered as it was before the 1939 White Paper. Thirdly, they stated that they would be prepared to recommend acceptance of a 'viable Jewish State in an adequate area of Palestine'.

The first of these suggestions, was, presumably, put forward to satisfy the 'Maximalists', for there can never have been any hope of it being accepted. The second was a position from which there could never be any retreat, for immigration and close settlement on the land were inherent in the Mandate. The last suggestion was in the nature of a reasonable compromise: a return to the policy of partition, 'half a loaf is better than no bread', as the Peel Commission had called it, a policy which had attracted Dr. Weizmann when it was first put forward, for he had realized that it might create a real possibility of coming to terms with the Arabs, for a Jewish State with definite boundaries internationally guaranteed would banish the ever-haunting fear that the Jews would absorb the whole of Palestine.[1]

Mr. Bevin, however, was not in favour of partition, and had already indicated that if no agreement could be reached with the Arabs and Jews he intended to submit the whole problem to the United Nations. Nevertheless, before doing this he would make one last desperate attempt to settle the question. On 7 February, therefore, the British delegates submitted a new set of proposals for a five-year period of British trusteeship over Palestine during which the country would be made ready for independence. This has since been known as the Bevin Plan.

The agreement may be summarized as follows:[2]

(1) In certain areas, so delimited as to include substantial Jewish or Arab majorities, there would be a substantial measure of local autonomy.

(2) The High Commissioner would protect minorities in these areas.

(3) The High Commissioner, though exercising supreme legislative

---

[1] See p. 129 above.
[2] *The Political History of Palestine under British Administration* (Jerusalem 1947), pp. 40–1.

and executive authority, would endeavour to form a representative Advisory Council.

(4) The local authorities would control land transfers.

(5) At the end of four years a Constituent Assembly would be elected and, provided a majority of both Arabs and Jews agreed, an independent State would be at once created. Otherwise the Trusteeship Council would be asked to advise on future procedure.

There remained the thorny question of immigration. The Bevin Plan provided for the admission of four thousand Jews a month for two years, that is to say ninety-six thousand in two years, as compared with Mr. Truman's immediate hundred thousand. For the remaining years of the trusteeship the threadbare doctrine of 'economic absorptive capacity' would be the yard-stick of Jewish immigration, and would be applied by the High Commissioner in consultation with his Advisory Council.

The Bevin Plan was rejected by all the Arab Delegations, which included representatives from the Arab Higher Executive, and by the Jewish Agency. Announcing the Government's decision to refer the whole question to the United Nations, the Foreign Secretary told the House of Commons on 18 February that H.M. Government had been faced with an irreconcilable conflict of principles. In Palestine the proportion of Arabs to Jews was two to one. The Jews wanted a sovereign Jewish State; the Arabs were determined to resist the establishment of Jewish sovereignty at all costs. Recent discussions had clearly shown that the two parties would never be likely to come to an agreement. The Mandatory was precluded by the Mandate from enforcing an arbitrary decision. The Government had, therefore, decided to submit the problem to the judgment of the United Nations but not to recommend any particular solution. It was, indeed, a tragic admission of failure.

CHAPTER XII

The United Nations Special Committee

IN pursuance of H.M. Government's decision to submit the problem to the judgment of the United Nations, a letter was addressed to the acting Secretary-General by the United Kingdom Delegation on 2 April asking that the question of Palestine be placed on the agenda of the next ordinary session of the General Assembly, and that a special session be summoned, with as little delay as possible, to set up and instruct a special committee to make recommendations for the General Assembly's consideration.

The letter intimated that H.M. Government would submit an account of its administration of the Palestine Mandate and ask the General Assembly to make recommendations under Article 10 of the Charter regarding the future government of Palestine.

In due course the special session was held. At one of its meetings Sir Alexander Cadogan, representing Britain, was questioned by the Indian representative about a statement which had been made on behalf of H.M. Government to the effect that whatever the recommendations of the United Nations, the United Kingdom was not prepared at that stage to say that it would accept them. Sir Alexander replied that what had been said by the speaker was, 'I cannot imagine H.M. Government carrying out a policy of which it does not approve.' That did not mean that the Government would not accept any recommendation of the Assembly, but only that it would not carry out a decision it felt to be wrong. At a subsequent meeting Sir Alexander further clarified his Government's attitude. 'We have tried for years,' he said, 'to solve this problem of Palestine. Having failed so far, we now bring it to the United Nations in the hope that they can succeed where we have not.

If the United Nations can find a just solution which will be accepted by both parties, it could hardly be expected that we should not welcome such a solution. All we say—and I made this reservation the other day—is that we should not have the sole responsibility of enforcing a solution which is not accepted by both parties, and which we cannot reconcile with our conscience.'

After much wrangling the General Assembly decided on the representation of the Special Committee and gave it some general instructions. Its report was to be submitted not later than 1 September so that it could be circulated to the Members of the United Nations in time for consideration at the next regular session of the General Assembly. It was to investigate all questions and issues relevant to the Palestine problem, giving particular attention to the religious interests there of Islam, Judaism and Christianity, and to submit such proposals as might be considered appropriate for the solution of the Palestine problem.

The Special Committee held its first meeting at Lake Success on 26 May, and later sat in Jerusalem, Beirut and Geneva. Before making its final recommendations the Committee weighed up the conflicting claims of both the Arabs and the Jews.

When appraising the Jewish case the Committee referred to the obligation upon the Mandatory Power to establish a Jewish National Home and develop self-governing institutions. Were these two obligations of equal weight? Were they consistent with one another? Some had taken the view that neither had priority and that they were in no way irreconcilable. Others had taken the opposite view. The practical significance of this controversy, as it appeared to the Committee, was that if the country were placed under such political conditions as would secure the development of self-governing institutions, that would, in fact, destroy the National Home. Although it was not contemplated, at the time the Mandate was confirmed, that these obligations would prove incompatible the Committee found that in practice they had proved irreconcilable. The idea of the National Home was expressed in both the Balfour Declaration and the Mandate. Both documents promised the establishment of a Jewish National Home but neither defined its meaning. The Committee came to what it considered was an 'inescapable' conclusion that the vagueness in the wording of both instruments was intentional. That the words 'National

Home' were used instead of 'State' or 'Commonwealth' surely indicated that it was always intended to place a restrictive construction on the National Home plan from the start. No one knew exactly what was in the minds of the authors of the Declaration, but as early as 1922 the British Colonial Office had placed a restrictive construction upon it. This was, of course, a reference to the Churchill Memorandum. In that document the 'ancient historic connexion' of the Jews with Palestine was, it is true, recognized, and they were declared to be there 'as of right and not on sufferance'. Nevertheless, it was made clear that in the eyes of the Mandatory Power the Jewish National Home was to be founded in Palestine, and not that the whole country was to be converted into a Jewish National Home.

But it was not as simple as that, for though neither the Balfour Declaration nor the Mandate specifically referred to the establishment of a Jewish State they did not categorically preclude its eventual creation. By creating the obligation upon the Mandatory to facilitate immigration, the Mandate's Preamble conferred upon the Jews an opportunity to create eventually, by large-scale immigration, a State with a Jewish majority.

The terms of the Declaration and the Mandate were not limited solely to the Yishuv and it could, therefore, be argued that every Jew in the world had a right to go to Palestine if he wished. The Committee, however, thought that this was an unrealistic argument because 'a country as small and poor as Palestine could never accommodate all the Jews in the world'.

The Arab case was also carefully considered by the Committee. The representatives of the Arab Higher Committee, who were heard during the early meetings of the special session of the General Assembly earlier in the year at Lake Success, and the delegates of the Arab States, who appeared before the Committee itself in Beirut and Geneva, wanted the immediate creation of an independent Arab Palestine west of the Jordan.

They made this claim upon the following grounds:

(1) They were in a majority of two to one.

(2) They considered themselves as having a 'natural right' to the country. This claim was based on the contention that the Arabs have

been connected with Palestine, without interruption, for centuries, as the term 'Arab' refers, not to the seventh-century invaders of Palestine from the Arabian peninsula, but to the indigenous population which intermarried with the invaders and became permanently Arabicized.

(3) They had been made certain promises and given certain pledges, in particular the McMahon–Hussein correspondence and other letters, messages and declarations.[1] In their view these various undertakings recognized Arab political rights in Palestine which the British were under an obligation to accept and uphold, but about which they had done nothing.

(4) The Mandate for Palestine was itself illegal and had no validity.

The Committee considered that there were no grounds for this last contention. The terms of the Mandate for Palestine formulated by the Supreme Council of the Principal Allied Powers, as a part of the settlement of the First World War, were subsequently approved and confirmed by the Council of the League of Nations.

Finally, the Committee gave, in accordance with their instructions, 'most careful consideration to the religious interests in Palestine of Islam, Judaism and Christianity', and hoped that the new State (or States) to be created in Palestine would be ready to accept undertakings aiming at preserving existing rights as regards the Holy Places and other religious interests.

The Committee need have had no doubt that the Jews would be prepared to preserve such rights, for one of the duties of the Ministry of Religions in the Israeli Government of today is to see that the pledges contained in the Declaration of Independence are carried out 'to guarantee freedom of religion, conscience, education and culture, and to safeguard the Holy Places of all religions'. The Ministry carries out these duties in a spirit of complete tolerance, and every religious community in Israel is free to practise its own religion.

Before the Committee went to Beirut to hear the views on the Palestine problem put forward by representatives of the Governments of Egypt, Iraq, the Lebanon, Saudi Arabia, Syria and the Yemen, it spent two months in Palestine. There it heard spokesmen from the Jewish Agency, the Jewish National Council, and a small minority

[1] All these have been discussed in Chapter III.

who wanted a bi-national State under international trusteeship before proceeding to full independence.

It was while the Committee was still in Palestine that an incident occurred which severed any cords of sympathy and friendship that still remained between the Jewish community and the British Government. Two ship loads of about 4,500 displaced persons from Central Europe had been seized off the coast of Palestine whilst trying to land refugees as illegal immigrants. Since the war such immigrants had been sent to a detention camp in Cyprus, and these displaced persons, too, would have been sent there had the usual practice been carried out. On this occasion the British Foreign Secretary, Mr. Ernest Bevin, had refused to let them be sent to Cyprus, and ordered that they should be returned to France whence they had sailed. On arriving in France they refused to disembark, and the French authorities very properly refused to compel them by force to land. Mr. Bevin then gave orders that they should be taken to the British Zone of Germany and forcibly disembarked at Hamburg.

He could not have made a more unfortunate decision. The bulk of these refugees had been made homeless through Nazi aggression, many of their parents and grandparents, their brothers, their sisters, their sons and their daughters had been 'liquidated' in the gas-chambers of Auschwitz and Dachau. All they wanted was to reach the hospitable shores of their fatherland to live, and work, and die in peace. They had all but attained their desire when they found themselves returned to the very land which had been the cradle of their misfortune. It is small wonder that agitation and terrorism broke out afresh in Palestine, or that the greater part of the civilized world was profoundly shocked.

The Committee completed its task within the fixed time limit of three months and made recommendations on a problem which for years had puzzled many with far more experience of Palestine affairs than the Committee's members possessed. This they realized and frankly admitted, but they did not think that it was a problem which would be solved from an accumulation of detailed information. Had any other country been the subject of more enquiries? There had been a plethora of Committees and a flood of White Papers, and they had all led nowhere. The problem, as the Committee saw it, was one of human relationships and political rights.

During its deliberations in Geneva the Committee discussed at length the many aspects of this troublesome problem. At an early stage in these discussions it became evident that there was but little support for the two extreme solutions, a single Arab or Jewish State. The Committee decided that they must produce a compromise solution and, at all costs, avoid satisfying one side at the expense of the other.

Once the Committee had discarded the two extreme solutions they next considered the bi-national State and cantonal proposals. Two cantonization proposals had been advanced during the past two years. These were the Morrison and Bevin Plans which have already been described.[1] It appeared to the Committee that both these schemes might well entail an excessive decentralization of governmental authority and prove to be quite unworkable. The bi-national solution, though it had some attraction for the Committee, was considered unwieldy and impracticable.

Almost the only possibilities left, therefore, were partition under a confederation arrangement, or a Federal State. After two informal working groups had studied these alternatives it was discovered that there was a substantial measure of agreement with regard to a number of the more important issues.

The following recommendations, among others, were unanimous:

(1) *That the Mandate for Palestine should be ended as soon as practicable.*

All directly interested, the Mandatory Power, the Arabs and the Jews, were agreed that there was an urgent need for a change in Palestine's status. The British representatives had told the Committee that in the Government's view the Mandate had proved to be unworkable in practice, and that the obligations undertaken in respect of the two communities in Palestine had been shown to be irreconcilable. If there was one thing absolutely clear at that time it was that there was a vital clash between the Jews and the Mandatory Power on the one hand, and tension between the Arabs and the Jews on the other. The rising tide of organized terrorism was evidence of this. It had steadily grown more intense since the end of the war, and had taken an ever-mounting toll of loss of life and destruction of property.

Both Arabs and Jews, however, were agreed on one point, that the

[1] See pp. 168 and 183 above.

Mandate should be terminated and that Palestine should be granted independence. As to the form that independence should take there was profound disagreement.

(2) *That independence should be granted in Palestine at the earliest practicable date.*

The Committee considered that the people of Palestine were sufficiently advanced to govern themselves independently, and that after more than a quarter of a century's guardianship under the Mandate both were seeking a means of effective expression of their national aspirations.

(3) *That there should be a short transitional period before the grant of independence.*

This seemed to the Committee to be essential. During such a period the machinery of government would have to be set up, and guarantees established for the protection of minorities and the safeguarding of the Holy Places and religious interests. The transitional period, however, must not be of long duration, and after its termination the final solution would have to be ready to go into operation at once.

(4) *That during the transitional period the authority entrusted with the administration of Palestine and preparing it for independence should be responsible to the United Nations.*

This responsibility, it was realized, would be heavy, for whatever solution was eventually adopted enforcement measures on quite a large scale might be necessary for a considerable time.

(5) *There were also four recommendations regarding the Holy Places and religious interests.*

(*a*) The sacred character of the Holy Places must be preserved, and access to them for the purposes of worship and pilgrimage guaranteed on the basis of the *status quo*.

(*b*) The existing rights of the various religious communities in Palestine must remain unimpaired.

(*c*) An adequate system for impartial settlement of religious disputes should be devised.

(*d*) If any independent Palestinian State or States were created, specific stipulations concerning the Holy Places, religious buildings or sites, and the rights of the several religious communities would have to be written into the constitution.

(6) *The General Assembly should bring about an international arrangement whereby the problem of the Jewish displaced persons estimated at about 250,000, would be dealt with as a matter of urgency for alleviation of their plight and of the Palestinian problem.*

The Committee recognized that these homeless Jews who were a legacy of Hitler's war, must be regarded as an international responsibility. The fact that most of them wanted to go to Palestine rendered them a difficult factor in the final solution. Any action which would ease the plight of the distressed Jews in Europe would lessen the pressure of the Palestinian immigration problem, and this would allay the fears of the Arabs that they were soon to be swamped by Jews from all over the world.

(7) *It must be understood beforehand that the political structure of any new independent State would be democratic, to the extent that its government would be representative of the people, and that its constitution would contain safeguards to protect the rights and interests of minorities.*

The Committee ended its unanimous recommendations by suggesting that the General Assembly should call on the peoples of Palestine to extend their fullest co-operation to the United Nations and, in the interest of peace and good order, to exert every effort to bring to an early end the acts of violence which had for too long beset that country.

The Special Committee was divided, however, on the question of whether to recommend partition of Palestine into two States or a Federal Unitary State, although a majority of seven to three, Australia being neutral, was in favour of the former alternative, and it was in principle this solution which in November secured a majority vote in the plenary session of the General Assembly at Lake Success.

The following is a short summary of the Plan on Partition with Economic Union.

(1) Palestine, as it then existed, was to be formed, after a transitional period of two years beginning on 1 September 1947, into an independent Arab State, a similar Jewish State, and the City of Jerusalem.[1]

(2) Independence was to be granted to each State on request, only after it had adopted a constitution complying with certain provisions which the Committee laid down. A declaration would also have to be

---

[1] See map on opposite page.

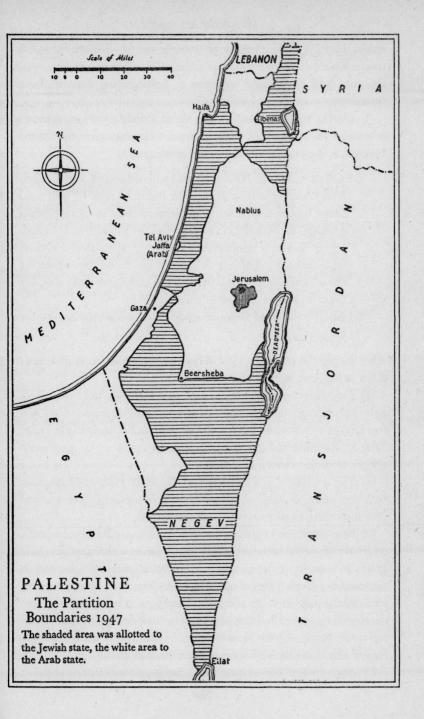

Scale of Miles

10 5 0   10   20   30   40

LEBANON

S Y R I A

Haifa

Tiberias

MEDITERRANEAN SEA

N

Nablus

Tel Aviv
Jaffa
(Arab)

Jerusalem

Gaza

DEAD SEA

T R A N S J O R D A N

Beersheba

E
G
Y
P
T

N E G E V

PALESTINE

The Partition
Boundaries 1947

The shaded area was allotted to
the Jewish state, the white area to
the Arab state.

Eilat

made to the United Nations containing certain guarantees, and a treaty would have to be signed creating the 'Economic Union of Palestine' and establishing a system of collaboration between both States.

(3) During the transitional period Great Britain would continue to administer the territory of Palestine, under the auspices of the United Nations, and carry out the following measures:

    (*a*) Admit within the borders of the proposed Jewish State 150,000 Jewish immigrants at a uniform monthly rate. Of this total thirty thousand were to be allowed to enter on humanitarian grounds. Were the transitional period, for any reason, extended, Jewish immigration should be continued at an annual rate of sixty thousand. The Jewish Agency was to be responsible for the selection and organization of this immigration as, also, for the care of the immigrants themselves.

    (*b*) Abolish the Land Regulations of 1940 within the borders of the Jewish State.

Also, during this period, no Jew would be permitted to establish residence in the Arab State or vice versa.

(4) The constituent assembly of each new State was to be elected by universal suffrage upon a basis of proportional representation, and freedom of transit and visit for all residents and citizens of the other State in Palestine and the City of Jerusalem was to be guaranteed subject to considerations of security.

(5) The existing rights in respect of the Holy Places and religious buildings and sites, and complete freedom of worship, language and education were to be preserved and guaranteed.

(6) Economic union between the two States was to be the subject of a treaty which would become binding immediately without ratifications. It was to include a customs union, a common currency, operation in the interests of both States of railways, inter-State roads, postal services, etc., and the ports of Haifa and Jaffa. There was to be a joint economic development, especially in respect of irrigation, land reclamation and soil conservation. A Joint Economic Board was to be formed to organize and administer the objectives of the economic union.

(7) After recognition, sympathetic consideration should be given to

the application by either or both the new States for admission to membership of the United Nations.

The Committee justified their recommendations of a plan for partition on the following grounds:

Of the claims which both Arabs and Jews laid to Palestine, both had validity, but were irreconcilable.

Partition was the most likely solution to provide a realistic and practicable settlement.

Both Arabs and Jews had historic roots in the country, and both made vital contributions to the economic and cultural life of the country. Partition took account of this.

Only by partition could the conflicting national aspirations of both find expression.

Only partition was likely to provide finality, which was vital. The creation of the Jewish State, under a partition scheme, was the sole way of removing the prickly issue of Jewish immigration from the arena of conflict between Arab and Jew.

Dr. Weizmann, who was always of the opinion that co-operation with the Arabs would only come about if the Jewish community in Palestine enjoyed equal status, pleaded for partition before the Special Committee while it was sitting in Jerusalem. That was one of the reasons why he had accepted the idea when it was suggested to him by the Peel Commission ten years earlier.[1] It seemed to him then, and many others later came to see it, that the creation of a Jewish State was the only way out of the rut into which they had got. He also thought, and he has written of this in his autobiography,[2] that it was the only way to begin restoring the former good relations between the Jews and Great Britain which had progressively worsened as the years rolled by.

Dr. Weizmann, even at times when he might well have been forgiven for so doing, never forgot to acknowledge that the Jewish people would be 'eternally grateful to Great Britain for the inauguration of that policy which the Balfour Declaration embodied'. Nor did he forget to do so before the Special Committee, even though the British

[1] See p.129 above.   [2] Trial and Error, pp. 557–8.

Government was doing its best to bring about a decision by the Committee unfavourable to the Jews. He felt compelled to do this 'by the feeling of historic justice'.

The partition plan was, of course, not to Mr. Bevin's liking. He had sponsored a scheme of cantonization, and the minority's Federal State plan somewhat resembled it. Partition, however, meant a reversal of the 1939 White Paper policy, for it made it encumbent on the Mandatory Power, during the transitional period, to carry out a large Jewish immigration and repeal the Land Regulations. When finally, to Mr. Bevin's chagrin, the General Assembly passed a resolution to the effect that the two new States should come into existence not later than 1 October 1948, the British Government proved to be bad losers.

CHAPTER XIII

The End of the Road

THE National Home was in sight at last, the long journey was nearly over. On 4 October the United Nations general debate opened, and continued with varying fortunes until 29 November when the final vote was taken and the famous resolution passed by thirty-three votes to thirteen, ten countries abstaining including the United Kingdom.

No one had known on which side the Soviet Union would come down, and when the head of the Russian delegation, Mr. Gromyko, declared his country's support for partition it came as a great surprise. Two days later the United States of America followed suit. It was the first time, but not the last, that these two great protagonists of the East and West found themselves strangely allied on an historic issue. On the first occasion they brought Israel into being; on the second they did her a grievous wrong.

Having made the momentous decision to back partition, after much vacillation, the U.S.A. then started to lobby for the necessary two-thirds majority, but it was not until the day before the vote was taken that the Americans managed to swing the wobblers into line.

Great Britain, however, had already made it quite clear as early as 17 October, through her delegate Mr. Creech Jones, that 'H.M. Government would not accept responsibility for the enforcement, either alone or in co-operation with other nations, of any settlement antagonistic to either the Jews or the Arabs or both, which was likely to necessitate the use of force'. If there were any doubt about the exact meaning of that announcement it was dispelled by an answer which the Foreign Secretary gave to a question put by one of his Socialist colleagues in the House of Commons on 2 January 1948. Mr. Bevin was asked whether it meant that if the Security Council were to decide that collective enforcement action was necessary in respect of Palestine, Great Britain would not take its share as one of the members of the United Nations. He answered that it meant exactly that.

Creech Jones's announcement, when it was made, had put the cat among the pigeons, for the U.S.A. then found themselves in the position of having to side with Russia against Britain. It is difficult to understand what prompted the British Government to adopt the attitude of a spoilt child. It had already decided to surrender the Mandate, and a solution by the United Nations of a problem that had proved so intractable for over a quarter of a century would relieve it of any further obligations to either Arab or Jew. It was little more than two years since the United Nations Organization had been heralded in with a flourish of trumpets, yet here was one of its chief members already refusing to assist in implementing a majority decision. Furthermore, there was not even unanimity within the Commonwealth on the subject, for Great Britain alone abstained. All the other members of the Commonwealth voted for the resolution.

The resolution of 29 November 1947 appealed to all governments and all peoples to refrain from taking any action which might hamper or delay the carrying out of its plan. It declared that the Mandate for Palestine was to terminate 'as soon as possible, but in any case not later than 1 August 1948'. Independent Arab and Jewish States, and a specific international régime for the City of Jerusalem were to come into existence in Palestine two months after the evacuation of the armed forces of the Mandatory Power had been completed, but in any case not later than 1 October 1948.

Until the Mandatory Power finally withdrew, certain obligations were placed upon it by the resolution:

(1) Not later than 1 February 1948, to evacuate and provide a seaport and hinterland adequate for substantial Jewish immigration.

(2) To turn over to the Adminstration the Palestine Commission *pari passu* with evacuation.

(3) Not to take any action to prevent or delay implementation.

It was announced by the Foreign Secretary in the House of Commons on 11 and 12 December 1947 that the Mandate would end on 15 May 1948 and evacuation would be completed by 1 August.

The Colonial Secretary, however, had stated that until the Mandate was finally surrendered, the Palestine Government would be responsible for law and order, and as there were not less than a hundred thousand British troops still in Palestine it was reasonable to suppose that this could be done. Events turned out differently, and the spate of outrages let loose when the terms of the U.N. resolution became known was never got under control.

Jewish motor convoys were attacked by Arabs on the main roads; there was street fighting on the adjoining boundaries of Jaffa and Tel-Aviv, and in the ancient city of Jerusalem. Bombs were exploded in the streets and other public places. The attacks upon Jewish convoys on the road from Tel-Aviv were particularly serious, for they cut the lines of communication between Jerusalem and the coast and prevented many isolated settlements in Galilee and the Negev from receiving essential supplies. The Palestine Government would neither provide escorts, for that 'might be interpreted as British implementation of partition', nor allow the Jews to carry arms for self-defence on such occasions.

At the same time Syrian guerrilla bands were operating in Palestine and an 'Arab Liberation Army', as it was called, armed with medium tanks was ranging throughout the length and breadth of Palestine from the Lebanon to Transjordan. The infiltration of an Arab fifth column continued daily without let or hindrance. The United Nations Palestine Commission reported to the Security Council in the middle of February that powerful Arab interests, both inside and outside Palestine, were defying the resolution of the General Assembly, and were engaged in a deliberate effort to alter by force the settlement envisaged therein.

This was no less than the truth. Furthermore, a sober and objective review of all the evidence which is available today leads to one conclusion only, namely that the British Government was completely disinterested in the outcome of the U.N. resolution and did all it could, by devious means, to sabotage the formation of a Jewish State.

It should have occasioned no surprise, therefore, when the Jewish Agency, in a memorandum to the U.N. Palestine Commission, stated that the Jewish people in Palestine had come to recognize that only their own forces stood between them and annihilation. Faced with the

Government's neutrality on the issue of their survival or extermination the Jews of Palestine had now assumed a responsibility which formally rested on the Mandatory Power.

Meanwhile, at Lake Success, things were not going too well in the Security Council. During a meeting on 24 February, the U.S.A. delegate expressed the opinion that the Council was not bound to follow the lead of the General Assembly, had no power to enforce a political settlement, and that a Five-Power Committee of permanent members should be set up 'to consult the Palestine Commission, the Mandatory, and representatives of the principal parties concerned to endeavour to get an agreement on the basis of the General Assembly's resolution'.

There is no doubt that the real situation in Palestine was being deliberately misrepresented in some quarters. It had even been reported in the United States that all good Jews were leaving Palestine, that the Red flag was flying there alongside the Star of David, and that Israel would be organized as a Communistic State.[1] Perhaps the fact that Russia had so surprisingly and consistently supported the U.N. resolution was, in some degree, responsible for this canard.

In the middle of March, Senator Austin, the American representative in the Security Council, proposed that the implementation of the policy contained in the resolution should be suspended, that a truce in Palestine should be arranged, and a special session of the General Assembly called to set up a trusteeship for Palestine with effect from 15 May, when the Mandate was due to end.

As Dr. Weizmann has written, this blow, despite all forewarnings, was 'sudden, bitter and, on the surface, fatal to our long-nurtured hopes'. To him the idea of another trusteeship was utterly unrealistic. All that had made the Mandate unworkable would operate again in the same way. He issued the following statement to the Press on 25 March: 'The plan worked out by the Assembly was the result of a long and careful process of deliberation in which the conflicting claims of the various parties were judged in the light of international equity. In order to achieve a compromise between the Jewish and Arab national claims, the Jews were asked to be content with one-eighth of the original area of the Palestine Mandate. They were called upon to co-operate in a settlement for Jerusalem which set the city's international associations above

---

[1] See *Israel* by Harry Sacher, p. 106.

its predominantly Jewish character. We accepted these limitations only because they were decreed by the supreme authority of international judgment, and because in the small area allotted to us we should be free to bring in our people, and enjoy the indispensable boon of sovereignty —a privilege conferred upon the Arabs in vast territories.'[1] It was now being suggested, Dr. Weizmann continued, that the resolution should not be implemented because the policy declared in it had not got the agreement of all parties. This seemed a strange line to take, for it was entirely because the prospect of agreement was non-existent that the Mandatory Power had submitted the whole question to the United Nations in the first place.

Dr. Weizmann declared, and it could not really be disputed, that but for the admission into Palestine of foreign Arab forces, no problem of security would have arisen which the local militia, envisaged by the Assembly's decision, could not have controlled. He was unable to understand how the Mandatory Government could allow such forces to cross the frontiers into Palestine freely by bridge and road, and pre-pare, in their own time and without any interference, to make war against the Jews and against the settlement adopted by the United Nations.

Dr. Weizmann also appealed personally to President Truman. 'The choice for our people, Mr. President,' he wrote, 'is between statehood and extermination. History and providence have placed the issue in your hands, and I am confident that you will yet decide it in the spirit of the moral law.'

Weizmann's main attack, however, was reserved for the British Colonial Secretary, Mr. Creech Jones, who pleaded that the invasion of Palestine by 7,500 Arabs had taken the British Government by surprise. Nevertheless, they were there, and there was no disputing the fact, or that the Jews would have to deal with them. The Zionist leader, soon to be Israel's first President, answered that the Jews had no intention whatsoever of evacuating the territory which had been allotted to them. He was astounded that those who had been in the Palestine administra-tion for so many years could have made such a faulty appreciation of the situation, for they evidently imagined one of two things, either that the Arabs would overwhelm the Jews as soon as the Mandatory troops

---

[1] *Trial and Error*, pp. 577–8.

left the country, or that the Jews would give in without a fight. Whichever of these views the British held, events were soon to prove them wrong.

In April the General Assembly met again, but during the interval since its last meeting the situation had vastly changed. The so-called Army of Liberation had been routed at Mishmar Ha-Emek and in some districts the Jewish forces had assumed the offensive. Seven Arab villages had been taken. Simultaneously, a combined force of Irgun and the Stern Group attacked the village of Deir Yassin and killed not less than two hundred and fifty Arabs, including many women and children. This outrage was the worst atrocity ever committed by the Jewish terrorists, and although the Jewish Agency issued a statement expressing 'its horror and disgust at the barbarous manner in which this action was carried out', this disavowal carried little weight, for the not unreasonable retort was made that as the Jewish Agency spoke for all the Jews in Palestine it must take responsibility for their acts.[1]

By 29 April the Palestine Commission announced that partition was now an accomplished fact, and that the Jews were in control of large parts of the country. As it had now become clear that Mr. Austin's 'trusteeship' proposal could no longer be adopted, a 'temporary truce' was suggested, and a resolution was adopted by the Council calling upon both sides to cease fire, to stop bringing in arms or reinforcements, and to suspend all political activity. Both Arabs and Jews were to help in the maintenance of order and the Holy Places were to be respected.

The American, Belgian and French consuls in Jerusalem were appointed as a Truce Commission. It was clear from their report that the moment to call for a truce had already passed. The general situation in Palestine, they reported, had badly deteriorated. Government departments were daily closing down, and the normal activities of the country were rapidly coming to a standstill. The Jewish Agency was acting as a general organizing body for the Jewish areas, and attempting to replace suspended Government activities. Arab areas were depending on municipal authorities without any central authority. Telegraph facilities and telephone trunk lines no longer existed in most districts and, all the time, the intensity of the fighting was increasing. As soon as camps and other important installations were evacuated by

[1] *Promise and Fulfilment* by Arthur Koestler, p. 160.

the British they became the scene of severe fighting. Further military operations on a large scale were anticipated.

Despite the unlikelihood of it being successfully implemented the inherent dangers of the truce proposal were apparent to the Jewish leaders, and not least to Dr. Weizmann and Mr. Shertok, the Jews' chief spokesman at the United Nations. They realized that it might appeal to some of their friends and colleagues who feared that to proclaim a Jewish State, notwithstanding the terms of the November resolution, against the wishes of America, might well estrange a powerful friend and potential ally. These faint-hearts were not in evidence in Palestine where there was never any question of relinquishing the rights conferred by the United Nations General Assembly.

Two days before the Mandate was due to come to an end Dr. Weizmann made one last attempt, in a letter to the President of the United States, to obtain American recognition for the Jewish State as soon as it was proclaimed. In a letter dated 13 May he expressed the hope that the unhappy events of the past few months would not obscure the very great contribution which Mr. Truman had made towards a final and just solution of the Palestine question which had been a source of trouble for so long. At midnight the following day the British Mandate would end, and the Provisional Government of the Jewish State would assume full responsibility for preserving law and order within its boundaries, defending it from external aggression, and discharging its obligations to the other nations of the world in accordance with international law. Dr. Weizmann hoped that the United States, which under their President's leadership had done so much to find a just solution, would promptly recognize the new State. The world would regard it as especially appropriate that the greatest living democracy should be the first to welcome the newest into the family of nations.[1]

At midnight on 14 May the British High Commissioner left Haifa and the Mandate was over. At the same hour the proclamation of the State of Israel became effective and, according to Mr. Truman, the White House announcement of recognition was made public eleven minutes later. It ran as follows: 'This Government has been informed that a Jewish State has been proclaimed in Palestine and recognition has

[1] *Trial and Error*, pp. 583–4.

been requested by the Provisional Government thereof. The United States recognizes the Provisional Government as the *de facto* authority of the new State of Israel.' The full and complete extent of this recognition, which took the General Assembly by surprise, was clarified seven months later by the United States delegate in the Security Council. Some confusion, he said, had perhaps arisen between the recognition of the State of Israel and the Provisional Government of Israel. 'So far as recognition of the State of Israel is concerned,' he continued, 'the recognition accorded by the United States Government to the State of Israel was immediate and full recognition. There was no qualification. It was not conditional; it was not *de facto* recognition; it was full recognition. So far as the Provisional Government of Israel is concerned the United States did extend *de facto* recognition to that Government.'

The new State had been proclaimed at 4 p.m. on 14 May when the following Declaration of Independence was read out by Mr. Ben Gurion:

The Land of Israel was the birthplace of the Jewish People. Here their spiritual, religious and national identity was formed. Here they achieved independence and created a culture of national and universal significance. Here they wrote and gave the Bible to the world.

Exiled from the Land of Israel, the Jewish people remained faithful to it in all the countries of their dispersion, never ceasing to pray and hope for their return and the restoration of their national freedom.

Impelled by this historic association, Jews strove throughout the centuries to go back to the land of their fathers and regain their statehood. In recent decades they returned in their masses. They reclaimed the wilderness, revived their language, built cities and villages, and established a vigorous and ever-growing community with its own economic and cultural life. They sought peace, yet were prepared to defend themselves. They brought the blessings of progress to all inhabitants of the country, and looked forward to sovereign independence.

In the year 1897 the First Zionist Congress, inspired by Theodor Herzl's vision of the Jewish State, proclaimed the right of the Jewish people to national revival in their own country.

This right was acknowledged by the Balfour Declaration of November 2nd, 1917 and reaffirmed by the Mandate of the League of Nations, which gave explicit international recognition to the historic connexion of the Jewish people with Palestine and their right to reconstitute their National Home.

The recent holocaust, which engulfed millions of Jews in Europe, proved anew the need to solve the problem of the homelessness and lack of independence of the Jewish people by means of the re-establishment of the Jewish State, which would open the gates to all Jews and endow the Jewish people with equality of status among the family of Nations.

The survivors of the disastrous slaughter in Europe, and also Jews from other lands, have not desisted from their efforts to reach Eretz Israel[1] in face of difficulties, obstacles and perils; and have not ceased to urge their right to a life of dignity, freedom and honest toil in their ancestral land.

In the Second World War the Jewish people in Palestine made their full contribution to the struggle of the freedom-loving nations against the Nazi evil. The sacrifices of their soldiers and their war effort gained them the right to rank with the nations which founded the United Nations.

On November 29th, 1947 the General Assembly of the United Nations adopted a Resolution requiring the establishment of a Jewish State in Palestine. The General Assembly called upon the inhabitants of the country to take all the necessary steps on their part to put the plan into effect. This recognition by the United Nations of the right of the Jewish people to establish their independent State is unassailable.

It is the natural right of the Jewish people to lead, as do all other nations, an independent existence in its sovereign State.

ACCORDINGLY WE, the members of the National Council, representing the Jewish people in Palestine and the World Zionist Movement, are met together in solemn assembly today, the day of the termination of the British Mandate for Palestine; and by virtue of the natural and historic right of the Jewish people and of the Resolution of the General Assembly of the United Nations.

I HEREBY PROCLAIM the establishment of the Jewish State in Palestine to be called Medinath Yisrael (The State of Israel).

WE HEREBY DECLARE that, as from the termination of the Mandate at midnight, the 14th–15th May, 1948, and pending the setting up of the duly elected bodies of the State in accordance with a Constitution to be drawn up by the Constituent Assembly not later than the 1st October 1948, the National Council shall act as the Provisional State Council, and that the National Administration shall constitute the Provisional Government of the Jewish State, which shall be known as Israel.

THE STATE OF ISRAEL will be open to the immigration of Jews from all countries of their dispersion; will promote the development of the country for the benefit of all its inhabitants; will be based on the principles of liberty, justice and peace as conceived by the Prophets of Israel; will uphold the full social and political equality of all citizens, without distinction of religion, race or sex; will guarantee freedom of religion, conscience, education and culture; will safeguard the Holy Places of all religions; and will loyally uphold the principles of the United Nations Charter.

THE STATE OF ISRAEL will be ready to co-operate with the organs and

---

[1] The State of Israel.

representatives of the United Nations in the implementations of the Resolution of the Assembly of November 29th, 1947, and will take steps to bring about the Economic Union over the whole of Palestine.

We appeal to the United Nations to assist the Jewish people in the building of its State, and to admit Israel into the family of nations.

In the midst of wanton aggression, we yet call upon the Arab inhabitants of the State of Israel to preserve the ways of peace and play their part in the development of the State, on the basis of full and equal citizenship and due representation in all its bodies and institutions, provisional and permanent.

We extend our hand in peace and neighbourliness to all the neighbouring states and their peoples, and invite them to co-operate with the independent Jewish nation for the common good of all. The State of Israel is prepared to make its contribution to the progress of the Middle East as a whole.

Our call goes out to the Jewish people all over the world to rally to our side in the task of immigration and development, and to stand by us in the great struggle for the fulfilment of the dream of generations for the redemption of Israel.

With trust in Almighty God, we set our hand to this Declaration, at this Session of the Provisional State Council, on the soil of the Homeland, in the City of Tel-Aviv, on this Sabbath Eve, the fifth of Iyar, 5708, the fourteenth day of May, 1948.

When David Ben Gurion rose in the Jewish National Council to read that Proclamation, a large portrait of Theodor Herzl hung behind him on the wall. On his return to Vienna, after the First Zionist Conference, Herzl had written in his diary, 'If I were to sum up the Basle Congress in a single phrase—which I would not dare to make public—I would say this. In Basle I created the Jewish State. Were I to say this aloud I would be greeted by universal laughter. But perhaps five years hence, in any case certainly fifty years hence, everyone will perceive it.' As the events proved he was only a few months out in his final estimate, and on this historic occasion his spirit cannot have been far away.

LONDON
1959

APPENDIX I

Extracts from the McMahon Correspondence of 1915-16

This correspondence consists of ten letters exchanged between Sir Henry McMahon, who was then His Majesty's High Commissioner for Egypt, and the Sharif Hussein of Mecca. They were written between July 1915 and March 1916. The correspondence was published in a White Paper (Cmd. 5957) in 1939. The Report of a Committee set up to consider this correspondence was published as a White Paper in the same year (Cmd. 5974).

No. 1 *Letter from the Sharif of Mecca to Sir H. McMahon, 14 July 1915:*

To his Honour:

Whereas the whole of the Arab nation without any exception have decided in these last years to live, and to accomplish their freedom, and grasp the reins of their administration both in theory and practice; and whereas they have found and felt that it is to the interest of the Government of Great Britain to support and aid them to the attainment of their firm and lawful intentions (which are based upon the maintenance of the honour and dignity of their life) without any ulterior motives whatsoever unconnected with this object;

And whereas it is to their (the Arabs') interest, also to prefer the assistance of the Government of Great Britain in consideration of their geographical position and economic interests, and also of the attitude of the above-mentioned Government, which is known to both nations and therefore need not be emphasized;

For these reasons the Arab nation see fit to limit themselves, as time is short, to asking the Government of Great Britain, if it should think fit, for the approval, through her deputy or representative, of the following fundamental propositions, leaving out all things considered secondary in comparison with these, so that it may prepare all means necessary for attaining this noble purpose, until such time as it finds occasion for making the actual negotiations:

Firstly—England to acknowledge the independence of the Arab countries, bounded on the north by Mersina and Adana up to the 37° of latitude, on which degree fall Birijik, Urfa, Mardin, Midiat, Jezirat (Ibn 'Umat), Amadia, up to the border of Persia up to the Gulf of Basra; on the south by the Indian Ocean, with the exception of the position of Aden to remain as it is; on the west by the Red Sea, the Mediterranean Sea up to Mersina.

England to approve of the proclamation of an Arab Khalifate of Islam . . . .

No. 2 *Letter from Sir H. McMahon to the Sharif of Mecca, 3 August 1915:*

We have the honour to thank you for your frank expressions of the sincerity of your feeling towards England. We rejoice, moreover, that Your Highness and your people are of one opinion—that Arab interests are English interests and English Arab. To this intent we confirm to you the terms of Lord Kitchener's message, which reached you by the hand of Ali Effendi, and in which was stated clearly our desire for the independence of Arabia and its inhabitants, together with our approval of the Arab Khalifate when it should be proclaimed. We declare once more that His Majesty's Government would welcome the resumption of the Khalifate by an Arab of true race.

With regard to the questions of limits and boundaries, it would appear to be premature to consume our time in discussing such details in the heat of war, and while, in many portions of them, the Turk is up to now in effective occupation . . . .

No. 3 *From the Sharif of Mecca to Sir H. McMahon, 9 September 1915:*

With great cheerfulness and delight I received your letter dated the 19th Shawal, 1933 (30 August 1915), and have given it great consideration and regard, in spite of the impression I received from it of ambiguity and its tone of coldness and hesitation with regard to our essential point.

It is necessary to make clear to Your Excellency our sincerity to-wards the illustrious British Empire and our confession of preference for it in all cases and matters and under all forms and circumstances.

Nevertheless, Your Excellency will pardon me and permit me to say clearly that the coolness and hesitation which you have displayed in the question of the limits and boundaries by saying that the discussion of these at present is of no use and is a loss of time, and that they are still in the hands of the Government which is ruling them, etc., might be taken to infer an estrangement or something of the sort....

No. 4 *From Sir H. McMahon to the Sharif of Mecca, 24 October 1915:*

... I regret that you should have received from my last letter the impression that I regarded the question of the limits and boundaries with coldness and hesitation; such was not the case, but it appeared to me that the time had not yet come when that question could be discussed in a conclusive manner.

I have realized, however, from your last letter that you regard this question as one of vital and urgent importance. I have, therefore, lost no time in informing the Government of Great Britain of the contents of your letter, and it is with great pleasure that I communicate to you on their behalf the following statement, which I am confident you will receive with satisfaction:

The two districts of Mersina and Alexandretta and portions of Syria lying to the west of the districts of Damascus, Homs, Hama and Aleppo cannot be said to be purely Arab, and should be excluded from the limits demanded.

With the above modification, and without prejudice to our existing treaties with Arab chiefs, we accept those limits.

As for those regions lying within those frontiers wherein Great Britain is free to act without detriment to the interests of her ally, France, I am empowered in the name of the Government of Great Britain to give the following assurances and make the following reply to your letter:

(1) Subject to the above modifications, Great Britain is prepared to recognize and support the independence of the Arabs in all the regions within the limits demanded by the Sharif of Mecca.

(2) Great Britain will guarantee the Holy Places against all external aggression and will recognize their inviolability.

(3) When the situation admits, Great Britain will give to the Arabs her advice and will assist them to establish what may appear to be the most suitable forms of government in those various territories.

(4) On the other hand, it is understood that the Arabs have decided to seek the advice and guidance of Great Britain only, and that such European advisers and officials as may be required for the formation of a sound form of administration will be British.

(5) With regard to the Vilayets of Baghdad and Basra, the Arabs will recognize that the established position and interests of Great Britain necessitate special administrative arrangements in order to secure these territories from foreign aggression, to promote the welfare of the local populations and to safeguard our mutual economic interests. . . .

No. 5 *From the Sharif of Mecca to Sir H. McMahon, 15 November 1915:*

I received with great pleasure your honoured letter, dated the 15th Zil Hijja (24 October 1915), to which I beg to answer as follows:

In order to facilitate an agreement and to render a service to Islam, and at the same time to avoid all that may cause Islam troubles and hardships—seeing moreover that we have great consideration for the distinguished qualities and dispositions of the Government of Great Britain—we renounce our insistence on the inclusion of the Vilayets of Mersina and Adana in the Arab Kingdom. But the two Vilayets of Aleppo and Beirut and their sea coasts are purely Arab Vilayets, and there is no difference between a Moslem and a Christian Arab; they are both descendants of one forefather. . . .

No. 6 *From Sir H. McMahon to the Sharif of Mecca, 14 December 1915:*

I am gratified to observe that you agree to the exclusion of the districts of Mersina and Adana from boundaries of the Arab territories.

. . . With regard to the Vilayets of Aleppo and Beirut, the Government of Great Britain have fully understood and taken careful note of your observations, but, as the interests of our ally, France, are involved in them both, the question will require careful consideration and a further communication on the subject will be addressed to you in due course. . . .

No. 7 *From the Sharif of Mecca to Sir H. McMahon, 1 January 1916:*

We received from the bearer your letter, dated the 9th Safar (14 December 1915) with great respect and honour, and I have understood its contents, which caused me the greatest pleasure and satisfaction, as it removed that which had made me uneasy. . . . As regards the northern parts and their coasts, we have already stated in our previous letter what were the utmost possible modifications, and all this was only done so to fulfil those aspirations whose attainment is desired by the will of the Blessed and Supreme God. It is this same feeling and desire which impelled us to avoid what may possibly injure the alliance of Great Britain and France and the agreement made between them during the present wars and calamities; yet we find it our duty that the eminent Minister should be sure that, at the first opportunity after this war is finished, we shall ask you (what we avert our eyes from today) for what we now leave to France in Beirut and its coasts.

I do not find it necessary to draw your attention to the fact that our plan is of greater security to the interests and protection of the rights of Great Britain than it is to us, and will necessarily be so whatever may happen, so that Great Britain may finally see her friends in that contentment and advancement which she is endeavouring to establish for them now, especially as her Allies being neighbours to us will be the germ of difficulties and discussion with which there will be no peaceful conditions. In addition to which the citizens of Beirut will decidedly never accept such dismemberment, and they may oblige us to undertake new measures which may exercise Great Britain, certainly not less than her present troubles, because of our belief and certainty in the reciprocity and indeed the identity of our interests, which is the only cause that caused us never to care to negotiate with any other Power but you. Consequently, it is impossible to allow any derogation that gives France, or any other Power, a span of land in those regions. . . .

No. 8 *From Sir H. McMahon to the Sharif of Mecca, 25 January 1916:*

. . . As regards the northern parts, we note with satisfaction your desire to avoid anything which might possibly injure the alliance of Great Britain and France. It is, as you know, our fixed determination that nothing shall be permitted to interfere in the slightest degree with our united prosecution of this war to a victorious conclusion. Moreover, when the victory has been won, the friendship of Great Britain and France will become yet more firm and enduring, cemented by the blood of Englishmen and Frenchmen who have died side by side fighting for the cause of right and liberty . . . .

APPENDIX II

The Committee set up by H.M. Government at the time of the Palestine Conference in 1939 considered a number of documents which might shed light on the meaning or intention of the McMahon correspondence. These included the 'Hogarth Message', the 'Declaration to the Seven', certain assurances given by General Sir Edmund (later Viscount) Allenby when commanding the Allied Forces in Syria and Palestine, and the Anglo-French Declaration or 7 November 1918. All these documents are set out below.

A. THE HOGARTH MESSAGE

The following are the terms of the message which Commander Hogarth was instructed to deliver to King Husain when he visited Jedda in January, 1918:

(1) The Entente Powers are determined that the Arab race shall be given full opportunity of once again forming a nation in the world. This can only be achieved by the Arabs themselves uniting, and Great Britain and her Allies will pursue a policy with this ultimate unity in view.

(2) So far as Palestine is concerned we are determined that no people shall be subject to another, but

(a) in view of the fact that there are in Palestine shrines, Wakfs and Holy places, sacred in some cases to Moslems alone, to Jews alone, to Christians alone, and in others to two or all three, and inasmuch as these places are of interest to vast masses of people outside Palestine and Arabia, there must be a special régime to deal with these places approved of by the world.

(b) As regards the Mosque of Omar it shall be considered as a Moslem concern alone and shall not be subjected directly or indirectly to any non-Moslem authority.

(3) Since the Jewish opinion of the world is in favour of a return of Jews to Palestine and inasmuch as this opinion must remain a constant factor, and further as His Majesty's Government view with

favour the realization of this aspiration, His Majesty's Government are determined that in so far as is compatible with the freedom of the existing population both economic and political, no obstacle should be put in the way of the realization of this ideal.

In this connexion the friendship of world Jewry to the Arab cause is equivalent to support in all States where Jews have a political influence. The leaders of the movement are determined to bring about the success of Zionism by friendship and co-operation with the Arabs, and such an offer is not one to be lightly thrown aside.

B. THE DECLARATION TO THE SEVEN

His Majesty's Government have considered the memorial of the seven with the greatest care. His Majesty's Government fully appreciate the reasons why the memorialists desire to retain their anonymity, and the fact that the memorial is anonymous has not in any way detracted from the importance which His Majesty's Government attribute to the document. The areas mentioned in the memorandum fall into four categories:

(1) Areas in Arabia which were free and independent before the outbreak of war;

(2) Areas emancipated from Turkish control by the action of the Arabs themselves during the present war;

(3) Areas formerly under Ottoman dominion, occupied by the Allied forces during the present war;

(4) Areas still under Turkish control.

In regard to the first two categories, His Majesty's Government recognize the complete and sovereign independence of the Arabs inhabiting these areas and support them in their struggle for freedom.

In regard to the areas occupied by Allied forces, His Majesty's Government draw the attention of the memorialists to the texts of the proclamations issued respectively by the General Officers Commanding in Chief on the taking of Baghdad and Jerusalem. These proclamations embody the policy of His Majesty's Government towards the inhabitants of those regions. It is the wish and desire of His Majesty's Government that the future government of these regions should be based upon the principle of the consent of the governed and this policy has and will continue to have the support of His Majesty's Government.

In regard to the areas mentioned in the fourth category, it is the wish and desire of His Majesty's Government that the oppressed peoples of these areas should obtain their freedom and independence and towards the achievement of this object His Majesty's Government continue to labour.

His Majesty's Government are fully aware of, and take into consideration, the difficulties and dangers which beset those who work for the regeneration of the populations of the areas specified.

In spite, however, of these obstacles His Majesty's Government trust and believe that they can and will be overcome, and wish to give all support to those who desire to overcome them. They are prepared to consider any scheme of co-operation which is compatible with existing military operations and consistent with the political principles of His Majesty's Government and the Allies.
June 1918.

C. SIR EDMUND ALLENBY'S ASSURANCE TO THE AMIR FAISAL

The following are the terms in which General Sir Edmund Allenby reported to His Majesty's Government on the 17 October 1918 a communication which he made to the Amir Faisal:

I gave the Amir Faisal an official assurance that whatever measures might be taken during the period of military administration they were purely provisional and could not be allowed to prejudice the final settlement by the peace conference, at which no doubt the Arabs would have a representative. I added that the instructions to the military governors would preclude their mixing in political affairs, and that I should remove them if I found any of them contravening these orders. I reminded the Amir Faisal that the Allies were in honour bound to endeavour to reach a settlement in accordance with the wishes of the peoples concerned and urged him to place his trust wholeheartedly in their good faith.

D. THE ANGLO-FRENCH DECLARATION OF 7 NOVEMBER 1918

The object aimed at by France and Great Britain in prosecuting in the East the War let loose by the ambition of Germany is the complete and definite emancipation of the peoples so long oppressed by the Turks and the establishment of national governments and administrations deriving their authority from the initiative and free choice of the indigenous populations.

In order to carry out these intentions France and Great Britain are at one in encouraging and assisting the establishment of indigenous governments and administrations in Syria and Mesopotamia, now liberated by the Allies, and in the territories the liberation of which they are engaged in securing and recognizing these as soon as they are actually established.

Far from wishing to impose on the populations of these regions any particular institutions they are only concerned to ensure by their support and by adequate assistance the regular working of governments and administrations freely chosen by the populations themselves. To secure impartial and equal justice for all, to facilitate the economic development of the country by inspiring and encouraging local initiative, to favour the diffusion of education, to put an end to dissensions that have too long been taken advantage of by Turkish policy, such is the policy which the two Allied governments uphold in the liberated territories.

APPENDIX III

Article 22 of the Covenant of the League of Nations

1. To those colonies and territories which as a consequence of the late War have ceased to be under the sovereignty of the States which formerly governed them and which are inhabited by peoples not yet able to stand by themselves under the strenuous conditions of the modern world, there should be applied the principle that the well-being and development of such peoples form a sacred trust of civilization and that securities for the performance of this trust should be embodied in this Covenant.

2. The best method of giving practical effect to this principle is that the tutelage of such peoples should be entrusted to advanced nations who by reason of their resources, their experience or their geographical position can best undertake this responsibility, and who are willing to accept it, and that this tutelage should be exercised by them as Mandatories on behalf of the League.

3. The character of the Mandate must differ according to the stage of the development of the people, the geographical situation of the territory, its economic conditions and other similar circumstances.

4. Certain communities formerly belonging to the Turkish Empire have reached a stage of development where their existence as independent nations can be provisionally recognized subject to the rendering of administrative advice and assistance by a Mandatory until such time as they are able to stand alone. The wishes of these communities must be a principal consideration in the selection of the Mandatory.

5. Other peoples, especially those of Central Africa, are at such a

stage that the Mandatory must be responsible for the administration of the territory under conditions which will guarantee freedom of conscience and religion, subject only to the maintenance of public order and morals, the prohibition of abuses such as the slave trade, and arms traffic and the liquor traffic, and the prevention of the establishment of fortifications or military and naval bases and of military training of the natives for other than police purposes and the defence of territory, and will also secure equal opportunities for the trade and commerce of other Members of the League.

6. There are territories, such as South-West Africa and certain of the South Pacific Islands, which, owing to the sparseness of their population, or their small size, or their remoteness from the centres of civilization, or their geographical contiguity to the territory of the Mandatory, and other circumstances, can be best administered under the laws of the Mandatory as integral portions of its territory, subject to the safeguards above-mentioned in the interests of the indigenous population.

7. In every case of Mandate, the Mandatory shall render to the Council an annual report in reference to the territory committed to it charge.

8. The degree of authority, control, or administration to be exercised by the Mandatory shall, if not previously agreed upon by the Members of the League, be explicitly defined in each case by the Council.

9. A permanent Commission shall be constituted to receive and examine the annual reports of the Mandatories and to advise the Council on all matters relating to the observance of the Mandates.

APPENDIX IV

The Mandate for Palestine

The Council of the League of Nations:

Whereas the Principal Allied Powers have agreed, for the purpose of giving effect to the provisions of Article 22 of the Covenant of the League of Nations to entrust to a Mandatory selected by the said Powers the administration of the territory of Palestine, which formerly belonged to the Turkish Empire, within such boundaries as may be fixed by them; and

Whereas the Principal Allied Powers have also agreed that the Mandatory should be responsible for putting into effect the declaration originally made on November 2, 1917 by the Government of His Britannic Majesty, and adopted by the said Powers, in favour of the establishment in Palestine of a National Home for the Jewish people, it being clearly understood that nothing should be done which might prejudice the civil and religious rights of existing non-Jewish communities in Palestine, or the rights and political status enjoyed by Jews in any other country; and

Whereas recognition has thereby been given to the historical connection of the Jewish people with Palestine and to the grounds for reconstituting their National Home in that country; and

Whereas the Principal Allied Powers have selected His Britannic Majesty as the Mandatory for Palestine; and

Whereas the Mandate in respect of Palestine has been formulated in the following terms and submitted to the Council of the League for approval; and

Whereas His Britannic Majesty has accepted the Mandate in respect of Palestine and undertaken to exercise it on behalf of the League of Nations in conformity with the following provisions; and

Whereas by the afore-mentioned Article 22 (paragraph 8), it is provided that the degree of authority, control or administration to be exercised by the Mandatory, not having been previously agreed upon by the Members of the League, shall be explicitly defined by the Council of the League of Nations;

Confirming the said Mandate, defines its terms as follows:

Article 1.   The Mandatory shall have full powers of legislation and of administration, save as they may be limited by the terms of this Mandate.

Article 2.   The Mandatory shall be responsible for placing the country under such political, administrative and economic conditions as will secure the establishment of the Jewish National Home, as laid down in the preamble, and the development of self-governing institutions, and also for safeguarding the civil and religious rights of all the inhabitants of Palestine, irrespective of race and religion.

Article 3.   The Mandatory shall, so far as circumstances permit, encourage local autonomy.

Article 4.   An appropriate Jewish Agency shall be recognized as a public body for the purpose of advising and co-operating with the Administration of Palestine in such economic, social and other matters as may affect the establishment of the Jewish National Home and the interests of the Jewish population in Palestine and, subject always to the control of the Administration, to assist and take part in the development of the country. The Zionist Organization, so long as its organization and constitution are in the opinion of the Mandatory appropriate, shall be recognized as such agency. It shall take steps in consultation with His Britannic Majesty's Government to secure the co-operation of all Jews who are willing to assist in the establishment of the Jewish National Home.

Article 5.   The Mandatory shall be responsible for seeing that no Palestine territory shall be ceded or leased to, or in any way placed under the control of, the Government of any foreign power.

Article 6.   The Administration of Palestine, while ensuring that the rights and position of other sections of the population are not prejudiced, shall facilitate Jewish immigration under suitable conditions and shall encourage, in co-operation with the Jewish Agency referred to in Article 4, close settlement by Jews on the land, including State lands and waste lands not required for public purposes.

Article 7.   The Administration of Palestine shall be responsible for enacting a nationality law. There shall be included in this law provisions framed so as to facilitate the acquisition of Palestinian citizenship by Jews who take up their permanent residence in Palestine.

Article 8.   The privileges and immunities of foreigners, including the benefits of consular jurisdiction and protection as formerly enjoyed by Capitulation or usage in the Ottoman Empire, shall not be applicable in Palestine.

Unless the Powers whose nationals enjoyed the aforementioned privileges and immunities on August 1, 1914, shall have previously renounced the right to their re-establishment, or shall have agreed to their non-application for a specified period, these privileges and immunities shall, at the expiration of the Mandate, be immediately re-established in their entirety or with such modifications as may have been agreed upon between the Powers concerned.

Article 9.   The Mandatory shall be responsible for seeing that the judicial system established in Palestine shall assure to foreigners, as well as to natives, a complete guarantee of their rights.

Respect for the personal status of the various peoples and communities and for their religious interests shall be fully guaranteed. In particular, the control and administration of Waqfs shall be exercised in accordance with religious law and the dispositions of the founders.

Article 10.   Pending the making of special extradition agreements relating to Palestine, the extradition treaties in force between the Mandatory and other foreign Powers shall apply to Palestine.

Article 11. The Administration of Palestine shall take all necessary measures to safeguard the interests of the community in connection with the development of the country, and, subject to any international obligations accepted by the Mandatory, shall have full power to provide for public ownership or control of any of the natural resources of the country or of the public works, services and utilities established or to be established therein.

It shall introduce a land system appropriate to the needs of the country, having regard, among other things, to the desirability of promoting the close settlement and intensive cultivation of the land.

The Administration may arrange with the Jewish Agency mentioned in Article 4 to construct or operate, upon fair and equitable terms, any public works, services and utilities, and to develop any of the natural resources of the country, in so far as these matters are not directly undertaken by the Administration. Any such arrangements shall provide that no profits distributed by such Agency, directly or indirectly, shall exceed a reasonable rate of interest on the capital, and any further profits shall be utilized by it for the benefit of the country in a manner approved by the Administration.

Article 12. The Mandatory shall be entrusted with the control of the foreign relations of Palestine and the right to issue exequaturs to consuls appointed by foreign Powers. He shall also be entitled to afford diplomatic and consular protection to citizens of Palestine when outside its territorial limits.

Article 13. All responsibility in connection with the Holy Places and religious buildings or sites in Palestine, including that of preserving rights existing and of securing free access to the Holy Places, religious buildings, and sites, and the free exercise of worship, while ensuring the requirements of public order and decorum, is assumed by the Mandatory, who shall be responsible solely to the League of Nations in all matters connected herewith, provided that nothing in this Article shall prevent the Mandatory from entering into such arrangements as he may deem reasonable with the Administration for the purpose of carrying the provisions of this Article into effect; and provided also that nothing in this Mandate shall be construed as conferring upon the Mandatory authority to interfere with the fabric or the management of purely Moslem sacred shrines, the immunities of which are guaranteed.

Article 14. A special Commission shall be appointed by the Mandatory to study, define and determine the rights and claims in connection with the Holy Places and the rights and claims relating to the different religious communities in Palestine. The method of nomination, the composition and the functions of this Commission shall be submitted to the Council of the League for its approval, and the Commission shall not be appointed or enter upon its functions without the approval of the Council.

Article 15. The Mandatory shall see that complete freedom of conscience and the free exercise of all forms of worship, subject only to the maintenance of public order and morals, are ensured to all. No discrimination of any kind shall be made between the inhabitants of Palestine on the ground of race, religion or language. No person shall be excluded from Palestine on the sole ground of his religious belief. The right of each community to maintain its own schools for the education of its own members in its own language, while conforming to such educational requirements of a general nature as the Administration may impose, shall not be denied or impaired.

Article 16. The Mandatory shall be responsible for exercising such supervision over religious or eleemosynary bodies of all faiths in Palestine as may be required for the maintenance of public order and good government. Subject to such supervision, no measures shall be taken in Palestine to obstruct or interfere with the enterprise of such bodies or to discriminate against any representative or member of them on the ground of his religion or nationality.

Article 17. The Administration of Palestine may organize on a voluntary basis the forces necessary for the preservation of peace and order, and also for the defence of the country, subject, however, to the supervision of the Mandatory, but shall not use them for purposes other than those specified save with the consent of the Mandatory. Except for such purposes, no military, naval or air forces shall be raised or maintained by the Administration of Palestine.

Nothing in this Article shall preclude the Administration of Palestine from contributing to the cost of the maintenance of the force of the Mandatory in Palestine.

The Mandatory shall be entitled at all times to use the roads, railways and ports of Palestine for the movement of armed forces and the carriage of fuel and supplies.

Article 18. The Mandatory shall see that there is no discrimination in Palestine against the nationals of any State Member of the League of Nations (including companies incorporated under its laws) as compared with those of the Mandatory or of any foreign State in matters concerning taxation, commerce or navigation, the exercise of industries or professions, or in the treatment of merchant vessels or civil aircraft. Similarly, there shall be no discrimination in Palestine against goods originating in or destined for any of the said States, and there shall be freedom of transit under equitable conditions across the Mandated area.

Subject as aforesaid and to the other provisions of this Mandate, the Administration of Palestine may, on the advice of the Mandatory, impose such taxes and Customs duties as it may consider necessary, and take such steps as it may think best to promote the development of the natural resources of the country and to safeguard the interests of the population. It may also, on the advice of the Mandatory, conclude a special Customs agreement with any State the territory of which in 1914 was wholly included in Asiatic Turkey or Arabia.

Article 19. The Mandatory shall adhere on behalf of the Administration of Palestine to any general international conventions already existing, or which may be concluded hereafter with the approval of the League of Nations, respecting the slave traffic, the traffic in arms and ammunition, or the traffic in drugs, or relating to commercial equality, freedom of transit and navigation, aerial navigation and postal, telegraphic and wireless communication or literary, artistic or industrial property.

Article 20. The Mandatory shall co-operate on behalf of the Administration of Palestine, so far as religious, social and other conditions may permit, in the execution of any common policy adopted by the League of Nations for preventing and combating disease, including diseases of plants and animals.

Article 21. The Mandatory shall secure the enactment within twelve months from this date, and shall ensure the execution of a law of antiquities based on the following rules. This law shall ensure equality of treatment in the matter of excavations and archæological research to the nations of all States Members of the League of Nations.

(1) 'Antiquity' means any construction or any product of human activity earlier than the year A.D. 1700.

(2) The law for the protection of antiquities shall proceed by encouragement rather than by threat.

Any person, who, having discovered an antiquity without being furnished with the authorization referred to in paragraph 5, reports the same to an official of the competent Department, shall be rewarded according to the value of the discovery.

(3) No antiquity may be disposed of except to the competent Department, unless this Department renounces the acquisition of any such antiquity. No antiquity may leave the country without an export licence from the said Department.

(4) Any person who maliciously or negligently destroys or damages an antiquity shall be liable to a penalty to be fixed.

(5) No clearing of ground or digging with the object of finding antiquities shall be permitted, under penalty of fine, except to persons authorized by the competent Department.

(6) Equitable terms shall be fixed for expropriation, temporary or permanent, of lands which might be of historical or archæological interest.

(7) Authorization to excavate shall only be granted to persons who show sufficient guarantees of archæological experience. The Administration of Palestine shall not, in granting these authorizations, act in such a way as to exclude scholars of any nation without good grounds.

(8) The proceeds of excavations may be divided between the excavator and the competent Department in a proportion fixed by that Department. If division seems impossible for scientific reasons, the excavator shall receive a fair indemnity in lieu of a part of the find.

Article 22. English, Arabic and Hebrew shall be the official languages of Palestine. Any statement or inscription in Arabic on stamps or money in Palestine shall be repeated in Hebrew, and any statement or inscription in Hebrew shall be repeated in Arabic.

Article 23. The Administration of Palestine shall recognize the holy days of the respective communities in Palestine as legal days of rest for the members of such communities.

Article 24. The Mandatory shall make to the Council of the League of Nations an annual report to the satisfaction of the Council as to the measures taken during the year to carry out the provisions of the Mandate. Copies of all laws and regulations promulgated or issued during the year shall be communicated with the report.

Article 25. In the territories lying between the Jordan and the eastern boundary of Palestine as ultimately determined, the Mandatory shall be entitled, with the consent of the Council of the League of Nations, to postpone or withhold application of such provisions of this Mandate as he may consider inapplicable to the existing local conditions, and to make such provision for the administration of the territories as he may consider suitable to those conditions, provided that no action shall be taken which is inconsistent with the provisions of Articles 15, 16, and 18.

Article 26. The Mandatory agrees that if any dispute whatever should arise between the Mandatory and another Member of the League of Nations relating to the interpretation or the application of the provisions of the Mandate, such dispute, if it cannot be settled by negotiation, shall be submitted to the Permanent Court of International Justice provided for by Article 14 of the Covenant of the League of Nations.

Article 27. The consent of the Council of the League of Nations is required for any modification of the terms of this Mandate.

Article 28. In the event of the termination of the Mandate hereby conferred upon the Mandatory, the Council of the League of Nations shall make such arrangements as may be deemed necessary for safeguarding in perpetuity, under guarantee of the League, the rights secured by Articles 13 and 14, and shall use its influence for securing, under the guarantee of the League, that the Government of Palestine will fully honour the financial obligations legitimately incurred by the Administration of Palestine during the period of the Mandate, including the rights of public servants to pensions or gratuities.

The present instrument shall be deposited in original in the archives of the League of Nations and certified copies shall be forwarded by the Secretary-General of the League of Nations to all Members of the League.

Done at London the twenty-fourth day of July, one thousand nine hundred and twenty-two.

Certified true copy:

For the SECRETARY-GENERAL
RAPPARD,
Director of the Mandates Section.

Bibliography

The official and non-official documents, books and pamphlets on this subject are legion. The following is only a short list of some of the more important sources of information used by the author when writing this book.

Official Documents

Great Britain, Parliamentary Command Papers

An Interim Report on the Civil Administration of Palestine during the Period 1st July 1920–30th June 1921, Cmd. 1499, 1921. The First Samuel Report.

Palestine: Disturbances in May, 1921. Report of the Commission of Inquiry with Correspondence relating thereto, Cmd. 1540, 1921. The Haycraft Report.

Correspondence with the Palestine Arab Delegation and the Zionist Organization, Cmd. 1700, 1922. The Churchill White Paper.

Mandate for Palestine: Letter from the Secretary of the Cabinet to the Secretary-General of the League of Nations regarding the Mandate of Palestine and the Holy Places Commission, Cmd. 1708, 1922.

League of Nations: Mandate for Palestine, together with a Note by the Secretary-General relating to Its Application to the Territory Known as Transjordan, Cmd. 1785, 1922.

Palestine: Proposed Formation of an Arab Agency. Correspondence with the High Commissioner for Palestine, Cmd. 1939, 1923.

The Western or Wailing Wall in Jerusalem: Memorandum by the Secretary of State for the Colonies, Cmd. 3229, 1928.

Report of the Commission on the Palestine Disturbances of August, 1929, Cmd. 3530, 1930. The Shaw Report.

Palestine: Statement with regard to British Policy, Cmd. 3582, 1930. The White Paper on the Shaw Report.

Palestine: Statement of Policy by His Majesty's Government in the United Kingdom, Cmd. 3692, 1930. The Passfield White Paper.

Palestine: Royal Commission Report, Cmd. 5479, 1937. Peel Report.

Palestine: Statement of Policy by His Majesty's Government in the United Kingdom, Cmd. 5513, 1937. White Paper on Partition.

Policy in Palestine: Despatch Dated 23rd December 1937, from the Secretary of State for the Colonies to the High Commissioner for Palestine, Cmd. 5634, 1938. The terms of reference of the Partition Commission.

Palestine: Partition Commission Report, Cmd. 5854, 1938. The Woodhead Report.

Palestine: Statement by His Majesty's Government in the United Kingdom, Cmd. 5893, 1938. Revoked Partition and announced Round Table Conference.

Correspondence between Sir Henry McMahon and the Sharif Hussein of Mecca, July 1915–March 1916, Cmd. 5957 (Miscellaneous No. 3), 1939.

Report of a Committee Set Up to Consider Certain Correspondence between Sir Henry McMahon and the Sharif of Mecca in 1915 and 1916, Cmd. 5974, 1939.

Palestine: Statement of Policy, Cmd. 6019, 1939. The White Paper of May, 1939.

International Commission on the Wailing Wall

Report of the Commission Appointed by His Majesty's Government in the United Kingdom of Great Britain and Northern Ireland, with the Approval of the Council of the League of Nations, to Determine the Rights and Claims of Moslems and Jews in Connexion with the Western or Wailing Wall at Jerusalem, December 1930, London, 1931.

Jewish Agency

America Speaks: a Free Jewish Palestine, London, 1942.

An Appeal to the British People, London, 1939.

The Balfour Declaration: Origins and Background by Blanche Elizabeth Dugdale, London, 1940.

The Development of the Jewish National Home in Palestine: Memorandum Submitted to His Majesty's Government by the Jewish Agency for Palestine, May, 1930.

Documents relating to the Balfour Declaration and the Palestine Mandate, London, 1939.

Documents relating to the McMahon Letters, London, 1939.

Documents relating to the Palestine Problem, 1945.

The Jewish Case against the Palestine White Paper, London, 1939.

Memorandum Submitted to the Palestine Royal Commission, London, 1936.

The Palestinian Arabs under the Mandate, London, 1930.

League of Nations, Permanent Mandates Commission

Minutes of the First Session Held in Geneva, October 4th to 8th, 1921. C.416, M.296, 1921. VI.

Mandate for Palestine and Transjordan. C.P.M. 269, 1922. VI.

Mandate for Palestine. C.259, M.314, 1922. VI.

Mandate for Palestine. C.P.M. 466, C.667, M.396, 1922. VI. (Same as Cmd. 1785, 1922).

Minutes of the Sixteenth Session Held in Geneva, November 6th to 26th, 1929. C.538, M.192, 1929. VI.

Palestine Arab Congress

Report on the State of Palestine, Presented to the Right Honourable Mr. Winston Churchill, P.C., M.P., by the Executive Committee of the Third Arab Palestine Congress. Jerusalem, March 28, 1921, Jerusalem, 1921.

Palestine Arab Delegation

The Arab Case: Statement by the Palestine Arab Delegation, London, 1936.

The Holy Land: the Moslem-Christian Case against Zionist Aggression, London, 1921.

Books and Pamphlets

Amery, L. S. *The Forward View*, London, 1935.

Antonius, George. *The Arab Awakening*, Philadelphia, 1939.

Arab Office. *Arab World and the Arab League*, London, 1945.

Balfour, Arthur James. *Speeches on Zionism*, Foreword by Sir Herbert Samuel, London, 1928.

Bein, Alex. *Theodor Herzl, a Biography*, 1941.

Ben Gurion, D. *Anachnu Ushchenenu* (*We and Our Neighbours*), Tel-Aviv, 1931.
   Palestine in the Post-War World, London, 1942.
   The Peel Report and the Jewish State, London, 1938.

Bentwich, N. *England in Palestine*, London, 1932.
   Fulfilment in the Promised Land, London, 1938.

Brandeis, Louis D. *Brandeis on Zionism; a Collection of Addresses and Statements*, Washington, 1942. Solomon Goldman, ed.

Churchill, Winston S. *The Aftermath*, London, 1929.
   The Second World War, London, 1948–54. 6 vols.

Cocks, F. Seymour. *The Secret Treaties*, London, 1918.

Cohen, Israel. *The Zionist Movement*, London, 1945.

de Haas, Jacob. *History of Palestine, the Last Two Thousand Years*, New York, 1934.

Dugdale, Blanche E. C. *Arthur James Balfour*, London, 1937. 2 vols.

Esco Foundation for Palestine, Inc. *Palestine, a Study of Jewish, Arab and British Policies*, New Haven. 2 vols.

Garnett, David (ed.). *The Letters of T. E. Lawrence*, London, 1938.

Gibb, H. A. R. *The Arabs*, Oxford, 1941.

Gollancz, V. *Nowhere to Lay Their Heads*, London, 1945.

Goodman, Paul (ed.). *The Jewish National Home, 2nd November, 1917–1942*, London, 1943.

Graves, Philip. *Palestine, the Land of Three Faiths*, London, 1923.

Hanna, Paul L. *British Policy in Palestine*, Washington, 1942.

Herzl, Theodor. *The Jewish State*, New York, 1934.
  Old-New Land, New York, 1941.
Hogarth, D. G. *The Nearer East*, London, 1902.
Horowitz, P. *The Jewish Question and Zionism*, London, 1927.
Kisch, Frederick H. *Palestine Diary*, London, 1938.
Lawrence, T. E. *Revolt in the Desert*, London, 1927.
  Seven Pillars of Wisdom, London, 1935.
Lloyd George, David. *The Truth about the Peace Treaties*, London, 1938. 2 vols.
Lowdermilk, W. C. *Palestine, Land of Promise*, New York, 1944.
Lytton, The Earl of. *The Problem of the Mandate in Palestine*, Nottingham, 1931.
Naiditch, Isaac. *Edmond de Rothschild*, Washington, 1945.
Nordau, Max. *Zionistische Schriften*, Berlin, 1923.
Oxford and Asquith, The Earl of. *Memories and Reflections 1852–1927*, Boston, 1928. 2 vols.
Ronaldshay, The Earl of. *The Life of Curzon*, London, 1928. 3 vols.
Royal Institute of International Affairs, The. *Great Britain and Palestine 1915–1939*, London, 1939. Third ed. (*1915–1945*), 1946.
Royden, Maude. *The Problem of Palestine*, London, 1939.
Samuel, Herbert. *Great Britain and Palestine*, London, 1935.
  Memoirs, London, 1945.
Sidebotham, Herbert. *Great Britain and Palestine*, London, 1937.
Simson, H. J. *British Rule and Rebellion*, London, 1937.
Smuts, J. C. *The League of Nations—a Practical Suggestion*, London, 1918.
Sokolow, Nahum. *Hibbath Zion (The Love for Zion)*, Jerusalem, 1934.
  History of Zionism 1600–1918, London, 1919. 2 vols.
Spring Rice, Cecil Arthur. *Letters and Friendship*, London, 1929. 2 vols.
Storrs, Sir Ronald. *The Memoirs of Sir Ronald Storrs*, London, 1937.
Temperley, H. W. V. *England and the Near East*, London, 1936.
  A History of the Peace Conference of Paris, London, 1920–1924. Vol. 6.
Weizmann, Chaim. *Trial and Error*, London, 1950.

INDEX

Abdul Hamid, Sultan, 10, 11, 13, 15

Abdullah, Emir of Transjordan, 66, 118

Ahad Ha'am. *See* Ginsberg, Asher

Alexander, Mr., 44, 45

Allenby, General Sir Edmund (later Viscount), 36, 62, 65, 213, 215

Allgemeine Zeitung, 4

Altneuland (Herzl), 16

American Zionists. *See* Zionist Organization of America

Amery, Leopold, 80, 104, 115, 138–9, 140, 151

Andrews, Mr., 131

Anglo-American Committee, 161–6

Anglo-Jewish Association, 44

Anti-Semitism: in France, 1, 2; in Austria-Hungary, 1; in Germany, 1, 110, 148; in Russia, 1, 18; in Poland, 144, 147

Arab League, 180

Arab Nationalism: the Hussein–McMahon correspondence, 27, 29–34, 207–12 (Appendix I); the Sykes–Picot Agreement, 34–6; and the Balfour Declaration, 51–2, 55–9; agitation for an independent Arab Palestine, 67; the Arab Committee's demands, 67–8; and Jewish immigration, 69–71; and the Churchill Memorandum, 72; Arab refusal to co-operate with British Government, 73–5; the Hogarth Message to Hussein, 213–14; the Declaration of the Seven, 214–15; Allenby's assurance to Feisal, 215; Anglo-French Declaration of 1918, 215–16

Asquith, H. H., 38

Attlee, C. R.: and the Anglo-American Committee's Report, 165, 166; on the seizure of Jewish Agency H. Q., 170

Austin, Senator, 200, 202

Austria, Jews from, 148

Baden, Grand Duke of, 6, 15

Baldwin, Stanley, 103–4

Balfour, A. J., 16, 24, 39–41, 43, 45, 54–5, 61, 76, 83, 95, 139

Balfour, Lady Blanche, 54

Balfour Declaration, 36, 39, 45–8; varying interpretations of, 48; endorsed by President Wilson, 50; motives for, 50–5; Arab opposition, 55–6, 67–8

Barker, General Sir Evelyn, 177

Basle Charter, 8, 23

Ben Gurion, David: opposes setting up of Legislative Council, 113–14; urges departure from Weizmann policy, 143; reads Declaration of Independence, 204, 206

Bertie, Lord, 37, 38

Bevin, Ernest: his Statement on Government Policy, 159, 160; and the Anglo-American Committee, 165; on cost of Jewish immigration, 167; and the Morrison Plan, 169; his Plan for Palestine, 183–4, 190; orders displaced persons to Germany, 189; opposes partition, 196; and collective enforcement of partition, 198

Board of Deputies of British Jews, 44

Brandeis, Louis (later Justice), 43

Bridges, Sir Edward, 153

Brodetzky, Professor, 104

Cadogan, Sir Alexander, 185

Cafferata, Mr., 92

Cecil, Lord Robert (later Lord Cecil of Chelwood), 45, 102–3

Chamberlain, Austen, 104

Chamberlain, Joseph, 13, 16–20

Chamberlain, Neville, 49–50, 134, 138, 150

Chancellor, Sir John, 75; High Commissioner for Palestine, 81; and the Wailing Wall incident, 88; his proclamation during the 1929 disturbances, 94–5

235